KT-442-106

B.S.U.C. - LIBRARY

00250301

AMERICAN MEMORY IN HENRY JAMES
VOID AND VALUE

American Memory
in Henry James
Void and Value

WILLIAM RIGHTER

Edited by Rosemary Righter

ASHGATE

© William Righter 2004
　Edited by Rosemary Righter

All rights reserved. No part of this publication may be reproduced, stored in a retrieval system, or transmitted in any form or by any means electronic, mechanical, photocopying, recording or otherwise without the prior permission of the publisher.

The editor has asserted her moral right under the Copyright, Designs and Patents Act, 1988, to be identified as the editor of this work.

Published by
Ashgate Publishing Limited
Gower House
Croft Road
Aldershot
Hampshire GU11 3HR
England

Ashgate Publishing Company
Suite 420
101 Cherry Street
Burlington, VT 05401-4405
USA

Ashgate website: http://www.ashgate.com

British Library Cataloguing in Publication Data
Righter, William
　American memory in Henry James: Void and Value 1. James, Henry, 1843–1916 – Criticism and interpretation 2. History in literature 3. America – in literature I. Title
　II. Righter, Rosemary 813.4

Library of Congress Cataloging-in-Publication Data
Righter, William,
　American memory in Henry James: Void and Value / William Righter; edited by
　Rosemary Righter
　　　p. cm.
　Includes bibliographical references.
　ISBN 0-7546-3674-7 (alk. paper)
　　1. James, Henry, 1843–1916 – Knowledge – History. 2. James, Henry, 1843–1916 – Knowledge – History – United States. 3. National characteristics, American, in literature. 4. Literature and history – United States. 5. United States – in literature. 6. History in literature. 7. Memory in literature. I. Righter, Rosemary. II. Title

PS2127.H5R54 2003
813′.4–dc21
　　　　　　　　　　　　　　　　　　　　　　　　　　2003045332

ISBN 0 7546 3674 7

Typeset by MHL Production Services Ltd, Cov
Printed and bound in Great Britain by MPG Bo

BATH SPA UNIVERSITY
COLLEGE
NEWTON PARK LIBRARY
Class No.
813.4 JAM R
Phil Dutch 13 MAY 2005

Contents

List of Illustrations   vii
Author's note   ix
Acknowledgements, in Memoriam, by Rosemary Righter   xi

Part One: America Deconstructed

1 The Jamesian Perspective   5
2 The Composite Light   9
3 America and the Pathos of Desire   22
   Notes to Part One   44

Part Two: The Note of Europe

4 An Encounter in Nôtre Dame   49
5 'There to Reconstruct'   56
6 The Comedy of Moral Terms   64
7 Strether's Reasons   72
8 Values in Collision   79
9 Nihilism and Decorum   86
   Notes to Part Two   94

Part Three: Amerigo in an American Nowhere

10 Characters in a Void   99
11 The Shaping of the Prince   104
12 Anomalies of Place and Time   112
   Notes to Part Three   120

Part Four: A Dark Fable of Love and Power

13 The Perilous Equilibrium   125
14 The Triumph of the Will   136
15 A Map of Incommensurability   144

16 Fictive Resolutions   158
    Notes to Part Four   163

Part Five: Form and Contingency

17 From Portland Place to American City   169
18 In the Museum   179
19 The Elusive Synthesis   193
20 Coda: The 'Complex Fate'   207
    Notes to Part Five   212

Bibliography   214
Index   216

Author's Note

In my own country I haunt museums. It is not that the great museums of the Old World contain objects of less importance or allure. But in the New their meaning is transformed. Their relation to the surrounding culture acquires an urgency which is linked to detachment. So in New York, Chicago or Washington the great museums have a character quite different from the Louvre or the Uffizi, for rather than representing a continuous tradition through the masterpieces which embody it those works are an alien presence. The museums bring the fragments, icons, the surplus value of other worlds to a new form of creation, a strange mixture of quickening and withdrawal which that assembly offers to a place that is not its own. They oppose rather than underwrite, confront rather than confirm. The moments passed in them are committed to an unspoken discontinuity. And for me the great galleries of America become the compelling point of reference and refuge, above all in my own birthplace, in Kansas City, where the Nelson Gallery, marvellous in its absurd eclecticism, rises like a marble island from the sprawl.

Such islands have their magic, but it is ambiguous. The enterprise of implanting the beautiful and the edifying may intend a cultural transformation. But one's overwhelming impression is of something apart and hence an implication of conflict, a conflict surely not envisaged by those who conceive the movement of civilization as an unbroken progression, a steady advance of something like Arnold's sweetness and light. If a version of this latter gleams for Lambert Strether on the banks of the Seine, it is the vision of its transplantation, of creating a new world of culture in the vast spaces beyond the Hudson which hovers in the background of *The Golden Bowl*, spaces in which culture's mission mingles with the darkness of exile. That mixture of darkness and light, seldom in a controlled *chiaroscuro*, but in hidden implications, disturbing vistas, moments of discovery and of loss – even of terror – fills those late works of Henry James that attempt, however unevenly, a final assessment of an America which does not reflect the world of his youth but alien forces reaching to an unknown future. 'One discovers Europe to know America' said F.O. Matthiessen, in a replay of a saying of Emerson. But what

America? One perhaps whose opacity grows for the sequence of discoverers whose most reflective representative is Lambert Strether. It will of course include James himself, for it is above all *The American Scene* which gives 'the restless analyst' his own voice.

If the relation of culture to the new America escapes both artistic and intellectual resolution, it remains the focus of James's final years, where his creative powers had both their greatest triumphs and their breaking point.

William Righter

Acknowledgements, *in Memoriam*

When cancer was diagnosed, my husband William Righter was in one of the most creative phases of his life. He had completed the first, manuscript, draft of this book and revised one section, Part II. He was also working on two further books – a further exploration of James's sense of history, and *Culture and Entropy*, which would have been his riposte to Matthew Arnold and an anatomy of what constitutes culture at the dawn of the twenty-first century. It may have been the rigours of therapy that caused him to cease work on the present text, but I think it was more that, knowing better than he would admit how fast the hands on his life's clock were now whirring towards midnight, he was determined to use what time remained on the other volumes. Before he died, only nine months later, I promised him that I would bring this book to completion. I am keenly aware how much he would have polished, as he always did at the revising stage. My own editing has been of the lightest; the greatest challenge was in interpreting the elegant but always almost indecipherable flow of his thick-nibbed fountain pen across the pages.

I have had unstintingly generous help in this labour of love. I owe a particular debt to Martin Warner, my husband's close colleague and friend at the philosophy department of Warwick University, who has kept steady watch over the project, solved puzzles that had eluded me and given invaluable guidance on structure. In Cambridge, Robert Lord gave early typescript versions the most meticulous and learned reading, and sat down with me to work out a reordering of some chapters and sections. From Princeton, Michael Wood gave enthusiastic encouragement and advice. To them, as indeed also to my colleagues at *The Times* who helped to sustain me in the abyss of loss, I am supremely grateful. The result is perhaps inevitably a half-hewn representation of the workings of a mind that bridged the Atlantic as few have, and that was too subtly *imprévisible* for an attempt to smooth out any rough edges to be other than an intellectual impertinence. But the insights in this text are, I think and hope, sufficiently rewarding for the reader to accept and to excuse any unavoidable element of the provisional.

Rosemary Righter

PART ONE

America Deconstructed

1. The Jamesian Perspective
2. The Composite Light
3. America and the Pathos of Desire

*Crowded Life on Mulberry Street, on New York's Lower East Side,
ca* 1900. © Bettmann/CORBIS

..ORI, DETROIT PHOTOGRAPHIC CO.

Chapter 1

The Jamesian Perspective[1]

James's concept of history was shaped by European culture; but the shaping took a number of stages. These move from the construction of Europe, to the recollection of America; then to the reconstruction of Europe in terms of America, and thus finally to the reconstruction of America, in terms of a Europe seen by way of America.

What we see at the end of his life is almost a fading of Europe, in a transformation of the international theme that had its most celebrated début in *The Portrait of a Lady*. His final phase moves from the quest for an intelligible past, to an evaluation that asks how the age of brass came about, and what to make of the post-Wharton America of the cultural pirates.

This is an intellectual journey that traces a complementary narrative to that of Henry Adams and the construction of the past in terms of general laws. There are two different versions of history in play, those of process (progress) and of residue (civilization). The landscape – and the relation between these concepts – shifts. James's early concern with culture and its mixture of attractions and dangers is absorbed into his ultimate struggle with the vertigo of process. It is as wrong as it is common therefore to see James as the novelist of the historiography of continuity; closer to his enterprise is the historiography of difference. What might be called the 'post-vulgar James' – the James that speaks, moreover, to us most eloquently – is concerned with an attempt to relate continuity to process.

James began in New England and the 'native tradition' of speculation that was a grafting of European idealism onto the traditions of the Puritan ministry. Eliot has largely the same inheritance. To an extent, this replaces the Enlightenment outlook of the founding fathers – who in any case were not predominantly New Englanders. It involves unitarianism and other forms of eclecticism, yet it can be seen as a tradition of a sort, which fuses a certain moral severity with a foggy sense of uplift. And it carries with it the sense of a more immediate continuity, from Emerson and his circle to the Harvard of 1890–1910. Parochial as this mixture of elements may be, it makes an identifiable ground, where this idealistic intellectual tradition was allied to a sense of community.

James's work spanning the turn of the century reflects the break-up of this tradition, the disappearance of an old order – a theme of course writ large in

5

Adams as well. There are affinities here with Santayana's 'genteel tradition'. And James's terror of a mindless and commercial outlook without a viable tradition, of a falling apart of form for which no prodigies of energy can compensate, is the underlying drama in *The American Scene* – his interpretation of the 'new' America he revisited in 1904, after a lapse of nearly a quarter of a century that gave him, he wrote, 'much of the freshness of eye' of 'an enquiring stranger'. The enquiry as to what can replace the old order is hardly launched there. But the awareness of the problem is pervasive. And the answer, insofar as there is one, does not lie in the past but in the sense of the past. By cultivating our memory, by seeing ourselves as part of a continuity rather than a moment, we avoid a philistine assimilation to that moment. We do not of course return to the past but, in the present, become another self through understanding and memory.

The difficulty is imagining a form that this can take. For James, this is probably what prevented the development of *The Sense of the Past*; he would have had to imagine a form of American life to which the young protagonist, once possessed of his past, could return. James's aim is to turn the moment, the fact of process, into a form of intelligible continuity. This is the opposite of Adams, who wishes to place continuity in process. The Adams version of process (the dynamo) devours the continuity: History is absorbed into its active principle. For James, there is no such escape.

His view of history has been shaped by the European vision of culture which informs his perspective on the bustle of late nineteenth-century America, in love with modernity, rapidly reinventing itself right down to the touchstones of its identity and shot through with ambiguities about the past. In his novels, the process of this shaping can be watched. There is the first great celebration of the romance and seductive force of European culture, in *The Portrait of a Lady*. There is then almost a fading of Europe, as he joins it; and the vision of America becomes more powerful.

The distancing has its power, opening up questions about memory, history, the present – questions about what Europe and America, the first with culture and the second with wealth and power, have in common – and about what they *cannot* have in common because their historical contexts and cultural antennae are so profoundly different. By the time he comes to *The Ambassadors*, it is with the comedies of aesthetic and moral conflict that he is concerned, with what Isaiah Berlin was to call the 'collisions of forms of life'. And throughout *The Golden Bowl*, the most concentratedly 'comparatist' of his novels even if implicitly so, runs the dramatic thread of the emptying out of the content of European civilization, into the Museum in American City which will be the dehistoricizing of culture. At work is a commitment to history as immediacy and action, not unreminiscent of *The Magic Mountain*; the move is from residue or product, to process.

And so he returns to what might be meant by an American historical sense. He finds it built of anecdotes, selections and reinventions, of failures of continuity, where tradition is a question of reincarnation, to create a meta-sense of recollection. There is something akin to the Byzantine vice of historiography at work, an obsession with the predominantly exemplary. All history becomes allegory, and fact a form of escape.

This is where the Jamesian novel, his 'prodigious form', faces its last and ultimately unsurmounted challenge. James oscillates between the notion of memory as a personal thing which places the individual in his perceived world, and a more generalized sense of the past that requires awareness of cultural depth. There is an implicit polemic between the disappearance of the sense of history and, in *The Sense of the Past*, its fantastical re-evocation in a physical journey into the past – a past, and a sense of history, that proves impossible to represent.

To what extent does the late Jamesian sense of loss of context, of the half-articulated crisis with its conversion of historical sense into things and place, talismanic objects, represent a retreat from a possible sense of history? And how far do the implications of the Jamesian dilemma stretch forward? The crisis delineated in *The American Scene* has dual components: the break-up of the 'native tradition'; and the emergence of modernism, seen as a serious social engagement that is inextricably bound up with the emergence of an 'outsider's culture'.

His modern America comprises two main elements. There is what we would now call wasp culture, an etiolated form of the old where culture is veneer, a suitable and decorative surface, the small change of 'the genteel tradition'. Then there is the alienated urban – largely Jewish – culture. This is the one that takes substantive matters seriously, from the Jewish cafés in *The American Scene*, redolent of 'the various possibilities of the waiting spring of intelligence' (p. 138[2]), to the *Partisan Review*. And there is a speed of assimilation which James notes in *The American Scene*. In the 'alien' newcomers to America, he pinpoints two things: the annihilation of memory in becoming American – although this is in some ways illusory; and the challenge, in the face of the huge diversity of this great migration, to the intelligibility of the concept of being 'American'.

Does the new America lie beyond clear conceptualization? He sifts this problem of identity with 'the impression of History all yet to be made' (p. 462), where the speed of metamorphosis undermines and qualifies description and identification. The universities are to emerge as receptacles for this mixture, an uneasy equilibrium of two cultural models. And this problem of synthesis

approaches the great question of American experience. What is to be made of
the implicit polemic? Can an intelligible order be imposed? For James, the
American experience is too much the falling apart of form. Its muse is tragic;
prodigy is not enough.

In a way the 'native tradition' understood its European origins, even when
defining its own departures. Does the internal reference of recent thinking
attempt a more self-enclosed tradition? Or does it, rather, adapt a European and
traditional conservatism to an American cultural context – and language? For
the paradoxical problem of 'inventing a tradition' produces a powerful urge to
assimilate the world – to make an all-embracing eclecticism into a principle. For
James, the gradual transformation in his own historical sense reflects personal
displacement and the loss of feeling for the kind of intellectual community that
is possible in America. James has shifted between the kind of representation that
is 'about' America, and the literary response. The journey that became *The
American Scene* was a crisis point, one that marks for him, as novelist, the need
to move beyond allegory, beyond the real or even the displacement of the real
into reconstruction – through narrative as pure creation. His final work is a
conscious putting-together – of an order beyond allegory.

Yet he is either too fatalistic, or too fastidious, to force this upon us. In both of
James's late masterpieces on this theme, *The Ambassadors* and *The Golden
Bowl*, the doubleness of conclusion is achieved through an extraordinary
tension between theme and form. At journey's end we have the conjunction of
opposites which we can read as alternative modes of interpretation. What he
draws together are the factors that might shape some necessary sense of
consequence. The economy of that shaping becomes in James the 'charm' –
particularly if we understand that with James, economy is the opposite of
simplicity and that what is claimed for form is not the arbitrary imposition of
order, but the most appropriate version of working out.

It may also suggest that, as the limits are pushed, the usual words which
convey the character of drama and form begin to fail, that at some point they
have run their course and are no longer useful. *The Ambassadors* ends not so
much in a contradiction as in the realization that the great social comedy is
played out, and that the final perspective cannot be usefully classified.

The 'intelligible continuity' can be taken far, at a personal level; as far as
construction and hypothesis can lead, but not so far as a synthesis of what
may not be compatible. With James, the conjunction of opposites in this
most prodigious of literary forms represents less a collision course, than the
coexistence which only the prodigious could accommodate; for only that
can contain the necessary scope of our delicious and bitter lives.

Chapter 2

The Composite Light

In James's autobiography the element of memory is of course primary. At moments James feels that it is all too much: 'I confess myself embarrassed by my very ease of re-capture of my young consciousness; so that I perforce try to encourage lapses and keep my abundance down' (*Autobiography*, p. 156). For the other texts it is more an interpretative frame. What I shall want to distinguish is the relation of this immediacy of personal memory to its cultural sense, to see it as part of the Jamesian pattern of understanding.

One can see all the present because one has known the past – the startling alien chatterers encountered on Boston Common in *The American Scene* have their far-reaching effect because of the extraordinary shock to expectations, to the awareness of what some continuity might have given to a Boston that had created a future out of its own past, rather than housing an all too improbable present. The accents of these 'new Americans', hardly recognized by the polyglot James, were the intrusion of the unexpected truth which the whole of that late American journey was to bear out: the America of his youth was transformed not only in degree but in kind. And so through memory, in places re-encountered after an absence of decades, the most banal observation takes on its power.

Part of this power comes from the almost invisible chain of implied comparison. For if memory is a basis, a point of departure, it becomes the counterpoint to the vast social transformation that James conveyed in the sequence of shocks and discontinuities to which memory gave a second order. Yet, in order to reach America, the construction of Europe is a necessary condition. And it is important that the early memories are as much of Europe as of America.

The extraordinary zigzag path of the James family, between America and Europe and from one European country to another, meant a past formed of continuous contrast, out of which any sense of the whole was to require the constant reabsorption of discontinuity. But the effect of the memory bank is the authenticity of a recollection that is neither American nor European, but which moves easily between the two. Moments of powerful impressions, both in terms of immediate sensation, and in the awareness of their personal importance, may arise beside Lake Geneva, in walks by the sea at Newport, or in the stroll up the rue de Tournon to the Luxembourg – a path that will be later, in *The*

Ambassadors, followed by Lambert Strether. And the early recollections of Paris, taken with his tutor to the Louvre, are the basis of that extraordinary dream of terror and of glory which returned to him in his later years. In the Galerie d'Apollon or before Couture's famous painting of the decadence of Ancient Rome, a vision of imperial grandeur and of its perils created an historical awareness that remained an imaginative factor throughout James's life, creating a sense of the past that was based on the immediacy of the European experiences.

Hence a point of departure quite unlike that of Henry Adams, who posits the beginning of natural awareness in the Adams family, their involvement with the public affairs of first colony, then republic. Adams is 'located' in a sense that James could not be. In place of an overpowering family past with its historical greatness and local depth, for James there was a sequence of fragments, calling for interpretation and construction. And this process was lifelong. Of course the James who reflected on his own experience was not the James who experienced. The authenticity of those experiences is modified by memory – and memory implies necessarily a double perspective. With James this is complicated by the variable sources of memory itself. Without the centring of his being on a particular sense of situation, but in the presence of the dazzling fragments of the multiple sources of impression, the most primitive memories involve the elements of difference – marked in its spatial as well as temporal form.

When a reflective process began to play upon this, in his early literary experiments in the late 1860s and in his first adult visit to Europe in 1869, the elements of comparison were already in play. What followed was a complex process of re-framing, replacing, of continual interpretation, which would extend until the final dictation in the year of his death. I shall try, not to describe this in a comprehensive way, which would be the task of a large-scale work on these threads alone, but to suggest two forms through which this process can be seen. One will lie in the conceptual coordinates through which it might take place. What was there that made the essential set of stages in this reflective journey work as they did? How did interpretations work through the set of implied questions that such a life had begun to pose? The second will refer to the reflection of that process in the works themselves, in their effective form of representation. The former is hypothetical, while the latter, an indication of the stages in such a process in the novels, will be necessarily extremely selective. But what matters is simply the indications of the way in which Jamesian reflection worked.

The mature curiosity began with a construction of Europe that was of course a reconstruction. But the impressions themselves were new. His interpretation arose from the double comparison of the present moment with his American, and European, pasts. And of course there is a reflexive element present in the form of the continuous criss-crossing of his frames of reference. The first person he encounters in London is Charles Eliot Norton, who led to William Morris and to Ruskin. The imaginative picture arising from Gothic structures, grass and gardens and dreaming spires is punctuated by connections made in Boston, such as Leslie Stephen. The London impressions of 1869, the only fragment of *The Middle Years*, are emphatic about the force of the impact: 'This doom of inordinate exposure to appearances, aspects, images, every protrusive item almost, in the great beheld sum of things' (*ibid.*, p. 549). This, whether it is the arrangement of a buttered muffin, or 'the damp and darksome light washed in from the steep, black, bricky street' or the firmly grasped synoptic vision:

> The unaccommodating and unaccommodated city remains none the less closely consecrated to one's fondest notion of her – the city too indifferent, too proud, too unaware, too stupid even if one will, to enter any lists that involved her moving from her base and that thereby, when one approached her from the alien *positive* places (I don't speak of the American, in those days too negative to be related at all) enjoyed the enormous 'pull,' for making her impression, of ignoring everything but her own perversities and then of driving these home with an emphasis not to be gainsaid. Since she didn't emulate, as I have termed it, so she practised her own arts altogether, and both these ways and these consequences were in the flattest opposition (*that* was the happy point!) to foreign felicities or foreign standards ... *Her* idiosyncrasy was never in the least to have been inferred or presumed; it could only, in general, make the outsider provisionally gape. (*ibid.*, p. 557)

The direct comparison suggests a construction of England – or in this case London – by way of an American absence. Just as a visual response to Rome, later in the same visit, is the dramatic celebration of a physical response which would be impossible in the circumstances of American life: 'At last – for the time – I live' he wrote to his brother William. 'It beats everything; it leaves the Rome of your fancy – your education – nowhere.' (Edel, 1985, p. 102) The impression is formed like Hume's building blocks. But what the impression marks is the world in which those impressions do not exist.

If there are American impressions, at least at this stage, they are scattered and diffuse. Between the year of this journey and the return to a more extended residence in Europe, James spent two years with his family in Cambridge, Massachusetts. These follow the death of Minnie Temple which at the close of *Notes of a Son and Brother* he marks as the end of 'our youth', both for him and William. Her death is anticipated in the narrative and placed before the beginning of *The Middle Years*, and that manuscript does not reach the Cambridge intellects.

His biographer Leon Edel makes much of this period, certainly rightly so. James's attitude to America was clearly marked by the European stay of 1869–70. As the awareness of his 'gains' from the year in Europe began to fade his sense of alienation within America, which he described closing '*bunchily* over them as flesh over a bullet', became a clear feature of his life (*ibid.*, pp. 118–119). Much that Edel draws upon is retrospective, but there is no reason to doubt the assessment. The moral requirement of 'knowing America' was based on a growing knowledge of Europe, and the American travel sketches became part of the justification of the subsequent European stay.

Reviewing for the *Nation* Hawthorne's stay in France and Italy early in 1872, he notes the absence in his understanding of 'that composite historic light which forms the atmosphere of many imaginations ... We seem to see him strolling through churches and galleries as the last pure American – attesting by his shy responses to canvas and cold marble his loyalty to a simpler and less encumbered civilization.' (*ibid.*, p. 121)

To composite light, nothing is ever pure. Although the fantasy of 'the last pure American' fails to anticipate the subsequent forms of American innocence. And in Lambert Strether he would invent the last vehicle of a conflict between 'composite light' and what is, if not purity, a self-denying integrity which is the Puritan inheritance. There will of course never be 'the last Puritan' or 'the last innocent' but one may wonder if the Jamesian 'composite light' is not a more special and contingent product of time. For the steps in that composition can go wildly awry, and one catches James carefully setting up an American awareness as perhaps a sop to conscience, but also as a foil. The European experience required a certain, but not excessive, American counterpart – which in turn called into being a further element of the composition.

However conscious a dialectic this may have been it responded to a variety of presences and needs, some of them no doubt based on the local and familial circumstances one might expect. But others more importantly lie in an imaginative structuring by which American awareness was a product of European experience, with the understanding of both conditioned by each other. The travel sketches seem rather insubstantial in themselves. But they create an angle from which the eye can operate – both to perceive, but also to create the ground of further observation. It is the ground from which the 'international theme' will quite naturally arise. And that will, in one sense, require a Europe that is made in America. For it will require understanding to create the misunderstandings on which doubtful commitments and false expectations may rest.

This reciprocal process, where the perspective changes have a relational model, is open to unlimited extensions. James at this crucial early time was beginning to find, in the simplest setting out of difference, the basis of an inexhaustible series of variants – not simply on a limited number of thematic lines, but on the nuances of cultural imprint which open their way to the endless modifications which desire and expectation can produce. But the rich consequences were far in the future.

The primitive realization that one place could supply the perspective for interpreting another set up a reflexive model, for the analysis of place and character certainly, but also for the interpretation of the past. One has of course the European sense of the depth of the past, and the mixture of freshness and volatility of the American cultural reaches. Also what is conveyed with respect to Hawthorne as 'pure'. There is a strange and unworldly distinction in figures like Emerson that belong in the remoter sort of backwater, yet retain their perfect apartness in the greater world. There is a moment of watching Emerson, in a joint visit to the Louvre in 1872, when his grandeur consists in having nothing to say (*ibid.*, pp. 135–136). Though perhaps the purity is preserved by the very absence of utterance.

The problems of the consequences of 'composite light' work through the travel sketches of this period. And a slightly later essay, 'Occasional Paris', in which the principles of comparison are sketched with a relatively light-hearted touch, nevertheless implies a substantial reflection on the 'cosmopolite'.[3] The best thing to be is a rooted – 'concentrated' – patriot, perhaps a sentiment he feels his readers will expect from him, or which depresses the natural suspicion they might have of the cosmopolitan stance. James is immensely skilful at showing the cosmopolitan vision as something of a fatality, the inevitable product of having 'lived about', of having reached the point 'when one set of customs, wherever it may be found, grows to seem to you about as provincial as another'. The reader is carefully protected from the imputation that he is any more of a dim backwoodsman than anyone else, and the cosmopolite, far from an ideal, is simply the result of having comparisons forced upon him so that he sees everything in relation to everything else. 'You have formed the habit of comparing, of looking for points of difference and resemblance.' This is done with an easy natural touch. Go somewhere else and we all compare, generalize, have attachments and revulsions, form opinions – often on the slightest ground. But a little reflection leads further. A moment comes when you see all circumstances in a comparative light and see yourself, your own country, as you see others. And the effect is a breadth of view: 'the consequence of the cosmopolite spirit is to initiate you into the merits of all peoples'.

This has an amiable and up-beat quality which is deceptive as to its implications. The comparative mentality is irreversible, and your perspective will become ineluctably relational. And the imaginative process, through the exposure to place and the immediate sensations of the other, is by an easy change of focus extended to time itself. We cannot directly experience the past, as an immediate impression. But we can do so through memory, indirect evidence. The projective process through which we move back and forth in terms of our own experiences and expectations is equally natural to us. Evocations of the past with golden-age beauties or dark-age horrors come quite as easily to the less literate and untravelled, although simplified by the bounds of knowledge and imagination. And these two simple movements of mind, the one the easy-come product of travel, the other the most casual evocation of a remembered past, continue in James to provide immense analytic power.

One effect of these movements of mind is to project a version of the past, of his total cultural inheritance, to which one can relate in an intelligible way. He discovers Europe through the power of the immediate impression, but he interprets this impression through a recognition of distance, both in the qualification that an American perspective involves and in the further dimension of historical time. Indeed, the awareness of distance is part of the impression. This pushes James towards a view of the past in terms of its collected artefacts and residue, towards what Nietzsche called 'monumental' history – history in terms of sites and exemplarity. These may turn culture into a collection of aesthetic traps or moral injunctions, for they turn the mind away from causality and process towards the result of that process – to the value implicit in the cultural endproduct.

This is of course subject to a further valuation. How are we to take the impressions of Lambert Strether? Some of them seem amiably harmless, but the grand scene in Nôtre Dame evokes the serious spiritual quality of the past. Are we, on the other hand, to take Chad Newsome's 'eye', his aesthetic education, as a genuine accomplishment or as the smoothing of a social surface? Isabel Archer, for all her intelligence and discrimination, is taken in by a rather superficial version of culture, one which is shown at the end of *Portrait of a Lady* as the veneer on a cold and manipulative world. Filtering the observation of the cultural conquests of the past through further observers and users has produced another set of variables. The romance of culture has many relations to the projected monumental. And a pervasive irony may season the aspiration or the nostalgia.

But this very contemplation of the monumental shows a profound difference from Henry Adams – not that *Mont St. Michel and Chartres* is lacking in monumental reverence. But Adams's interest lies in cause, process and in the grand laws that govern them. What totality of conditions created the medieval unity? and what sequence of transformations the depth? This sort of question is quite alien to James. Cultural depth, the sense of the past, are the objects of personal quest. One searches out the connections, but might also probe the discontinuities.

So construction does not lead to a fixed pattern either of cultural relativism or of the continuities which would bridge the cultural and historical gaps. The young James, most vividly in the early 1870s, may have saturated himself in the phenomena that Europe had to offer him with an eagerness and excitability that can almost touch the comic: museums, castles, galleries, atmospheric corners, physical appearances of both places and persons, rooms, houses, social circles, literary presences, above all the presence of the literary great. Especially the simple exposure to George Eliot and Tennyson. But a moment with Frederick Harrison 'beside Mrs Charles Norton's tea-room' gives an idea of the breathless shock: or at least a phenomenology of a complex perception:

> Has any gilding ray since that happy season rested here and there with the sovereign charm of interest, of drollery, of felicity and infelicity taken on by scattered selected objects in that writer's bright critical dawn? – an element in which we had the sense of sitting gratefully bathed, so that we fairly took out our young minds and dabbled and soaked them in it as we were to do again in no other. The beauty was thus at such a rate that ... one seemed likely to perceive figures here and there, whether animate or not, quite groan under the accumulation and the weight .... One had scarcely met it before – that I now understood. (*Autobiography*, pp. 562–563)

And standing by Titian's 'Bacchus and Ariadne' in the National Gallery he is startled, indeed 'thrilled' to find Swinburne standing beside him. But it is not the simple delight in the presence of celebrity. It is the recognition that, in admiring Titian as the poet admires him, he somehow shares in the mental process, identifies himself with the poet, finds Titian the common ground of a changing inner condition.

It is always the presence of the concrete, whether object or person, that gives that mental jolt, that momentary or lasting shifting of ground which prevents a diffuse and entropic assimilation. It will resist Nietzsche's vision of the conventional pattern by which culture is smoothed out to end in losing its vitality: 'we modern men race through art galleries and listen to concerts. We feel that one thing sounds different from another, that one thing produces a different effect from another: increasingly to lose this sense of strangeness, no longer to be very much surprised at anything, finally to be pleased with everything – that is then no doubt called the historical sense, historical culture.' (Nietzsche, *Untimely Meditations*, p. 98) The Jamesian perception is based on a certain resistance to accumulation, a respect for the difference which cultural identity implies. Only in the incarnation of the Museum is the levelling effect to be found. *The Golden Bowl* places this project in curious inverted commas, holding the grandiose cultural transposition in a cold and ironic light.

Perhaps too there is in James's life, seen as a whole, a shift from the discovery of Europe to a gradual accommodation, for which the return to America that produced *The American Scene* provided the mixed shock of the old and the new. And certainly the literary investigation of a European world continues to bring him closer to it, to the point that a distinctively American perspective seems to show an ease and familiarity which steps out of that special degree of 'otherness' which some have seen as distinguishing American literature itself. The great novels of his last phase have lost none of that perspective, though they have largely complicated it. The effect of James's irony is to draw multiple perspectives together without their oppositions cancelling each other in any way. It is a layering of awareness that does not blur the totality of effect.

This oscillation between interpretative frames and the original European attachment, projected upon the totality of James's work, inhibits any approach to the problem of the 'American' James – even if we value Matthiessen's 'major phase' and regard the critical views of Van Wyck Brooks as simply missing the point in the attempt to assimilate a highly individual achievement to a general model of a cultural development. Not to be part of the distinct 'otherness' of the American experience was to make an implicit betrayal. But that 'otherness' too is a construction. And one must remember James's exemplary good sense in believing that one must write about what one knows. Hence the advice to Edith Wharton to write about New York. The aim, of course, is not a weary mimeticism but a respect for the artist's necessary knowledge.

For him, knowledge required a new basis, a repositioning that gave a new vantage point, an intellectual and artistic podium from which further investigation could proceed. And it followed not from a rejection of one's own country and one's private past but from a realization, as personal conviction, that only through that alternative can the values that compose one's original life be put to the tests that reveal their interest. It is quite the contrary of the Nietzschean desire to break with one's past, to shed it so as not to be a prisoner of it – 'to confront our inherited and hereditary nature with our knowledge of it, and through a new, stern discipline combat our inborn heritage and implant in ourselves a new habit, a new instinct, a second nature, so that our first nature withers away ... to give oneself, as it were *a posteriori*, a past in which one would like to originate' (*ibid.,* p. 76).

Of course it is clear that James was driven by a positive sense of affinity. A primary desire and the excitement surrounding it are vividly manifest in everything that refers to the experience of the European stays in the early 1870s. But rather than shedding his past he created an alluring complement.

The integral presence of his American origin undergoes its own metamorphosis. From the construction of a European alternative, the mind doubles back to the reconstruction of America in terms of a Europe which has been more and more fully internalized. The internalization marks the process by which both culture and character are observed to grow in complexity. And it is precisely in the relational observation which these forms of 'aspect seeing' make possible that James finds his true subject matter. Of course its evolution takes him far from the enthusiasm of the 1870s. And if *The Golden Bowl* shows this internalization to the point that the actual presence of Europe has disappeared, so that the Prince's old-world paraphernalia is a mere hypothesis and the English foreground is the sketchiest of formalities, the value is still there and it is an absolute value. James has not yet taken his excursion to American City – it is a few months away – but there is a clear vision of its terrors. For it represents an America which is untouchable by the accommodations of memory, but is a strange beast in a jungle which is projected from indirect knowledge, an irredeemable transformation of the America which once belonged to the private sphere of personal feeling and observation – where the formation was clearly represented by memory.

The vast intellectual distance travelled in the years covered by the development of James's major works may have seemed to him to promise a large-scale cultural rapprochement, mediated through those civilized Americans whose talents and interests attuned them to a wider culture. Or he may have simply watched with ironic delight the nuances of difference, while accepting that the Nortons were with one always, and those who attained the advantage of the 'composite light' would always be a rather special minority. Or perhaps he saw his interpretative role as something unique, even if circumstances had made it possible, and those circumstances were indeed open to others, with whom the double vision could be shared.

There were of course two parts. The European part with its depth, its multiple layers of resonance, its translation into the rich diffusion of cultural objects which gave pleasure to the eye. The other in its simplicity and directness, in its appeal to the immediate conquest of a natural world which may be an undependable veneer. And both of them appealed to a memory bank. But the distinction between the culture-laden and the natural immediacy is not a direct Rousseau-esque contrast between nature and culture. The directness with which the natural world was to be felt in America was rapidly translated into human response.

The attempt to transpose, to absorb and utilize European culture would be the natural form of a relation. But it would become a form that altered the nature of the substance. In its translation to America the European past would become another, it would become that abstract thing 'culture', would be historicized, turned into the fodder of the universities, and its physical manifestations into the content of museums. James would live to see the beginning of this process, but not to realize its scope. The European past would become, in this transformation, a curious sort of timeless present. The American present would thus absorb that past, but qualify its force, and turn it into the tribute that culture invariably pays to wealth and power.

Perhaps this process in James can be represented as three phases. The first is a period of discovery and assessment, a gradual undertaking to enter into the cultural milieux of Europe in terms of language, styles, social modalities, artistic accomplishments, works of art, and the atmospheric surroundings that convince one of the distinctive quality of experience, of its depth, of its many possibilities, of its richness. James records the directness of this experience more in letters, conversations and his travel writings although those values have a fragmentary presence in the earlier fictions and their retrospective glory in *The Ambassadors*.

A second phase involves the complex equilibrium of the 'middle years' when the interest lies in balancing the authenticity and innocence of America with the dangers they imply, with the misfit of expectation, the corruption that the arid and superficial use of an older culture may produce. What rapport can the American consciousness find with a past that both is and is not its own? What will the effect of discovery be? Is the problem of interpretation one that lends itself to self-deception? This is balanced by a number of tales in which the experience of Europe is curiously evoked by the sense of its aftermath. These tales, largely from a later period, show the importance of the European experience, but without it being seriously represented. In 'Europe', 'Crapy Cornelia', 'The Jolly Corner' and more importantly in *The Ivory Tower* the absence in Europe provides no sense of a cultural depth, of the historical affinities that the past can offer, but is merely an escape from, or an interlude in, an American destiny which impoverishes or threatens.

These tales point to a final phase in which the European past has remained a constant but with familiarity has become invisible. There is the continuing American heiress figure, Millie Theale in *The Wings of the Dove* and Maggie Verver, but we are far from the self-consciousness of discovery, and the connection with the 'international theme' is no more than circumstantial. Only Strether conveys a synoptic view that unites the three phases I have suggested through the mixture of experience and memory, by which each comparison becomes a form of re-experience.

If at no particular point has the middle phase of such a movement suggested the outlines of a synthesis, it is perhaps partly because the very notion of such a synthesis would suggest a general conceptual overview somewhat alien to James – whose notebooks show a continuous reinvention in terms of immediate situations, personal relationships, points of enquiry and of conflict, even in the genesis of the larger fictions. After all, what is the beginning of fiction if not in conflict, desire, disequilibrium, misapprehension, false expectations and other forms of difference? Where the temptation to larger connections might reasonably appear, it is avoided. And if *The Ambassadors* raises the principle of comparison in such an overview it is to assert the necessary failure of synthesis. The two worlds of one's experience may touch, but the necessity of choice will ultimately require that the composite vision is not the basis of the eclectic and composite self.

In a personal sense however, James was surrounded by evidence of the opposite. His life was rich in figures who appeared with equal ease on both sides of the Atlantic, whose presence was as natural in Sussex as in Cape Cod, Newport or Geneva, in Boston as in Venice. And his large friendship included numerous transatlantic marriages. European society, with some qualifications in France, found an acceptable presence in the class of American known to James and represented by his characters. If there were limits to such an integration they were not such as to alienate the American sensibility that saw in Europe a natural and responsive setting to a life. Whether or not such a life was limited to its social forms, and found in cultural riches mere décor, was a matter of individual commitment which might be worthy of a novelist's observation. In the problematic of such involvement there are many testing grounds. But the inner rewards that are promised have a different status from the quotidian and social.

While it has its most vivid realization in Gloriani's Paris garden, Europe as quest, with its magical and transforming power, becomes a form of myth whose realistic representation is almost forbidden in its evocation. One can point to it and see it from afar like Pilgrim's city on a hill. One can point, can detail aspects of aspiration, but the consummation resists its spelling out. And in any case it is the lure, the struggle, the deception, the sacrifice that make the stuff of the novelist's work. Such a total transformation as the life and work of William Wetmore Story[4] has little to offer to the novelist's enquiring mind. Unless there were conflicts and self-deceptions whose interest took him well beyond the role of Story's ever discreet biographer. Part of the wisdom necessary to the 'composite light' was in knowing the uses of courtesy and hence what to omit.

The alternative, which lies both within and outside the situations of fiction, and is hence another element in the composite, is in the representation of place, or rather in the registering of the psychic space that the feeling for place occupies. Two forms of this abound. One is the large framework of cities themselves, the other is their drawing rooms.

Perhaps London is too close to him and the vast 'unaccommodating city', powerful as its presence is, has a grandeur too diffuse to provide the 'objective correlative' – excepting perhaps *The Princess Casamassima* – or other metonymic factor for the indication of a distinctively personal form of life. And as we shall see in *The Golden Bowl*, that London becomes shadowy to the point of dissolution. Its evocation is less concrete and immediate than the Venice of *The Aspern Papers* or *The Wings of the Dove*, where the curious fusion of physical beauty with hints of corruption, sexuality and the flavour of mortality itself provides a dense integument to frame the inner quality of the action.[5] And of course the Paris of *The Ambassadors* is a driving force, both in the implication of the details of life – sunlight on the *quai* or Mme de Vionnet's drawing room – and in the constant pressure of its evocation. Not necessarily in the slightly comic sighs about 'dear old Paris' but in the active and continuous summons to the meaning of the difference. Here you are in a different world, and are made to know it, characters constantly refer to it as a value, a presence, a fresh point of feeling and understanding: 'Don't you like it here?' asks Little Bilham as if Strether were called to make a judgment, take a side which the city defined for him, to use civilization's 'either/or'. But of course this is the most explicit case, and James's *summum* of the nature and working of impression, as it is of the two cultures and two pasts.

Within this urban framework lie houses and rooms. The movement within houses, the discovery of what is not merely a fragment of personal past but evokes broader affinities, may yet open up the conflict of values in a way that pushes towards the explicit. The modest rooms of Crapy Cornelia contain for the protagonist the comforting seriousness of the 'serene and sturdy' old New York he has seen vanish, while the 'swaggering' expensive novelties of Mrs Worthington inspire a kind of terror.[6] This is a familiar theme, sometimes explicit to the point of being a touch overdeterminate. But these arrangements reveal the moral and aesthetic qualities of their occupants. Or they can represent an aspect of their conception of themselves: Millie Theale wants her Venetian apartment to express the character of the old city – unlike the vulgar novelty of an hotel. She wishes to find some setting that is a correlative to her conception of herself and an inner state. It is almost as if history is borrowed, and fitted to the measure of a mixture of inner quality and hypothetical need. A need to fix upon a certain dimension of oneself, to produce the inner past. If it were a different story – that is, came out in a different way – the adaptation might have lent itself to some other recreation, rather than to a 'destructive element'.

Here, as for Strether if less elaborately, is the virtual history, the pointing out of possible selves, the suggestion of the connection which is swiftly aborted. Is it possible that only the rare fortunate like Maggie Verver can insert herself into the borrowed past? It is almost Maggie's lack of a reflective sense, a natural serendipity – even if it almost betrays her – that allows her into a paradise from which others are expelled. But here James is concerned with the evanescent nature of a transformation where the triumph and insulation are the product of the silky power of vast wealth. We shall, in any case, see her next year at Newport, and she may even stay with Mrs Wharton at Lenox; winter will take her to St Moritz and to drift on through the world of great houses and grand hotels. The consummation of serendipity is not in a constructed past or engagement with its cultural life, but in the 'floating world' of the international rich. But here is a corner that James does not turn.

This may represent a transformation which he had not quite registered, which generates problems that works subsequent to *The Golden Bowl* endeavoured to formulate. The change lies partly in the alteration he will see in Newport itself. And the travels of the 1870s, while comfortable enough, were not part of the Verver scene and scale. James recognized that a pursuit of the arts, as of the understanding and observation of what the arts have created, requires reasonable affluence and the leisure that goes with it. But his unease with great wealth and the special conditions of life it creates grows with the turn of the century.

I mean American wealth. The dangers of earlier days were the stuffy conversations of the displaced Bostonians and somewhere he remarks that he did not come to – was it Rome, Florence, or Venice – for a succession of Cambridge tea parties. The world of William Wetmore Story was, in spite of the 42 rooms in the Palazzo Barbarini, devoted to a consistently pursued creative effort. In his memoir of Story the elegant evasion and lightly touched irony with respect to Story's work does not mask the provincial earnestness of the great cosmopolitan. And while Edith Wharton's seriousness was never in doubt a certain hurdle was present in her lavish style.

The move from the high-minded New Englanders of his youth gave way to something inviting further explanation. The Story world chose quite consciously an expatriation that contained its contradictions but might also take one back to the aspirations implicit in Hawthorne's *The Marble Fawn*. Somehow the imperceptible leaving of this world meant a further distancing from two versions of the past, however artificial their point of fusion. For James the return to America in 1904, at the age of 61, was seemingly a necessary threshold. A new lens for the composite light required that shift in the kaleidoscope, that experimental basis for a further perspective.

Chapter 3

America and the Pathos of Desire

'When once you have interpreted the ... inordinate *desire for taste*, a desire breaking into a greater number of quaint and candid forms, probably, than have ever been known upon earth ... doesn't the question then become, almost thrillingly, that of the degree to which this pathos of desire may be condemned to remain a mere heartbreak to the historic muse? *Is* that to be, possibly, the American future ...?' Henry James, *The American Scene*, p. 446.

In both *The Ambassadors* and *The Golden Bowl*, the presence of America is powerfully conveyed from its measured distance. Woollett and American City are no less real for being far away, and their presence broods over the action. However distant and shadowy, they are an all-powerful determinant. If they produce the passing shudder, that moment of inspired resistance, of pained recognition, theirs is nevertheless the kingdom and the form of destiny. The Prince and Maggie Verver may escape, but at the cost of being powerless dependents.

There was a certain power in this vagueness, in the awareness of that distant compelling note to which it would perhaps have been dangerous to give a more palpable form. Therefore one cannot confront the immediacy of *The American Scene* without the danger of the vanishing distance, the investment in a foregrounding which works in an unpredictable way on understanding, sensibility, above all on the possibility of the artist's work. Perhaps the intensity of the need for this monumental perspective shift would account for the risk taken on such a grand scale. And whether or not James saw the venture in terms of artistic risk, it is clear that a more densely textured and immediate America was becoming an imaginative necessity. He saw it of course as a project which involved the conscious working out of an investigation and assessment. The imagined book was intended as a 'work of art' whose title could possibly be *The Return of the Novelist*. 'It *describes* really my point of view – the current of observation, feeling etc., that can float me further than any other,' he wrote to his publisher, Colonel George Harvey, in October 1904.[7] 'I'm so very much more of a Novelist than of anything else and am all things as such.' And the consequent artistic task was to be that of representing that flow of observation and of feeling – into a coherent form that gave the American experience some definitive and destructive force.

Yet James seems to eschew form in any obvious sense. *The American Scene* begins at the beginning and follows the course of a journey – although with a rearrangement of its sequence. It seems the most casually ordered travelogue, not far from the recording of a diary. There is no suggestion of a grand design or interpretative key and the work unfolds with a diffidence that may mask its concentration and power. Only gradually and indirectly does one come to any large and general understanding, which may appear unexpectedly and out of the particular circumstance. The diffidence is constantly present and the usual Jamesian reluctance to schematize or to make any comprehensive observations according to anything that resembles a general principle is steadfastly maintained.

And yet it is a book in which a total and coherent vision can be grasped, a more personal and far-reaching analysis of American life than any – with the possible exception of Tocqueville which in so many ways it complements. For if Tocqueville holds the great experiment of American democracy up to the Enlightenment dreams of human perfectibility, for better or for worse, James proceeds from the deeply conservative view of a community and its values, a community which exists largely in memory, in the accomplishments of a generation which has passed or is passing. These values are in a sense quite personal, embodied in the life and work of family and friends. To extract their general character too literally would in some degree falsify their quality. But we shall see an emerging 'scene' in all of the grandeur of its implications – something fully articulated in the same letter to Colonel Harvey claiming the power to write the 'best book (of social and pictorial and, as it were, human observation) ever devoted to this country' and then 'why not say frankly *the* Best? – ever devoted to any country at all'.

This project of course required, however obliquely and informally, the terms of play in which intelligible points of reference could be found. For the social modes that may prevail in any one place are marked by their difference. So the implied point of reference shows an ambiguity in the conception, for one must consider the imagined readership.[8] The very terms of understanding might not be the same for his English and his American readers. And whatever even-handedness may have been intended, the critical tone is pervasive enough.

One wonders about his expectations of the American response. The principle of comparison could of course have worked otherwise: the pleasures of American freedom from the constraint of tradition. And the persisting emphasis on manners seems to ignore the possibility that the casual style of a democratic society is in one sense 'manners', quite as much as the more formal codes of more traditional societies. So when enquiring into the life concealed by Cape Cod bungalows, too opaque almost for 'the story seeker', he almost pleads: ' "The *manners*, the manners: where and what are they, and what have they to tell" – that haunting curiosity, essential to the honour of his office, yet making it much of a burden, fairly buzzes about his head the more pressingly in proportion as the social mystery, the lurking human secret, seems more shy.' (*The American Scene*, p. 35)

Such absence may give an indistinct sense of 'a supreme queerness on Cape Cod' but the directness of enquiry into a mode of human relations predisposes his sense of where the interest of 'story' might lie. The density of relationships would seem to require two aspects of manners: codification as a principle of both distancing and communication, and the presence of a sense of form which gives social behaviour a restraint and style lacking in the 'summer girls' whose colossal and innocent immodesty and total inanity 'started, for the restless analyst, innumerable questions, amid which he felt himself sink beyond his depth'. (p. 33) The burst of talk, laughter indicated the movement of life without real experience, and 'how was the human and social function at all compatible with the *degree* of the inanity?' What opens is a formless outpouring of life's activity which lies beyond the world of manners, and hence beyond any possible significance.

The traveller can recollect an American quality to which a high value was attached, a 'naturalness'. It indicated a lack of affectation or self-consciousness but not a lack of the courtesies of being 'well brought up'. The problem for the 'restless analyst' is to distinguish the lack of form from the absence of convention, or the simple indifference to public appearance from a mindlessness which has no special social meaning. There are other spin-offs from his conundrum. But there is nowhere a recognition of that conventional American stance, an element both in Mark Twain and Melville, that there is interest in man as stripped of his social forms, before the corruption Rousseau discerned in all social relations.

The comment of Lévi-Strauss has its grand measure of truth: 'Qui dit homme dit langage et qui dit langage dit société.' The notion of man without a social formation, without culture, without the structure of attitudes and verbal devices which constitute manners – for better or for worse – is inconceivable and Rousseau's concept of the state of nature is not speculative anthropology but pure hypothesis. Yet the experience of the vast, the formless, the seemingly empty spaces, the felt social dissociation produced a powerful sense of cultural divide. Of course all was relative; passing through Albany on his way to New York from the American West James, had 'the absurdest sense of meeting again a ripe old civilisation and travelling through a country that showed the mark of established manners'. The return to Manhattan evoked his pleasure in 'having (approximately) done with Barbarism'. (Edel, 1985, p. 611) However, we shall see, he is not always this kind to New York.

The imaginative polarities are not formally considered, nor their possible meanings explored. Rough headings make their casual appearances. We can recognize the contrast of nature and culture, of barbarism and civilization, new and old. On what set of contrasts was the comparison of America and its alienated European past to be most revealing of what that cultural change could mean to mankind? Loose, imprecise coordinates continually reposition themselves to give the surrounding phenomenal whirl the passing sense of its own significant form.

Yet the powerful conviction of knowing how the coordinates work is there. The flash of recognition comes, as I have mentioned, even on Boston Common where, on Beacon Hill, he meets a language totally alien to that of the Brahmins: 'For no sound of English, in a single instance, escaped their lips ... No note of any shade of American speech struck my ear, save in so far as the sounds in question represent to-day so much of the substance of that idiom ... the people before me were aliens to a man, and they were in serene and triumphant possession.' (*The American Scene*, p. 231) They are in fact Europeans. And among tones that are 'some outland dialect unknown to me' James hears what he has to admit is Italian, but an Italian of a 'rude form' quite unlike the civilized Tuscan of his Italian friends. And one of the great themes of *The American Scene* is the transformation of Europe into its Americanized form, of the alien's passage from his culture into a strange movement of obliteration.

This adds to the complex pattern of cultural confrontation and reciprocities, to the perspective shifts which constitute the journey's pleasure, excitement and tension. For this European migration is a penetration of America by products of another world whose primary aim is to lose all contact with their previous selves. To see America as the twentieth century dawns is to see a new America where Europe is dying to be born again. But the shape of that new birth is vague and indeterminate. And at times heavy with an indistinct threat. Why does the Americanized Italian lack the charm and responsiveness of his own country and seem sunk in a dim *ressentiment*? Is there a cultural loss without gain, the vanishing of forms into an entropic haze? And how is one to relate this to the old America whose shapes the new will palpably, he feels, fail to match – or even desire to match? It is the movement of incommensurates to fill the vast spatial emptiness. But the incommensurate elements do not meet, or engage with each other, but have a *lumpen* coexistence in which the specific gravity of both Europe and America gradually vanishes. Fragments of dignity remain: in the German beer-hall in uptown New York where aged men like flies in amber play at dominoes. Yet in the Jewish Café Royal on the lower East Side the churn of ideas and opinions, in the bastardized language of an English with multiple origins, shows the energy of an unformed and ungraspable version of the new.

The alien seems remote from what James expected to discover. But he is the key to many things and provides the coloration of many of James's most vivid and immediate experiences. Above all in the persistence of a certain shock of displacement; the rough and unintelligible syllables heard on Boston Common replace a world accessible to memory. The task of the 'restless analyst' might have seemed that of relating his past to the movement observed in what was his own society. But it was no longer his, and in ways that were unpredicted. The problem of interpretation has changed. It is no longer the internal transformations of the world he had left behind. Of course those people are still there, and their descendants, their works, their accumulated social consequences. But they are no longer the possessors of their world and are submerged by unfamiliar faces, by languages and cultural formations which mean an open-ended process whose very terms are difficult to recognize.

James's fascination seems to focus on two points at once, which seem to cancel each other but do not. One is the annihilation of memory through which the alien becomes American, not through assimilating the manners and values of the earlier Americans, but merely by shedding his own – a process of self-negation without corresponding gains. Hence an openness to possibility which seems to have no definite character at all.

Yet the obvious other face of this negative process is the diversity of its sources. Here is the variety that eludes any distinctive social form, any recognizable configuration that would make possible the identification of actions, manners, marked features of behaviour. James regards this diversity as a subversion of the notion of what it is to be American, denying the possible unity of the national identity even to the point of putting in question its intelligibility. The concept has become too diffuse, making any attempt to identify and describe things American strangely indeterminate. Attempts to explain similarity and difference are therefore subject to mutual undermining and unpredictable metamorphoses, something marked in the provisional nature of the cities – the great houses built for a day, the sky-scrapers assigned an almost aggressively transitory role.

This awareness of the gap which discrepancy proposes constantly recurs in the variety of particular circumstances that arise at random, but is also the subject of several expanded meditations including one where the alien, 'the great "ethnic" question', is treated with an almost unJamesian directness:

The sense of the elements in the cauldron – the cauldron of the 'American' character – becomes thus about as vivid a thing as you can at all quietly manage, and the question settles into a form which makes the intelligible answer further and further recede. 'What meaning, in the presence of such impressions, can continue to attach to such a term as the "American" character? – what type, as the result of such a prodigious amalgam, is to be conceived as shaping itself?' (pp. 120–121)

Questions posed as in themselves unanswerable, so that enquiry must necessarily renounce 'any direct satisfaction or solution' and drop 'the immediate need of conclusions' for 'the blest general feeling for the impossibility of them, to which the philosophy of any really fine observation of the American spectacle must reduce itself'. The move is from the scientific to the aesthetic, from prediction based on the immediate 'impression' to the contemplation of the whole spectacle, a shift in perspective that implies a change in what might be an answer to a question. It is a change forced by the awareness of scale, which defies interpretation. The spectator must make his move before the spectacle becomes a substitute for what he cannot know. And his experience is to be repeated again and again when scale defeats sense, where the variety, or incongruity or the evanescence of the impressions fail to add up or propose a distancing that is more in awe than understanding. 'There is too much of the whole thing, he sighs, for the personal relation with it.' (p. 122)

Yet our imagination requires a sense of shape and of limit. And the idea of community is felt to involve something more than the satisfaction of rudimentary economic needs; 'the human imagination absolutely declines everywhere to go to sleep without some apology at least for a supper'. The presence of Independence Hall in Philadelphia has suggested the need of a 'social *point de repère*' and a reflection on that 'lucky legacy of the past' which seems to have 'a real, a moral value'. Around this forms a reflection on the nature of community: 'The collective consciousness, in however empty an air, gasps for a relation, as intimate as possible, to something superior, something as central as possible, from which it may more or less have proceeded and around which its life may resolve.' (p. 290) The desideratum is romantic or heroic, although he reflects that in most of America, where hotel, school, factory 'or, for climax of desperation, the house of the biggest billionaire' have had to stand in for the non-existent historical monument, the 'general imagination' can be captured, by necessity, at the level of any 'coloured rag' with which to clothe its doll.

It is the awareness of the imagination's necessity, of the *point de repère*, which gives some form to the notion of community. And it is between the bastion of such a focal point and the distanced overview that James's mind oscillates. It is in the search for the former, for which some physical presence so often gives James his 'objective correlative', that a second level is discovered, that hint of depth which is indicative of something to which consciousness can hold. It is the awareness of something 'behind', something 'within', that provides texture. The visual sense of relation which gives 'thickness' or 'complexity' comes to stand for some inner sense of what mental states the notion of community might imply. The visual correlations touch the centre of association, or the felt sense of being somewhere. This sense of focal point will also point up its absence and indicate the incoherence of the unformed world that sprawls about it, where Matthew Arnold's 'vast edges drear and naked shingles' are the norm.

If many subjects and places reflect this kind of polarity it is still not a rigorous conceptual frame. One's contemplation is to be as impressionistic as James's, but at least some of the force of *The American Scene* can be represented thematically. To start with the sense of community itself is to see that the paradox of James's journey has many dimensions – too many perhaps for the novelist of intelligible form. One might find, as Tocqueville did, a nation with strong claims to its identity and still find that identity difficult to fix, so loose and vague are the indicators. Certainly those who, like his brother William, or Clover Harper Adams who criticized James's 'Europeanized' angle of vision, believed, however vaguely, that there was a rich American subject matter for the novelist of manners. William's obtuseness and resentment show far more of what he dislikes than of the awareness of the potential power of the American subject. One implied task of *The American Scene* is to find in the community some pattern of relationships that would awaken the interest of the subject – something perhaps tentatively and abortively undertaken in *The Ivory Tower*.

So there is a continuous search for coherent areas of relationship, in which the interplay of character and quality of life would engage the novelist's imaginative power. But of course James is not creating but observing. The passing scene perhaps slides by too rapidly to make the sense of possible interaction cohesive. So the interpretation must push outward to the shape of the whole, to the sense of how a particular community shapes and works. One must extract a sense of the whole from the immediacy and intensity of the impression.

We will return in other circumstances to the overwhelming effect of scale. This is perhaps not so much a thematic development but a conditioning factor, transforming the aspect of the thematic contents, of the ways in which American life is distinctive. The vastness, the necessity of the machinery of society being on an enormous scale not only defeats analysis, where the variety of phenomena resist interpretation; that diversity has the strange effect of sameness. I can find no evidence that James had read Tocqueville but there are close analogies with Tocqueville's observations of seventy years before where, in the United States: 'Fortunes, opinions, and laws are there in ceaseless variation; it is as if immutable Nature herself were mutable, such are the changes worked upon her by the hand of man. Yet in the end the spectacle of this excited community becomes monotonous, and after having watched the moving pageant for a time, the spectator is tired of it.'[9]

The terms are not identical, but the experience seems the same: under the enormous diversity and changeability there is a wearing sameness. At the beginning of his journey, James notes that a question about the condition of life, put to 'a resident of a large city of the middle West' had received the reply: 'The conditions of the life? Why, the same conditions as everywhere else.' (*The American Scene*, p. 42) And he recollects this in a New England landscape, reflecting how the 'restless analyst' whose social study is 'too baffling in many a case' is thrown back upon the land, and where the very working of it, the very movement through 'the visible vacancy', 'is everywhere a large contribution to one's impression of a kind of monotony of acquiescence'. (*ibid.*, pp. 44–45) The pervasive monotony is expressed again as a tentative formula: 'There are no "kinds" of people; there are simply people.' Is it the opacity of the New England village that registers its propensity to give away very little and, conversely, to suggest that there probably is nothing to give?

'The uniformity of type' returns as he approaches a series of sketches that use his oblique manner of summing up, of gathering of impressions to which one can put a general character. 'It is of the nature of many American impressions, accepted at the time as a whole of the particular story, simply to cease to be, as soon as your back is turned – to fade, to pass away, to leave not a wreck [sic] behind. This happens not least when the image, whatever it may have been, has exacted the tribute of wonder or pleasure: it has displayed every virtue but the virtue of being able to remain with you.' It lacks the property or quality 'that makes for the authority of a figure, for the complexity of a scene'. European experience is more deeply etched. On the other hand, 'That doubtless is the matter, in the States, with the vast peaceful and prosperous human show – in conditions, especially, in which its peace and prosperity most shine out: it registers itself on the plate with an incision too vague and, above all, too uniform.' (p. 454)

Uniformity mixes with simplicity, and with the indistinctness of evanescence. It is an evanescence that has been seen in the impermanence of manners, institutions, the very cloud-capped towers of New York. In a spirit similar to Tocqueville's, everything changes yet remains the same. One cloud-capped tower will be replaced by another which will be similar only taller. Giganticism of scale may be implicit in the ambitions of the social order as a whole, but as such it serves largely to efface the character of any accomplishment.

The social body which is blanketed by this effacing power is partly the product of a de-historicizing process – the disappearance of the 'references' that the past might evoke – and partly the effect of democracy. Partly too, however, the productive process, the industrious movement and change, reflect a levelling world of commerce: 'the usual, in our vast crude democracy of trade, is the new, the simple, the cheap, the common, the commercial, the immediate, and, all too often, the ugly'. (p. 67) This associates democracy, which he distinguishes from the English version as being social as well as political (p. 250), with the crasser aspects of American life. And it is seen from the beginning as a source of alarm. The very moment of arrival is enough to make the awareness almost overwhelming.

> That, moreover, was but another name for the largest and straightest perception the restless analyst had yet risen to – the perception that awaits the returning absentee from this great country, on the wharf of disembarcation, with an embodied intensity that no superficial confusion, no extremity of chaos any more than any brief mercy of accident, avails to mitigate. The waiting observer need be little enough of an analyst, in truth, to arrive at that consciousness, for the phenomenon is vivid in direct proportion as the ship draws near. The great presence that bristles for him on the sounding dock, and that shakes the planks, the loose boards of its theatric stage to an inordinate unprecedented rumble, is the monstrous form of Democracy, which is thereafter to project its shifting angular shadow, at one time and another, across every inch of the field of his vision. It is the huge democratic broom that has made the clearance and that one seems to see brandished in the empty sky.
>
> That is of course on one side no great discovery, for what does even the simplest soul ever sail westward for, at this time of day, if not to profit, so far as possible, by 'the working of democratic institutions'? The political, the civic, the economic view of them is a study that may be followed, more or less, at a distance; but the way in which they determine and qualify manners, feelings, communications, modes of contact and conceptions of life – this is a revelation that has its full force and its lively interest only on the spot, where, once caught, it becomes the only clue worth mentioning in the labyrinth. The condition, notoriously, represents an immense boon, but what does the enjoyment of the boon represent?

There is the Jamesian effect of distancing the grand and general problem into the complex tissue of particulars. It is not worthy of us, or even in any real sense possible for us, to consider the nature of the 'monstrous form'. You can only make sense of it in the observed features which 'may appear at the moment', the clues to its working 'are never out of your hand'. But the clues point to no single set of conclusions, nor are they of a single intelligible kind. They are simply pervasive: 'You may talk of other things, and you do, as much as possible; but you are really thinking of that one, which has everything else at its mercy.' The truth about America is contained in this: 'The democratic consistency, consummately and immitigably [sic] complete, shines through with its hard light, whatever equivocal gloss may happen momentarily to prevail.' (pp. 54–55) It is the 'hard light' of the democratic consistency which plays upon all aspects of society, through which all human phenomena are seen. It is the condition of life, but it does not so much exist in itself but as the focal length of whatever does exist. And the 'hard light' seems to have the capacity of observing all things in their raw and brutal immediacy. For James there seem to be two kinds of light, this bright immediacy and a softer, mellower light through which older cultures display themselves. It is like the varnish on old paintings, or the Claude glass through which the brightness of nature could be attenuated and civilized and the setting sun observed to best advantage.

Yet there is a curious inconclusive quality to this short meditation. The hard light again falls, to the occasional 'gasp' before the 'quantity of illustration'. And 'The illustration might be, enormously, of something deficient, absent – in which case it was for the aching void to be (as an aching void) striking and interesting. As an explication or an implication the democratic intensity could always figure.'

The last sentence is almost a throwaway. The character of the democratic involvement is left undetermined. Causal connections are tacitly abandoned. Explanation is left open. There is a vividly abiding presence, a presence of absence, a void within the mass of diffuse impression, and we do not find the hard democratic light capturing the precise elements of a visible landscape, but an indistinct feature of the void. James needs only suggestion and the play of figure. The mind turns to the immediate impression, to the impact of occasion on memory. Democracy will surround us, an omnipresent aspect of whatever we see. But James's own cultural distance responds to its alienating power. And sees it not as the natural and proper condition of life, but as one marked by the special terms of the American continent, by the curiosity of a great game, as if the *tabula rasa* had presented itself for the infinity of creation, and the myriad activities had failed to inscribe themselves and suggested the continuity of the void.

However, James is far from consistent in the use of the image. Many impressions show the depth of 'bile'. Perhaps the most vivid is the distinctive character of American women. It is with a startled excitement that he creates the American woman on her own cultural ground, a different kind of role from that indicated in many of his fictions because it asserts a large and general model of social behaviour, a counterpoint to the 'business man' in his *déformation professionnelle.* One has seen that the man who has made a perfectly vast amount of money is somehow impressive, set apart by a quantitative measure that is insulated against innerness. But the business world has no feature of intellect or culture. The women 'appear to be of a markedly finer texture than the men'. Physiognomy first, and a sense of its bearing, point to 'a queer deep split or chasm between the two stages of personal polish, the two levels of the conversible state, at which the sexes have arrived.' (p. 65)

Washington gives the strongest sense of the possibility of the 'conversible' because it is the one where men are not in business, so it was possible that 'The tone was, so to speak, of *conscious* self-consciousness, and the highest genius of conversation no doubt dwelt in the fact that the ironic spirit was ready always to give its very self away, fifty times over, for the love, or for any quickening of the theme.' The presence of Adams, Hay and their quite international circle no doubt gives a golden glow to this exceptional moment. For one must mark the distinctness of the contrast: 'The value here was at once that the place could offer to view a society, the only one in the country, in which Men existed, and that rich little fact became the key to everything.' Otherwise – elsewhere – the dead hand of the businessman falls on the social scene, producing an appalling emptiness. 'It lies there waiting, pleading from all its pores, to be occupied – the lonely waste, the boundless gaping void of "society"; which is but a rough name for all the *other* so numerous relations with the world he lives in that are imputable to the civilized being.' Much follows about the 'possession', 'conquest' and 'predominance' – 'two-thirds of the apparent life' and 'absolutely all of the social' – of the American woman. The conclusion is radical but difficult to fill out in terms of its consequences. 'The woman produced by a women-made society alone has obviously quite a new story'. But this story is little more than a grand hypothesis. A mention is made of the international social presence. And he glances for a moment to a world below his own social level and the effects of labour-saving devices. (pp. 344–345)

The brilliant rhetorical passage that follows suggests the revolution this creates both in the notion of a social structure and in the character of the implicit compact between the sexes. On the other hand the Washington model might gain in general importance and Men might come to exist. He thinks that such existence can be palpably felt in the 'City of Conversation' where there is a value of the European kind, with an equilibrium in which no one is effaced and the roles of the sexes have greater ease and reciprocity. It is tempting to take this as a delightful *scherzo* where comic charm lends itself to satire. The dour picture of the American male is relieved by this playful indication of the alternative. Certainly this does not look like more than an assessment of the best-chosen drawing rooms. Nor does the proposed transformation read well as a social prediction – least, indeed, for Washington. The act of pondering 'Is the man "up to it", up to the major heritage' dissolves in the speculative, or rather throws at us a question of such scope, and perhaps of such imprecision, that we can only regard it as a hopeful, if sceptical, gesture directed towards the great absence.

The effect of the city is annihilating in another way. From the first vision of the Jersey shore with its ostentatious display of wealth, and its concomitant impermanence – 'We are only instalments, symbols, stopgaps', say the houses that, as everywhere in this journey, talk to him, 'expensive as we are, we have nothing to do with continuity, responsibility' – to the renewed sight of Manhattan, this sense of the cities' continuous movement, of change, imposes a perpetual flux on the permanent, fixed *points de repère* of human consciousness. Therefore, the very coordinates that should shape our awareness of ourselves, the tissue of relations by which one recognizes one's place in the world, are themselves imperilled, subject to the flow of Heraclitus's river so that one can hardly say 'some' with any intelligibility. And again the 'great adventure of a society reaching out into the apparent void' poses the question of what it can find or construct that will take it beyond the triumph over necessity. James puts the original terms of his enquiry in such terms, 'to gouge an interest *out* of the vacancy' (p. 12).

The echo of change can be personal because the *point de repère* is memory. On this more intimate scale the most dramatic irony strikes in Boston, on revisiting Ashburton Place on Beacon Hill. So much has altered 'of the pleasant little complexity of the other time' where 'memory met that pang of loss' but he still found the house where he had spent the last years of the Civil War and, in the evocation of the Boston of his youth, a 'conscious memento'. But returning a month later the house had been demolished and he 'found but a gaping void, the brutal effacement, at a stroke, of every related object, of the whole precious past'. The unmaking of history is so much swifter than its making. 'It was as if the bottom had fallen out of one's own biography, and one plunged backwards into space without meeting anything.' (pp. 229–231) The sense of connection is replaced by 'the rupture'. And it is this moment of personal effacement which is followed by his encounter with the alien mass making their passage across Boston Common.

A milder recurrence of the same is to be found in New York, in the moments when, near Washington Square, the recollections of earlier years are obliterated by the shifting movements of commerce and fashion, above all by the desire to build large for the maximizing of profit. One can equally imagine his horror at the London which was transformed in inter-war and post-war development, where the utilitarian blankness of Victoria Street meets Westminster Abbey. For the reductive character of style available to the march of commerce lies a few decades beyond the moment of *The American Scene.* In the immediate environs of Washington Square the same conjunction of memory and the indifference of 'progress' has its passing moment of anguish or pathos, as the menaced church sinks into its surround. His demolished birthplace, 'ruthlessly suppressed' has the effect for him 'of having been amputated of half my history', and the 'supremely characteristic local note' is of the great city 'projected into its future as, practically, a huge, continuous fifty-floored conspiracy against the very idea of the ancient graces ... so traceable, at every turn ... are the heavy footprints, in the finer texture of life, of a great commercial democracy seeking to abound supremely in its own sense and having none to gainsay it'. (p. 92) But the overall response to 'the terrible town' is more impersonal, is the mixture of awe and of horror at its continuous transformation, at the spectacle of perpetual movement, punctuated by the odd presence of the anomalous monumental in Grant's tomb: 'a great democratic demonstration caught in the past, in the fact, the nakedest possible effort to strike the note of the august'. (p. 145)

He is haunted by the problem of the monumental. How can a democratic society honour its past? There is a simple eloquence in Independence Hall or Mount Vernon. But the number of 'references' is restricted, and it is precisely the search for the reference point that dramatizes the emptiness. The most striking case perhaps is Richmond, with the ambiguity of the 'immense, grotesque, defeated project ... to-day pathetic in its folly, of a vast Slave State' and the attempt to create a memory of a blighted, untenable past, where one feels 'the prison of the southern spirit' in the very presence of the black. The conflict operating through that 'haunting consciousness' qualifies the southern enterprise. Yet in the Museum, the printer's book seems the only distinctive thing and the notion of a renewed version of the old South would hit the grotesquely false note. But the most fully lost element is an awareness of the great historical cataclysm itself. And the only distinguished imaginative work to come from the South since the war is from the black writer DuBois.

As memory strains away from the point of departure the integument grows thin, the sensibility stretches to find its coordinates. One loses an authentic America for an observed hypothetical. The demands on reflection begin to struggle against the sense of the alien. At a weaker level James's observation begins to be assimilated to the mere travelogue which registers the quaintness, or charm or absence of it, of whatever the passing traveller may note. This is marked in the special pleasure in Charleston, 'a city of gardens and absolutely no men'. Yet, unlike the European travel sketches that had represented the curiosity, interest, difference of a particular place, the South seems to effect a diminishing return for the 'restless analyst'. He is somehow blocked in confronting the affluent of Palm Beach. 'Every obligation lay upon me to "study" them as so gathered in, and I did my utmost, I remember, to render them that respect; yet when I now, after an interval, consult my notes, I find the page a blank, and when I knock at the door of memory I find it perversely closed.' (pp. 453–454)

Of course it is a relative distancing, but different in kind from that which drew back at the shock of the immensity. Rather than the strange troubling scope there is the anodyne effect of duty in recording in Florida the vagueness of an insidious way of pleasing which 'was still an appeal. The vagueness was warm, the vagueness was bright, the vagueness was sweet, being scented and flowered and fruited; above all the vagueness was somehow consciously and confessedly weak'. And James finishes on the touch of gallantry that finds in vagueness a plea to one's tenderness and is hence 'adorable'. (p. 460) But over this whole falls a shadow of comparison. In a parting moment the boat trip on a lake, the shore at sunset suggests 'a Nile so simplified out of the various fine senses attachable'. It is the notional setting stripped of history and therefore of significance. A foretaste for him of California, 'where the general aspect of that wondrous realm kept suggesting to me a sort of prepared but unconscious and inexperienced Italy, the primitive *plate*, in perfect condition, but with the impression of History all yet to be made'. (p. 462)

We are at the point of breaking off, in the contemplation of hugeness again, in evoking the Mississippi, a frontier to be crossed, but where the record fails. The mind turns from the substance to the means, and evokes the intimate relation with the Pullman car itself, its vast windows, the rumble of its wheels the measure of the great spaces, like the isolation of the explorer Jules Verne, or a space traveller. An evocation as symbolic as Gogol's troika rumbling over the Russian steppes. But unlike the mystic troika, the machine arouses James's 'eloquence of my exasperation' which puts the question as 'one of the painted savages' might put it, a question which is an incantation. 'Beauty and charm would be for me in the solitude you have ravaged, and I should owe you my grudge for every disfigurement and every violence, for every wound with which you have caused the face of the land to bleed.' It is a 'pretended message of civilisation'. 'You touch the great lonely land – as one feels it still to be – only to plant upon it some ugliness about which, never dreaming of the grace of apology or contrition, you then proceed to brag with a cynicism all your own. You convert the large and noble sanities that I see around me, you convert them one after the other to crudities, to invalidities, hideous and unashamed.' All of this compounded by the failure to notice: 'the vast general unconsciousness and indifference'.

So in the end it is the romantic vision of solitude that accuses the American achievement, a sense of the raw and uncorrupted without the blemish of ugliness that has been imposed upon it, but also without the redemption of 'History'. The Pullman which is the object of James's abusive address represents the mechanism of conquest, of the submission to the laws that industries force on the past of a noble solitude. But unlike the construction of older culture it seems ahistorical, representing like Adams's a force, an instrument, rather than a state of being.

Its passive, and equally ahistorical, companion is the hotel. Hotels loom large in *The American Scene*, not merely because they represent a new form of social gathering, a kind of tent in the American desert he can identify as 'hotel-civilisation' or the 'hotel-spirit' to which an elaborate and ironic tribute is paid (pp. 438–441). It removes the necessity of individual choice, and produces that perfectly homogeneous collectivity which fulfils the needs of an uncertain and undifferentiated society, accepting fusion as the price of luxury, 'caged, positively thankful, in its vast vacancy, for the sense and the definite horizon of a cage'. It is the container for a continuous passage of those whose relation to each other is contingent and transitory. As such it is the symbolic centre of the American city, a substitute for a socially structured form of life, where the passing caravan is subject only to a connection which is random and meaningless, out of which, at its most extreme, has been drawn an extravagant grandeur. Although the truth lies in a substitution of a certain artifice for the world beyond it. 'There are endless things in "Europe", to your vision, behind and beyond the hotel, a multitudinous complicated life; in the States, on the other hand, you see the hotel itself as that life, as constituting for vast numbers of people the richest form of existence.' (p. 406)

The presence of the hotel-spirit is in the end, however elaborate its decorative carapace, reductive and levelling. The sense of the individual shape that might have directed a personal choice is devoured in 'a great cumulative sum', a sum in which the values that distinguish the human condition are seen as lost, even if the hotel-spirit achieves its visual apotheosis:

The jealous cultivation of the common mean, the common mean only, the reduction of everything to an average of decent suitability, the gospel of precaution against the tendency latent in many things to become too good for their context, so that persons partaking of them may become too good for their company – the idealised form of all this glimmered for me, as an admonition of a betrayal ... Definitely, one had made one's pilgrimage but to find the hotel-spirit in sole *articulate* possession, and, call this truth for the mind an anti-climax if one would, none of the various climaxes, the minor effects – those of Nature, for instance, since thereabouts, far and wide, was no hinted history – struck me as for a moment dispossessing it of supremacy. (p. 442)

The hotel as guardian spirit effectively marks the end of his journey, for the promise of the Pullman is not to be kept. The marble vision on the shore of Lake Worth is the last port of call that James will record. It is the problem of taste that dangles before him in the presence of luxurious excess, to put in question 'the boundless field, the endless gold, the habit of great enterprises'. The very desire for taste in the presence of these grandiose negations, 'brief moments of aesthetic arrest' and admonitory presence, arises as a hypothetical confrontation, a clearing of the air for a speculative wondering as to 'the degree to which this pathos of desire may be condemned to remain a mere heartbreak to the historic muse?' (p. 446) The eloquent speculation hangs in the air.

What may have darkened the historic muse can be put in terms of a reserve, a sense of history that directs James's project, while lying outside of it like a melancholy reminder of what has been revealed as a vast absence. One must formulate some of the terms in which the muse would hope to operate, to find itself beyond the pathos of desire, to find an America in which narrative is possible in human and aesthetic terms.

One of the difficulties with any sense of history is seeing it in terms of continuities, of the present in terms of the past. The present may be its product, in fact inevitably is, but the felt sense of that continuity, in terms of an intelligible narrative, supplies a sequence which gives the present a sense of depth, of form appropriate to its past. Such a view of history is necessary to civilization, not as single events, 'one damned thing after another'. James's sense of history is not schematized, but a matter of felt depth. Yet of course the European is the necessary model: that moment in the Galerie d'Apollon; that awareness of London or Paris, or even Rye, as having given to mankind a consistency which has value.

The romantic and reverential aspect of the past makes a momentary entry in his visit to Concord (pp. 260–265), where the 'deep Concord rusticity' recalls the 'rough black mementos' of Britain: 'We remember the small hard facts of the Shakespeare house at Stratford' and on to Edinburgh Castle's 'rude closet' where James VI of Scotland was born and Mary Stuart's 'other little black hole' at Holyrood. Small, dark, unpropitious beginnings perhaps. But the Concord moment of romance is deep-set in personal memory; evocations of Hawthorne, Thoreau and Emerson mingle in the 'thrilling clearness' with which 'that supreme site speaks'. There is the immediacy of fusion between an historical romance and a personal past. The effect is to enter an heroic age, and one rich in exemplary figures. But does it create the beginning of a form with a continuity America can use, like the closets and black holes of Edinburgh, or is it a fragment of the heroic age, belonging to a mythical America, where the noble beginnings are on the path to a future of some totally different order?

James's response is double: there is the powerful effect 'of the warm flood of appreciation, of reflection', yet 'the communicated spell falls, in its degree, into that pathetic oddity of the small aspect' – and hence the 'hard facts'. The mild air nevertheless engenders respect and waves away 'any closer assault of criticism'. Beyond this the values of Emerson and Thoreau remain intact, a happy equivalent for James of the Weimar of Goethe and Schiller. The literary value established seems to run on its own track, as if the books in his library in Rye were the true survivors. They are ancestors and historical presences but in some way transposed and borne off with him. It is as if the mythic and exemplary had departed from the scene and only in recollection did they play a part in the culture that had produced them, entering in such a way that the causal chain is broken.

Concord, fragments of Boston, Independence Hall are precious touchstones, but their relation to the real America is the subject of a speculative quest. One needs to invent a past that is less a natural succession than the subject of conceptual and imaginative art. Of course James did not need to reinvent Emerson as Harold Bloom has, an Emerson congested with cultural possibilities undreamed by James. For of course he knew him well, and the memory is present – both in Concord and at the house. But the precious touchstones are reassembled, and according to the necessities that James has found in himself, an implied genealogy that is part of the imaginative life.

Whether through mythologization, or the evanescence born of the speed of movement, or the indistinct and shallow 'bite' of the etching acid upon the plate, or the cult of the new, or the indifference to the physical aspects of the past, or the levelling device of the hotel as a substitute for distinguishable social forms, the whole of American life dulls and diffuses the historical sense. James's criteria for the latter are not systematically formulated, but are repeated and clear: a pattern of social relations; a distinctness of personal impression; a sense that the self is governed by intelligible form; an awareness that the present arises from the past in a visible and continuous way, not in a sprawl of shapeless discontinuities; and a traceable physical fabric where the objects that are at least a partial incarnation of the past do not sink casually into oblivion.

Two further classes of object are important touchstones. One is the attempt to create the reference points through the monumental. James treats this is a sympathetic curiosity. One has seen his response to Grant's tomb. But there is a sense that, set in the upper west side of Manhattan, even that substantial and solid object has a tentative presence. More moving still is the Lee monument in Richmond: French and 'the work of a master', the figure 'looks off into desolate space' which the setting creates. The object and its surroundings fall apart and this very dissociation is a clue to 'the riddle of the historical poverty of Richmond' which is also the failure of a false ideal:

> It is the poverty that *is*, exactly, historic: once take it for that and it puts on vividness. The condition attested is the condition – or, as may be, one of the later, fainter, weaker, stages – of having worshipped false gods. As I looked back, before leaving it, at Lee's stranded, bereft image, which time and fortune have so cheated of half the significance, and so, I think, of half the dignity, of great memorials, I recognised something more than the melancholy of a lost cause. The whole infelicity speaks of a cause that could never have been gained. (p. 394)

It is always context that qualifies the effect of the monumental. Saint-Gaudens's Sherman is placed before 'the most death-dealing, perhaps, of all the climaxes of electric car cross-currents' at the edge of Central Park. And James feels a diffidence before the ambiguity of its message as the triumph of destruction: 'monuments should always have a clean, clear meaning'. (pp. 171–174) And the 'effect of the fine Washington Obelisk rather spends or wastes itself (not a little as if some loud monosyllable had been uttered, in a preoccupied company, without a due production of sympathy or sense)'. (p. 355) Others fare better; the White House, where history is 'insistently seated', Jackson in Lafayette Square, Lafayette himself and Rochambeau. But the ' "artistic" Federal city' is angled to the civic consciousness of the American voter, which points to a hesitant if mildly sceptical meditation: to what extent can he respond to the creation of such a monumental centre? The new conditions imposed by the American scene are often open-ended and their consequences incalculable. There is, will be, an 'American way' with its own evolution, but dominated – and this seems like James's obsession – by the necessity imposed by an unprecedented scale. And 'phenomena of this order strike us mostly as occurring in the historical void, as having to present themselves in the hard light of that desert' (pp. 357–358). And the void, rather than lending them a quality of existential eloquence, undermines their own implicit message. For those monumental public presences, 'The danger "in Europe" is of their having too many things to say, and too many others to distinguish these from; the danger in the States is of their not having things enough – with enough tone and resonance furthermore to give them.'

The question for James is one of how, out of the democratic process, the flow of money from raw industrial sources, the variety of random objects, places, intentions, political and public divagations, can the grand and marvellous thing be formed. He fails to note that Washington is that rare thing, a planned city, with l'Enfant's design expressly aimed at the monumental proportion. But perhaps, again, the scale is too grand for the coherence of the whole and the eye gropes for connections, as it does in the Washington of today. He retains, however, within sceptical parentheses, his opening to the visionary element, to the thought that the nation is yet new and will, for better or worse, create something unforeseen.

Generosity, in a sense, requires this open-ended note. For it is that vast Margin which surrounds American life and explains the failure of the observer with open eyes to reach conclusions. There is so much in the matter of pure, unlimited possibility surrounding whatever observed phenomenon or event. 'Not by any means that the Margin always affects him as standing for the vision of a possible greater good than what he sees in the given case – any more than so standing for a possible greater evil; these differences are submerged in the immense fluidity; they lurk confused, disengaged, in the mere looming mass of the *more*, the more and more to come.' (p. 401)

Among the powers not easily attributable to the Margin, one is yet incontestably there. That is the power to transform the object, however remote its origins, through its very capacity of alienating context. The value of the object of art is strangely altered because the perception of it is altered, its very meaning becoming different in kind. We are accustomed to see this as the immediate effect of the Museum itself, the wrenching of the art object out of context, to contemplate in the cold detachment where its companions are other works and the public scrutiny is indiscriminate.

It is of course clear from *The Outcry* that James is happier with great works in the private collections of those in long possession. Second best is the National Collection where that establishment of ownership justifies its presence. But of course America is different. There is no long possession in the mellow private galleries of great houses. Whether bought or bequeathed, the presence of great works of art is of recent origin. The museum is less the gathering of a continuous patrimony than an invention – hence not the product of the fashions of many times, but of the inventor's own. He treads carefully around the weaknesses of the Metropolitan, where the evolving taste of many of its benefactors must be handled with a suitable courtesy. And discretion of another kind unquestionably inhibits an account of the Isabella Stewart Gardner collection in the mock Venetian palazzo just created in Fenway Bay. The grandiose and noble compliments fall short of any attempt to examine and value this most ambitious design in cultural transposition – this most self-contained and self-conscious project of implanting the alien. It is oddly the old Boston spirit of public generosity that is marked for us, not the character and success of the undertaking.

If we do not face Titian's 'Europa' in Boston, 'the restless analyst found work to his hand' in a small head of Aphrodite which catches 'in the American light the very fact of the genius of Greece'. (pp. 252–253) The refined observer should be told 'that he has not *seen* a fine Greek thing till he has seen it in America'. The effect of the 'merciless case of transplanting' is to double her impact: 'so far from having lost an iota of her power, she has gained unspeakably more, since what she stands for she here stands for alone, rising ineffably to the occasion'. And this transformation is double: 'Where was she ever more, where was she ever as much, a goddess – and who knows but that, being thus divine, she foresees the Time when, as she has "moved over", the place of her actual whereabouts will have become one of her shrines?' But where is this shrine: the Museum, Boston, the great republic itself? James's moment of fantasy ends in more practical reflections. Yet one wonders if some such light will radiate from the Museum of American City.

Further speculation will of course be inconclusive, and James himself is deeply tentative in his own glances down a road to which his imagination is strongly tempted. But we can try to read back from such moments to the way in which James sees certain concepts, or even sees the necessity of their use. In the pursuit of a characteristic form of American manners – 'where, where?' – it is gradually made clear that the pattern of relations which would constitute 'manners' in the European sense does not apply. It falls short of those criteria through the lack of deeply established and reasonably durable social forms. And personal relations are more desultory and fragmentary because the backgrounds are not shared, and the connnections between persons represent a flow of contingency rather than relations with any sense of depth in time. The rapid movement of persons, the swift change in their conditions indicate, however imprecisely, a new kind of social order, founded in this very volatility. There is neither the growth of social institutions nor the physical forms they might take – the continuity in time of houses, neighbourhoods, churches, social centres, and other means of deepening and perpetuating human contact. All give way to the laws of continuous change, or are swallowed up in greater scenes of social mass where the particular identity is so eroded as to lose its distinctive contours. It is a double process, of continuous movement, and of increase of scale.

The sense of scale is partly the response to natural conditions. In limited circumstances – in New Hampshire, at Newport, on Lake Worth or in California – there are what we might call 'eco-fragments' in which the natural world can show its beguiling and reassuring face. But this is not its true characteristic. These fragments are devoured in the vast and undifferentiated space. Again and again the sense of the strange mixture of the empty and the ugly acts as a pervasive threat. The Pullman heads through blank spaces which convey the alien cast of nature itself. Yet, as one has seen, there is the romance of wilderness, of the isolated world of the Red Indian destroyed by a crass and mindless development.

How can a form of life spread across such a space with a humanizing grace? James offers no hope, and his sensibility seems to shrink in the face of what resembles a dark continent. Here is the impression in its rawest, most direct form. So raw and forceful that it cuts off commentary to implicitly indicate limits to the human mind's interaction and response. Similarly the vanishing New York, the vanishing houses in Ashburton Place so swiftly bear away the possible fixed coordinates of life that we are running to stand still in the improbable flux. And to what end? Does the mind require these fixed coordinates as guarantees of personal identity? As far as James's passing contacts go, it would seem not to be so. Americans seemed happy with their world, quick to justify it, to proclaim its superiority to other societies, both in freedom and affluence. If affluence looms large – much too large for James's taste – the assumption is that it is the product of creativity. And James's contempt for business and a society devoted to business created an imaginative chasm he would never cross. For business is above all a commitment to the transitory; after today's work there is tomorrow's, and so *ad infinitum*. The 'thousand glassy eyes' of New York's skyscrapers are 'crowned not only with no history, but with no credible possibility of time for history, and consecrated by no uses save the commercial at any cost, they are simply the most piercing notes in the concert of the expensively provisional'. (p. 77) The only final product James could conceive was vulgar consumption and the crotchety embittered wealth of the unpleasant old men, assembling in their grand Newport mansions in the opening pages of *The Ivory Tower*. One would like to think that the consummation of the Ververs' wealth in the Museum, Adam's grand act of enlightenment, was a suitable final course. But James is at pains to emphasize how lightly the world of business had touched his character.

However, there is a relation, perhaps not wholly tangible. The world of the transitory may expend itself in trivia and work. But the accumulation of great wealth has also felt the need to memorialize itself, as did the princes of the past for their own glory. Hence Fenway Court and Verver's project. But unlike the Medici or Gonzagas or Mazarin, they are committed not to creation but to collection. The great residue is the Museum itself, for it is there that a world of flux can find its fixed point, for its effect is the abolition of time, the entry of culture into a timeless world where it is no longer the product of living relations but the arrangement of the alien world of the past. Every society may have its grandest product outside its own proper activity and unrelated to its social forms.

Hence, 'history' will be in inverted commas. The events of the turbulent flux will not enter into 'history' because they will not mark significant features or stages in civilization's development. More like biological or economic processes, they cannot become part of the evolving consciousness we call 'history'. Of course the assumption is here that one form of life has more value than another. The consciousness that enters into history bears the distinctive marks of the etcher's plate, while the less distinct are lost to us. The latter are strictly speaking insignificant, for they have nothing distinctive in social or cultural forms.

If this is the normal condition of American life there is nevertheless something which stands outside and even perhaps above the river of Heraclitus. The Museum is there and has a message. Our historical under-standing will not arise from our awareness of the changes or developments of our immediate world, but at a degree of remove, where civilization's marks are assembled. Our understanding will grasp what is compared with others; it will be distanced and academic. Value will reside within the walls of the magnificent artifice.

No doubt this is less than wholly welcome, a fatality rather than a sought conclusion. And it is far from the intellectual village of the New England worthies. The final stretch of palpable truth and the imagination's grasp is the one that has been abandoned as the Pullman took its westward course. What was there lay beyond any need for the continuing narration and indeed beyond one's immediate need for interpretation.

Notes to Part One

1. This opening passage was constructed by Rosemary Righter from notebooks.
2. Henry James, *The American Scene*, 1946 edition, New York, Charles Scribner's Sons. Further quotations will be indicated by a page number in the text.
3. Henry James, 'Occasional Paris', in *The Art of Travel* (ed.), 1958, pp. 213–215.
4. James's only biographical memoir, *William Wetmore Story and His Friends*, was published in 1903. It was undertaken at the Story family's behest, and the modesty of his interest in the American expatriate artist as a subject can be gauged from his laconic promise to Grace Norton to put 'all the Rome I can' into the book and 'as little Story as I can keep out'. Letter cited by Edel, *The Life of Henry James*, Vol IV, *The Treacherous Years*, p. 273.
5. See the excellent essay by Tony Tanner, 'Proust, Ruskin, James and "le désir de Venise"' in *Henry James e Venezia*, Florence, Leo S. Olschki Editore, 1987, pp. 65 ff. Also the essay by Glauco Cambon, 'The Mazes of Venice', pp. 95 ff. in the same volume.
6. Henry James: 'Crapy Cornelia', first published in *The Finer Grain* (1910); republished by Macmillan, London in 1923: pp. 352 and 354.
7. Henry James, *Letters*, Vol. IV, p. 328.
8. James's publisher, Colonel George Harvey at Harper, New York, had promised to arrange serialization of his travel journal in the *North American Review*, followed by publication. Edel, *The life of Henry James*, Vol. V, *The Master*, p. 235.
9. Alexis de Tocqueville, *Democracy in America*, trans. Reeve, 1948, Vol. II, p. 228. And see the whole section, 'How the Aspect of Society in the United States is at Once Excited and Monotonous', pp. 288 ff.

PART TWO

The Note of Europe

4. An Encounter in Nôtre Dame
5. 'There to Reconstruct'
6. The Comedy of Moral Terms
7. Strether's Reasons
8. Values in Collision
9. Nihilism and Decorum

John Singer Sargent, *In the Luxembourg Gardens*, Paris, 1879.
The John G Johnson Collection, Philadelphia Museum of Art.

Chapter 4

An Encounter in Nôtre Dame

He would have issued, our rueful worthy, from the very heart of New England
... he had come to Paris in some state of mind which was literally undergoing,
as a result of new and unexpected assaults and infusions, a change almost hour
by hour.

Preface to *The Ambassadors*[1]

On the European scene, the 'restless analyst' in James is most thoroughly
present not in his voluminous travel writings, penetratingly observant
though they often are, but in his great novels of trans-cultural exploration.
Everything in *The Ambassadors* begins in enquiry. In Lambert Strether's
embassy, the process of discovery is the necessary condition of a successful
outcome. There are so many things he must know about the objective of his
journey. There are also matters which might seem peripheral, connected
with his understanding of himself, which nevertheless condition the whole
enterprise. James has us note from the beginning the effect of ambiguity in
'the oddity of a double consciousness. There was detachment in his zeal
and curiosity in his indifference.' (*Ambassadors*, p. 56) And his moment of
heightened consciousness is with us right from the beginning, in his acute
awareness, mingled with a touch of uncertainty, of 'the note of Europe'
(p. 55) – a note which largely consists in the sense of personal freedom.

Strether has set out on the embassy entrusted to him by the formidable
Mrs Newsome of Woollett, Massachusetts, to recover her errant son Chad
and return him to his proper inheritance as a New England industrialist. But
Strether's landing in Europe implies for him something further: a moment's
liberty, romantic effects, memories of his much effaced youth, some sense
of the recovery of a lost self which sets in train another level of reflection.
So discovery is to move on a double track: one follows the threads that are
the essential clues for the recovery of Mrs Newsome's wayward son;
another follows his own indifferent curiosity.

The former begins in a tissue of matters of fact, necessary to handling the
case, above all to a strategy of persuasion. With such facts the right cards
will be to hand. Yet their brute existence is fraught with problems of
interpretation that erode the clear shape of the project. What will he find in

Paris? What is the attraction of the city of art, sin and inconsequence to a young man of great expectations? To the necessary enquiry into the facts of the case are added, as he rapidly discovers, a secondary process of interpretation which is forced upon him, and an inner meditation which touches him in a deeper sense. Thus these questions of understanding unevenly fuse with the circumambient flickers of the sense of freedom that is the elusive but omnipresent 'tone' of his embassy.

Our understanding of his journey is necessarily connected with the curious mixture of emotions with which many readers conclude *The Ambassadors* – one element in which may well be irritation. We observe a reasoning process, only to see its effects aborted. Why does someone in the end act in a way contrary to his interest and his liking, when every rational step in his enquiry, every reflection on his own life as well as his changing understanding of the world about him, would require otherwise? We see two modes of ethical thinking in conflict, one teleological which has a full realization, to borrow a word from Dr Leavis; the other, barely hinted at in the action, resting on a deontological principle where the determinant is an unanalysable ethical intuition.[2] And we can see this conflict as a cultural consequence of a solid and durable aspect of American life, with a clear ancestry in the New England consciousness. It is a conflict between the Enlightenment tradition of secular and progressive thought and the moral absolutism of the Puritans, a conflict all too visible in American life as much today as a century ago. One might wish to conceive of Strether's fate as the necessary consequence of such a discrepant dualism, and see in him James's representation of the irresolvable division in American culture and indeed political inheritance.

Perhaps a touch of quaintness enters the 'note of Europe' which is conveyed by the walls and alleys of Chester rather than the docks of Liverpool. But a crucial element in the sense of freedom is the escape from a workaday world, the finding of an atmospheric *mise-en-scène* that opens on an alternative world to that of Woollett. This first circumstance is sketched with a touch of arch comedy. But there is a succession of moments in which the note is captured, with lesser or greater gravity. And the most powerful and elaborately prepared evocation of the note takes place in Nôtre Dame. It comes at a moment when the elements of the dramatic conflict have fully shaped themselves. The great cathedral is seen as a 'refuge from the obsession with his problem' even in company (p. 271) and as a model of the power of place to subvert and transcend.

Strether enters the cathedral in the spirit of the higher tourism: the search for both sensation and reflection that is partly illuminating through an element of unfamiliarity. He has been there before, of course, but the process of discovery continues. Nôtre Dame has that rare depth and special intensity of experience that is as far from the quotidian demands of his friends as from Woollett itself. The 'mighty monument' has its spell: 'He might have been a student under the charm of a museum – which was exactly what, in a foreign town, in the afternoon of life, he would have liked to be free to be.' (p. 272) One feels the faint breath of a much mellowed Gidean *disponibilité*, shorn of course of its more alarming possibilities and largely restricted to the sensations arising from the 'long dim nave' or from a walk by the Seine. But they are sensations certainly, and through them is felt the beautiful impalpability of capturing 'the note'.

Circumstances however do not allow the experience its purity. His attention is drawn to a mysterious passive figure for whom he invents a romantic identity, as from 'an old story', and is markedly slow to notice that she is the efficient cause of his presence in Paris and the primary object of his interpretative problems, Mme de Vionnet. James makes a triumph of the total improbability of this, as he does of the multiple incongruities in the scene which follows. Slowly out of the darkness and failure of perception – it is in fact Mme de Vionnet who recognizes him – emerges the gradual shaping of the awareness and understanding that will serve the occasion and move the combination of the story's elements. The penumbra of the spiritual, the shared pleasure in old and musty places enable the aborted romantic dream to transfer to his real acquaintance. Her air of profound devotion, the restrained and elegant manner, colour deeply the quality of the person. Yet into it erupts Strether's persistent and anxious query as to the nature of her relationship with Chad Newsome: is it innocent and virtuous? Or is it the worst, tainted by a carnality which one deeply fears, but hardly dares envisage? The unstable combination of pious associations, images of propriety, carnal suspicions and primitive fears whirls through Strether's mind like a frantic bat. The problem of interpretation is forced upon him in its most dramatic form.

The incongruous mixture has both its moving and its comic dimensions. What will follow is a series of contrasts, perspective shifts and reappraisals that are treated with the utmost delicacy and high-seriousness, yet tinged by the sense of comic discrepancy. We move at our ease from the grandeur of the cathedral to the good cheer of a little restaurant on the *quai*. Sensation is to some degree in the foreground. Yet Strether's mental processes reflect a development which he has only begun to understand, even if this little episode seems one of the high points of illumination. One dimension of the novel lies in the learning curve, through a series of steps by a man whose intellect and moral will are wholly bent on getting it right, where the sorting out process suggests the *Bildungsroman*, a sentimental education which, however qualified or eroded, constitutes a, or even *the*, primary line of interest. The distinctions, the steps by which a process of reflection evolves, are the essential stages of the action. What transformation will be possible through this reflection?

At this stage, shot through with disparities as his encounter may be, Strether feels the authenticity of his moment of experience, and James's mixture of eloquence with the wryness of double focus brings out the complexity of his method. One aspect of Strether's path seems to be that the process of getting it right involves the comedy of getting it wrong. For as the book unfolds the most solid insights are ironized by a further flash of recognition or by the turned corner of another perspective. Here Strether takes measure of how far he has come. 'Strether was to feel that he had touched bottom. He was to feel many things on this occasion, and one of them was that he had travelled far since that evening in London, before the theatre, when his dinner with Maria Gostrey, between the pink-shaded candles, had struck him as requiring so many explanations.' (p. 278)

That opening stage of explanations partly reflects the simple difference in social custom from Woollett. How does one come to be dining in a restaurant with a lady one barely knows? It is something totally absent from the Woollett code. There have been a number of steps from the pink-shaded candles to the luncheon by the Seine. Those that have followed the path of enquiry have been revealing but inconclusive. But patterns of feeling and awareness have revealed themselves, to alter his sense of what that enquiry might be about. One may not understand more precisely the relations between Chad and Mme de Vionnet and her daughter, or what conditions govern them, but one's perspective has subtly changed to an imaginative involvement that is both nuanced and open-ended.

The meeting in Nôtre Dame, the interplay of observations and the subsequent conversation make Strether feel that he has crossed some line, entering an *ambiance* hitherto warily observed from outside. But the experience is a dual one, that of a degree of attraction to the world of Marie de Vionnet, and of his palpable submission to sensation as a primary value. The scene has moved from the grey obscurity of the great church to the 'bright clean ordered water-side life' which comes in through the restaurant window. This disturbing awareness of being open to sensation had begun at Chester and is to continue with increasing intensity and complication. The effect is both a cautious evolution of feeling and a distancing from Mrs Newsome and the void of Woollett. Here, he suddenly seems, or at least feels, situated, as if he had a genuine and physical existence in a world which has been evoked through imagined fragments. What had seemed wholly other has become vividly present.

Of course, it is largely an illusion; Strether is far from touching bottom, from seeing the matter through all the way to the end, and the romantic intensity of this particular episode will yield to further awareness. The expression will return and there will be further occasion to look at its meaning. But one vivid occasion of its use is in the pastoral scene which precedes the terrible revelation of Chad and Marie in the rowing boat. Here again it is attached to immersion in immediate sensation, an experience of being at one with landscape and the natural world – a sensation totally exploded a moment later. How are we to see this harmony through the consequences of the events that follow? What value will it have in the alienation that marks the return to Woollett? To what extent is it ironised in that which Strether will take away, what Maria Gostrey calls his 'wonderful impressions'? For in the end it will be the sense of not belonging, of alienation that will predominate and James will acknowledge as much in Strether's last conversations both with Maria and with Marie. Yet James has caught us in a disconcerting double focus. The quality of an experience may be in question, ironised, shaped in context, without somehow destroying its value.

The double track of enquiry points to what is at least a double sense of truth in Strether's undertaking. One lies in the obvious demands of the narrative: the nature of the real circumstances of Chad Newsome, of all the ties that attach him to his European life. On the surface this investigation seems factual, but the understanding of the persons and events that surround them creates another demand. For this is also an enquiry into value, into what it is like to live in Chad's adopted world; we must meet the *dramatis personae*; see the form of life; and reach an assessment of it all. This is the point of the embassy both in its narrower and its wider sense. The gloomy comedy of Waymarsh performs the kind of counterpoint which pushes alternative readings of whatever circumstance Strether's way, with the delightful touch of crassness dressed as honest common sense. Any chunk drawn from the form of life about one becomes like the stone thrown in a pool, surrounded by concentric rings of interpretation. Even taking up the literal terms of Mrs Newsome's commission makes the barest matter a claim on perception, on the capacity to sort and evaluate evidence, where so much depends on the ability to see one's way through one's own preconceptions.

But there is no way in which the process could be other than reflexive; and the further dimension of truth lies in the effect of his experiences on Strether's sense of himself. The succeeding jolts to one's preconceptions put in train a process of inner discovery, like a curious mid-life *rite de passage* whose history is fused with the process of interpretation. Certainly in the meeting in Nôtre Dame both orders of perception are fully engaged. The inner course of Strether's reflection moves easily on to the moral reassessment of Mme de Vionnet, both processes shaped by the atmospheric power of suggestion that surrounds them in the great church. And the conversational exchange uses setting for explanation, in a context where brightness gives 'reasons enough'. The effect mingles impression with verbal exploration, in the kind of double focus where discovery of the world and of self are inseparable.

One important aspect of the process depends less upon Strether than upon others. Mme de Vionnet has made a move which is central to James's narrative method in *The Ambassadors* and is the pivot for a number of the exchanges with his female interlocutors. The action turns from the problems of Chad, of Mrs Newsome, Woollett, Europe itself – and in the case of Mme de Vionnet, of herself – to place Strether's moral dilemma, his reflections on it, his very awareness of the weight of the occasion, on centre stage. Strether is made the focal point by the sense that others need him. They invest him with an importance he would be reluctant to claim. And this gives Strether a standing in the action that his own words often do not underwrite. Mme de Vionnet addresses him as 'a man in trouble' as if he were the central matter of concern. Such a displacement creates in him a curious form of 'negative capability' which exploits his essential passivity. He becomes the spectator as principal actor. It is *his* novel, through taking on the consequences of the actions of others in an equilibrium of involvement and withdrawal, although our own involvement depends on that very projection of others which effectively enlarges our sense of what he is and why he prompts so deep a concern.

The impressions may be direct, but much of the construction of the self is indirect. A strange fissure may seem to divide these two sources of his being but Strether is dependent on both. The world of sensation has an immediacy stronger than James usually allows. And the indirect effects of social interplay convey that filtering of responsiveness which the complex occasion requires. The construction of the new Strether therefore involves the equilibration of opposites. The opposing modes give James that perilous unity his theme requires. Both are necessary to the continuous revaluation which is the essential course of the novel. Take a moment in the conversation by the banks of the Seine when Strether is struck by an unexpected quality: 'Strange and beautiful to him was her soft acuteness. The thing that moved him most was that she was so deeply serious. She had none of the portentous forms of it, but he had never come in contact, it

entertaining each other and speculating about the sort of personal relations that are best mentioned in a hush – an essentially frivolous scene?

This question of value will return in a variety of forms. But the character of 'Paris' and its social *ambiance* requires some clarification. *The Ambassadors* is often taken as a major example of 'the international theme' and certainly the transformation of Strether's sensibility is put to the account of that 'note of Europe' and of course, particularly of Paris. James gestures towards a large and active social scene. But the thought of Dorothea Krook that it is here one would go for 'the fullest, most direct portrayal of the Europeans'[4] fails to note that there are almost no Europeans in the novel. The only European of any substance is Marie de Vionnet. Her daughter Jeanne is barely sketched and Gloriani, the artist, is no more than a grandiose icon (and based to some extent on the American painter James McNeill Whistler). And even with Marie de Vionnet there are moments that do not entirely ring true. A French countess in whose family her younger American lover has such influence and whose whole manner is dominated by a pathetic eagerness to please is perhaps not entirely a model of the type.

As one scans the cast list of those assembled for *The Ambassadors* one sees a certain modification of 'the international theme'. Looking about at the inhabitants of Gloriani's garden the European presence is only in the crowd of 'extras' who have been brought on for use as décor. The known figures are almost entirely American. But if the cast is so substantially American, it is precisely a group that has chosen Europe, a group whose common ground is the rejection of whatever Woollett lies in their own particular past. Paris is the result of flight and a place of golden refuge. If a choice has been made there is an implied value even if it may be negative. Although with Little Bilham – and to some extent with Chad – one keeps returning to the sense of a wonderful place that exercises some beneficent magic. They are there for a mixture of physical beauty and those conditions which may be in certain senses intangible but which promote the love and practice of art. And although some of the Parisian décor has that tone of genteel travelogue which infuriated Leavis, we must grant James the assumption that the collective images are the expression of civilization itself, an expression that embodies social forms, politeness, consideration, style, the pleasure of conversation and perhaps, by the most wary extrapolation, the possibility of love. In this the guests of Gloriani, the little circle of artists and the wandering and tentative recipient of sensations – we might almost call him 'the restless analyst' – are on common ground.

But in terms of the collision of cultures, 'the international theme' effectively awaits the second embassy of the Pococks, when the force of moral difference will be dramatized – or at least the passion generated by the presumption of such difference. And at this point Strether is reduced more and more to spectator. The social conflict with its concomitant comedy has its dramatic moments and then sinks into the routine behaviour of the American in Paris: rounds of entertainment and many purchases. Strether is doubly dismissed from the role Woollett has assigned to him without exactly finding that there is any structured alternative, and indeed without seeking one. Without formulating the contrasting features of two forms of life he almost drifts into the recognition that in distancing and withdrawal a certain integrity can be pursued.

Yet something lies outside of this cool and protective mode and works through the gradual unfolding of the world of sensation. There is the flash of sunlight, the moment of physical wellbeing, the touches of ease with their poignant suggestion of an approach to an ecstasy never quite reached and not to be approached through reasons. In the moment of pleasure when, lying in the grass before the traumatic discovery scene in Book XI, the vividness of sensation reaches its high point, pure experience without the entanglement of social reference. Yet James is acting out a pictorial idea derived from Impressionist painting, a self-conscious immersion in pastoral, the discovery of authentic experience in the natural order through a model that is rich in civilized association. Strether seems to have committed himself to a process of awakening, of self-discovery, which remains deeply passive, a passivity to be filled by an awareness of possibility which too easily eludes. Here the lyrical intensity moves through the recollection of a painting, and he 'lost himself anew in Lambinet'. (p. 445) How deeply is this intense scene ironized by the discovery that follows: the palpable evidence of the carnal relation of Chad and Marie de Vionnet? James gives little away and everything seems to rest on its face value. One might think of a similar lyrical intensity in the pastoral – the moment when Rodolphe seduces Emma Bovary. But Flaubert's irony is both obvious and pervasive. Every step by which Emma's fantasizing adapts to the world of sensation is meticulously and drily drawn. Strether's fictionalizing is weaker and not self-referential: a notion of ideal pastoral beauty shaped by a mediocre painting. Does James know that it is mediocre? It does not matter; it is Strether's touchstone, a lost ideal recovered from a passing moment in Tremont Street many years ago. Is there an analogy to Emma's reliving of romantic novels? Certainly Strether's is more restrained, in better taste. And even in restraint Strether's pastoral imaging has an eloquence of abandon which is touching rather than absurd.

James postpones the irony. This beautifully sprung piece of improbability is brought off with a mixture of elegance and comic brio. Strether's jumping up and down to announce his presence is one of the few occasions when he takes a decisive action. In an instant the lyricism is turned into social comedy which contains its agonized strands of *mauvaise foi*. There follows a resplendent display of perfectly controlled awkwardness and embarrassment created by the wildly fortuitous circumstance. Appearances are beautifully preserved. But in the night that follows, Strether absorbs the effect of the lie, of the make believe, and the depth of the intimacy which lay behind it, a realization which leaves him 'lonely and cold'. (p. 468)

Yet it is in the rhapsodic pastoral moment that again 'he was touching bottom'. (p. 455) He has, or thinks he has, worked through the terms and consequences of his embassy. 'He was kept luxuriously quiet, soothed and amused by the consciousness of what he had found at the end of his descent.' What that is, James does not specify, beyond the thought of the achievement of his freedom, the escape from the 'special shyness' that has inhibited Strether's pleasure in his Parisian connections. James handles this lightly, placing a lull before the *bouleversement*. It is a lapse from good faith that Strether has feared. He effects a gentle and tentative summing-up, an assessment of the commitments and consequences his embassy has involved. But 'the filthy truth', as Dostoevsky calls it, lies in wait: the irrelevance of beautiful moments, the brutal intransigence of the workaday world, the all too true carnality that he has done everything possible to evade. A little boat rounds the curve in the river and shows him that he has not yet begun to touch bottom and has in fact dressed the more disturbing possibilities in a protective vagueness, 'as a little girl might dress her doll'. (p. 468)

Has James placed this touch of dramatic irony so effectively that we feel an excess of force, even heaviness of hand? One cannot accept such outrageous fortuity without a smile and an awareness that the fictional game is pushed to the limits of the possible. Yet one may well think that for Strether the moment of intensity by the riverbank, when the immediacy of sensation had its force, embodies a value that will survive the devastating truth that rounds the bend of the river.

Of course for us, the outsiders, the readers of great novels, there is no way to touch bottom. A moment's reflection or an hour's rereading sees us safely afloat. Strether's effort to fix the value of his experience in all of his vulnerabilty commands both respectful sympathy and the cold eye that irony forces on us. But it is a perspective that will never entirely stand still. The dramatic movement from ecstasy to comedy to irony leaves none of the components untouched by the others, each phase re-read in terms of the subsequent, almost as if the sense of the narrative movement were to be read

backwards. And there is a doubling effect by which Strether's expectations
control our own, yet we know and understand things that he does not. So if
the main interest of the action is in the development of his consciousness,
our relation to that development is necessarily unstable. It is partly the
element of blindness in Strether's consciousness that is the invitation, the
empty spaces both in his character and in his grasp of a world whose
elements are both familiar and otherwise. When the ironical effect is forced
upon him, it touches us with sympathy and a further irony, more complex
than his could be.

Yet an effect analogous to our own, and which faintly pre-empts our own
sense of perspective, lies in the awareness of how the impression will live
on beyond the moment of its occurrence. At one point in the scene in
Gloriani's garden, Strether's mind is represented as living in a future which
we are largely forbidden to contemplate, from which the closure of the
narrative excludes us. Caught in the spell of Gloriani's presence he allows
'his grey interior' to 'drink in the sun of a clime not marked in his old
geography'. The memory bank from his earlier passage in Europe is too pale
and thin. But this memory will be projected beyond the limits of the novel.
'He was to remember again repeatedly the medal-like Italian face, in which
every line was an artist's own, in which time told only in tone and
consecration; and he was to recall in especial, as the penetrating radiance, as
the communication of the illustrious spirit itself, the manner in which, while
they stood briefly, in welcome and response, face to face, he was held by the
sculptor's eyes.' (pp. 199–200) Here the most powerful of impressions,
underlined by a rather overwrought rhetoric, has, without any precise
intellectual content, the force of 'the deepest intellectual sounding to which
he had ever been exposed'.

James projects this power into a future to which it will be wholly alien.
'He was in fact quite to cherish the vision of it, to play with it in idle hours;
only speaking of it to no one and quite aware he couldn't have spoken
without appearing to talk nonsense.' (p. 200) The message was, after all,
both overwhelmingly important and totally opaque. It was, of course, the
experience of a smile. Will it have some further value in the invisible years
to come? Whatever that may be, it will be altered by the distances of time,
place and culture.

And in this spirit of projection what could be made of the other high
moment in Gloriani's garden when Strether is seized by a passionate
recognition, when he weighs the problem of his own identity, not as it is but
as he might wish it to be? In whose image would that diffident self wish to
be recast? 'Gloriani?' suggests Little Bilham. But a figure at the side of a

young girl in a softly plumed white hat moves into centre focus. It is Chad and 'all vagueness vanished. It was the click of a spring – he saw the truth.' (p. 217) If Chad is this truth incarnate, James has not told us how to take the ricochet effects and measure the consequences. We can see the nostalgic call of his lost youth and the delight in imagining it reborn, recaptured in terms of physical beauty and cosmopolitan style in this urban Arcadia. Can we see also the object of desire in some deeper and more alarming sense than is accessible to the perception or vocabulary of Woollett? James is merciful and withholds whatever knowledge he might have. But the emulative passion is fully unleashed: 'it was that rare youth he would have enjoyed being "like" '. Here is the moment of recognition that an imagined future might wish to suppress, along perhaps with the sense of a falsification of any authentic self that might be pursued.

Such authenticity has little help in the way of substance from a past that we must nevertheless presuppose, and that is evoked from an early stage. The dusty yellow paperbacks of his youth that reach out to him again, the longing for some historical depth that the meditation in Nôtre Dame discloses, the shadowy and evanescent domestic world, give only a fragile role to memory. Hence the imperative is problematic. Strether has warned himself as the flow of sensations continues, as he grazes the edge of café tables by the Odéon that 'he wasn't there to dip, to consume – he was there to reconstruct. He wasn't there for his own profit – not, that is, the direct; he was there on some chance of feeling the brush of the wing of the stray spirit of youth.' (p. 122) He hears 'the faint sound, as from far off, of the wild waving of wings'. But it is like the distant trumpets of the Verdi *Requiem*, heard with an intermittent attention disturbed by the prospect of consequences that are immeasurable. For how can even the faintest brush be felt other than by substitution, by a form almost of projective memory? There will at least be the recounted events. But the project is diffused in the course of the action, as new awareness and possibility vary memory's terms.

What opens is a gulf between the imaginative life and the real where the most alluring visual perceptions and human connections seem to beckon, to frame a form of life that one might reasonably enter. And we have various fragmentary versions of such an entry floated before us in the tentative reflections of the *flâneur*: 'of feeling the general stirred life of connexions long since individually dropped. Strether had become acquainted even on this ground with short gusts of speculation – sudden flights of fancy in Louvre galleries' (p. 116) that should connect the past with the present.

But the past preserves its reticence and the bright impressions fall on dusty ground. The city itself, 'the vast bright Babylon, like some irridescent object, a jewel brilliant and hard', reveals itself in its excitement and alienness. And just as the jewel professes a unity that would resist the analysis of its components, so the slightest sensation, whether delicate or overwhelming, has a distinct unanalysable identity. Like Hume's simple impressions which become the building blocks of knowledge, they are irreducible, and beyond accountability or conceptual explanation.

How close to bottom do these impressions touch? There is nothing in Strether's reflective process that would turn the impressions into the elements of a moral code. To generalize from the impression is precisely the kind of move that Strether would necessarily refuse. For where would it lead? To value them for their own sake might point in the direction of a paganism where the role of sensation would predominate. And the term 'Pagan' is applied in an impulsive way to Chad (p. 170) without following up the implications, as if James thought to try the idea on and quickly abandoned it. However powerfully the moment of identification with Chad may touch upon the truth, there is no path to be followed. Much of Strether's experience seems, in this way, difficult of access and simply to be taken as given. Explanations would seem rationalizations at best. And as such they would hardly fit among the good reasons Strether ultimately seeks. This primary experience simply is, and its value is present in the moment of sensation. I do not mean something of Pater's intensity, or a Gidean notion of the moment. The impressions may be simple and vague. But James represents a quality of experience that eludes the moral design and would hardly be assimilated into it.

How then is Strether to work on his project of reconstruction, of capturing some viable version of his lost self that incorporates these sensory fragments? To generalize on such a ground, to make them the substance of a form of life, would be to move in the direction of a sensual paganism that would be in conflict with the spirit of his intellectual enquiry and would ring false in the whole Puritan sensibility. To move towards a Gidean equilibrium between the claims of sensation and Puritan severity would stretch the Strether persona beyond recognition.

Yet what is one to do with the discovery of that flow of sensation and personal awareness that Paris has opened up? Perhaps nothing beyond observation and understanding. Discovery is simply there to be registered as an end in itself. From the beginning he has absorbed 'the immediate and the sensible' (p. 56) and a 'sharper survey of the elements of Appearance than he had for a long time been moved to make'. (p. 59) Yes, one may even change one's own appearance to the extent of a hat and necktie. But his engagement with forms of life reflects the 'detachment in his zeal' that imposes its built-in limits. And between the immediacy of pleasure and the ultimate consummation in sexual desire lies the barrier reef of moral codes. They have, above all in their most severe Woollett mode, shaped Strether's sensibility. Yet it would be crass to see this as a simple conflict between Puritan, provincial America and the cynical hedonism of Europe. Everything becomes involved with its opposite and, above all, the terms of moral codes are themselves subject to continuous re-examination.

There is, of course, an ambiguity in 'reconstruct' which James has not set out to resolve. One sense, that of 'recapture' leaves us directed towards the past, while that of 'remake' would embody a process of transformation. We see both of these operative in Strether's experience of Europe. Yet while 'recapture' draws on a past so shadowy as to be almost hypothetical, 'remake' can, in the end, bear only the weight of the sharpening of awareness itself. To see and feel the claims of a form of life that could give substance to 'remake' becomes in itself substance enough. The protagonist as observer, moral register, 'sensor',[5] indicator and measure of response provides the whole scope and limit of remaking. Caught between two worlds and incompatible claims, it is the limit of what Strether can do, and even, in a sense, of what a novelist can do. But the terms of this must be examined.

Chapter 6

The Comedy of Moral Terms

For all its appearance of formal perfection *The Ambassadors* creates its coherence through diverse means. Nothing could be further from the lyricism of the river bank or the evocative shadows of Nôtre Dame than the brilliant, stylish comedy of much of the dialogue. It is here that James puts his *ficelle* to glittering use, for it is Maria Gostrey who sets the tone and pace of the verbal play which becomes an essential vehicle of Strether's exploration. The effect of James's theatrical years is seen quite fully. Some scenes, where the narrative takes on the sharpness and vividness of high comedy, resemble miniature implants from the theatre.

It begins in London with an evening at the theatre and dining by the light of candles with rose coloured shades, and begins by questioning the essential presupposition of the embassy: 'Are you sure she's so very bad for him?' (p. 93) Two or three kinds of effect are delicately fused; the lightness and charm of Maria's interrogation confront the stolidity and moral severity with which Strether views the case. The beloved son of Woollett is undoubtedly sunk in a depravity which could contain no compensating value. The object of desire must be 'base' and 'venal' while it is a 'wretched' and 'obstinate' boy who has darkened his admirable mother's life.

The rigid commitment to Woollett's moral code and terms sets up a dialectical game in which one sense of a phrase is undermined by another. That Mrs Newsome and her daughter are 'remarkably fine women' brings the enquiry 'Very handsome, you mean?' which produces a measured series of qualifications that end upon the daunting name of 'Pocock'. The notion that true character breeds a touch of fear, that the two ladies are formidable and intimidating, is reached by way of a fine balance of literalism and its comic subversion. As for the unmentionable product of Woollett, it passes fleetingly by as does the Review, whose green cover seems its most distinguishing feature except that it is Mrs Newsome's tribute to the ideal. ("You go in for tremendous things" remarks Maria.)

Like the superb playwright he never quite became James has concentrated threads, hints, promises, explanatory fragments and many twists and turns of tone into this marvellous scene and done so with incredible economy. (pp. 93–107) But aside from its complex explanatory and promissory functions, one

64

feature of the scene stands out. The play of irony is almost entirely at Strether's expense. Perhaps this cannot be helped, for the attempt to bring Woollett fully into view cannot be managed without a tonality that indicates both its weight and limitation. Nevertheless, Strether is played as the straight man whose assumptions, judgments and commitments are slowly invaded by a slight sense of the ridiculous. He comes through as serious, upright, innocent and reluctant to question – almost a little thick. It will be many steps before the sensibility of the moral register, the 'sensor', comes clearly into view.

Yet the scene is punctuated by the growing sense of adventure, and the Strether who will open himself to new experience and new understanding has been marked from the start. 'Nothing could have been odder than Strether's sense of himself as at that moment launched in something of which the sense would be quite disconnected from the sense of his past and which was literally beginning there and then.' (p. 59) These pasts are stratified. We have seen the importance of reaching out to an older and much forgotten past. To disconnect from the past of Mrs Newsome is, at least partly, to discover that tentative and buried past which preceded Woollett, where the long-since purchased yellow paperbound volumes moulder on a back shelf somewhere. If the break is effected through the impressions of Paris, through the awareness of another tone or quality of life, this putting in question of the codes of Woollett also operates from and within them. After all they are to a large degree himself and have to be the point of departure. That both Strethers, that of the deep past and of the immediate operative past, should come into this process is of course necessary. The buried Strether provides openings. Yet they are indicated lightly and delicately; and the role that the youthful Strether plays in any new sense of self is veiled. But the more immediate past of the Newsome connection will put formidable obstacles to that beginning which is so odd.

A large part of the dismantling of those obstacles will come through the *ficelle*'s capacity to give a new perspective to that immediate past, which at their early meeting in Chester hits upon the embarrassment Strether feels in enjoying himself so much. Yes, the failure of Woollett is the failure to enjoy. (p. 64) And this is the beginning of an amiable critique.

More important, however, is the way in which the moral language of Woollett is subjected to a playful repositioning. Maria and Strether have reached the point of accounting for the now admitted transformation of Chad, and hence of the female presence responsible:

> There must, behind every appearance to the contrary, still be somebody – somebody who's not a mere wretch, since we accept the miracle. What else but such a somebody can such a miracle be?

He took it in. 'Because the fact itself is the woman?'
'A woman. Some woman or other. It's one of those things that have to be.'
'But you mean at least a good one.'
'A good woman?' She threw up her arms with a laugh. 'I should call her excellent!' (p. 179)

The play on the moral, quasi-moral and extra-moral uses of 'good' is carried out with a delightful *sprezzatura*. Maria's game is directed at the rigidity of Strether's 'classifications' and more generally at the separation of the moral sense from the values implicit in other civilized 'goods'. And the ambiguity is exploited elsewhere – as say, in the warning about Chad, 'He's not as good as you think', where 'good' is precisely the loyalty to the dangerous connection and its civilizing force. She will see Strether through in all sorts of ways from that first long conversation. But part of guidance is destruction, and the most powerful of these destructive dislocations bear on the assumptions built into Strether's moral language – the pillars of his moral thought.

This opening out of moral perspective is doubled in the 'virtuous attachment' in the conversation with Little Bilham (p. 187) where a similar ambiguity is used by Bilham to reassure. He knows that Strether will mean something else by 'virtuous' but in the best of faith he overrides Strether's meaning with his own. It misleads Strether into some false constructions. But he cannot be told the whole truth for two reasons. If he knew, the narrow sense of the term would prevail, his embassy would come to an end and the world the *ficelle* holds out to him would be foreclosed. And then, he is not yet ready to face such implications. Perhaps in some sense he never is, but insofar as part of his learning curve consists in a sentimental education he must adhere to the principle of *festina lente*.

The absence of the raw truth may lead to the odd fantasy about Chad's future, about his relations with Jeanne, and there is a certain comic mileage in his misreadings, his serious, honourable, high-minded and largely inept efforts to work through the factual and moral maze. But they are gently handled. Maria mixes a touch of flattery with an appreciation of the material cause: 'No – you reason well! But of course there's always dear old Woollett.' (p. 190) It is somehow an end-stop which his imagination puts behind him in the construction of hypothetical cases. Of course one place where the solid reality of Woollett is brushed aside is in the failure to understand that a Parisian marriage – whether to Marie or Jeanne – would no more satisfy Woollett than life in Woollett would enhance the life of a Parisian. It is not merely a matter of his mistaking the circumstances, but of an unrealistic assessment, an excessive and perhaps romanticized instinct to invent the ideal solutions to the problems that surround him. 'Everything's possible' says Strether. (p. 193) And such imagining represents his struggle with the problem of interpretation. The future of Chad, the virtuous attachment, the character and position of the two ladies is sorted out – and of course, mistakenly – in traditional novelistic terms, the proper and suitably romantic marriage. 'He already saw himself discussing [with Mme de Vionnet] the attractions of Woollett as a residence for Chad's companion.' (p. 219)

It does not stop there. After marrying Chad to Jeanne he thinks to marry Bilham to Jeanne and later Bilham to Mamie. James exploits the comic possibilities of all this with a gentle discretion. It is the thought of a man of good will. The impulse to create the scenario, to solve the problems of others is only contingently grotesque and the moral seriousness is only lightly punctured by Maria or Bilham. But even the great scene of moral exhortation to Bilham – 'Live all you can' – followed by the epiphany of his vision of Chad, is touched by Bilham's wry remark: 'Well, you *are* amusing – to *me*.'

The narrative has been distanced by a reflexive irony in capturing the manner: 'Slowly and sociably, with full pauses and straight dashes, Strether had so delivered himself.' (p. 216) Whether this is a parody of Howells, the source of the exhortation, or of James himself, there is no doubt of the presence of a smile, to which Bilham's response adds another. We are aware of the seriousness of it all, of the grand moment of self discovery, of the inner turbulence which accompanies the awareness of lost selves and of the perils of rebirth, the pain of loss and the urgency of the message. But what is the force of the smile at such a high moment?

It is perhaps too natural to take this high moment at its face value, to privilege, so to speak, the innerness and the drama of the struggle that Strether undergoes. But this would be untrue to the balance *The Ambassadors* seems designed to achieve. For we are also aware that it is faintly ridiculous, if not in substance then in style and in the lack of any real understanding of the persons and contexts addressed, of the world in which his embassy must necessarily operate. The ironic signal is given on the climactic occasion. Strether's enquiry is far from over, and the examination of terms, values and the diverse understanding of those values flows steadily on. Miss Barrace finds the friendship of Chad and Marie 'beautiful' and ridicules the value of marriage which is Strether's model of life's best solution. Marriage in general does not cut that dazzling a figure in James. The Puritan moralist coexists with the aesthete and romantic in a character that picks up first one thread then another but is unsure what he can make of the mix. But the very attribution of beauty to the unmarried connection wrongfoots Strether again and leads him, with relief, to the moral conclusion that the relationship is 'innocent'. ' "It's innocent", he repeated – "I see the whole thing." ' And the conclusion is partly based on a misunderstanding of Miss Barrace and a muddle about the identity in question.

I have emphasized these comic aspects of Strether's quest partly because it is in this novel, with the sharp reversals and double-takes of theatrical dialogue, that James can extract the most from trial balloons, false hypotheses, multiple wrongfootedness on the path Strether must take to that mixture of enlightenment and pained discovery which will be the real outcome of his Parisian episode. The colouration of the whole by this method sets *The Ambassadors* apart from *The Wings of the Dove* and *The Golden Bowl*. It is provocatively amusing in a way that they are not. The bluff humour of Bob Assingham is usually awkward and makes him an outsider to *The Golden Bowl*'s tonality. But the many scenes in *The Ambassadors* that are played for comic effect do not diminish the seriousness. The mixed effect of 'all comically, all tragically' that we see at the end marks the interdependence of two modes, and a clearly intended sense of the whole.

A certain self-conscious placing of the interchanges at the right level of lightness enters into the description of the action itself to almost underline a special quality of the occasion: 'Strether laughed' or 'he laughed' or 'she laughed'; conversation is pursued 'cheerfully', concluded 'almost gaily'. Of course these are commonplaces that might well appear in many sorts of conversation, but it is their frequency and cumulative effect that seem to indicate an insistence on James's part that this lightness of verbal flow is both characteristic and significant. Yet it does not always point to the real sense of an exchange, for the lightly turned and witty occasion may point beyond itself. The tonalities of comedy are subversive and the laughter rubs off, qualifies both the New England high seriousness and the poignancy of the belated *Bildungsroman*. We have seen those moments in which Strether is in the last perception caught somewhat off balance, and the point of the comic dislocation is far from comic. The decentring effect of comedy is a means to the shock of discovery, and the process of gradually thickening perceptions derives from a strong sense of incongruity.

Incongruities are of many kinds and one of Strether's gifts is in the realization of difference. In Chad's flat he was to feel in 'the presence of new measures, other standards'. (p. 137) With Bilham and Barrace he is 'often at sea', so that 'his sense of the range of reference was merely general and ... on several different occasions he guessed and interpreted only to doubt'. (p. 139) And much of this slippage is in groping for the meaning of terms. In trying to get things straight he is also subjected to an irony which approaches the outrageous:

'I understand what a relation with such a woman – what such a fine high friendship – may be. It can't be vulgar or coarse – and that's the point.'

'Yes, that's the point', said Little Bilham. 'It can't be vulgar or coarse. And bless us and save us, *it isn't!* It's, upon my word, the very best thing I ever saw in my life, and the most distinguished.' (pp. 263–264)

And this version of the lie is a value statement, a marker which Strether will eventually come to understand.

The search for the right language, the right moral terms will go on, and the embassy of the Pococks will return him to the language of the Woollett absolute, perhaps not so much a moral code based on absolute principles as a series of absolute conventions which it is fatal to transgress and which are stated less in abstract terms than in social. Strether may believe in the early chapters that this code is his own, but the propaedeutic games may first unsettle, then open the way to an engagement with their terms which form a part of his real undertaking, one which has begun to infiltrate his more formal intentions by a necessity he is slow to understand. The continuous quest for the right description: 'good', 'bad', 'coarse', 'beautiful', 'virtuous' or otherwise, which moves through the dialogue evolves into the sort of modulation by which opposites lose their force and moral categories lose their precise form.

You can read much in *The Ambassadors* as the subversion of mindless moral stances and rigid categories. The Puritan tradition is systematically demolished and a prime weapon has been comedy. As the project advances the tone darkens and the comedy shifts its target to the Pococks. These characters themselves are almost colour-coded: Jim, ludicrous; Sarah, terrifying; Mamie, sympathetic. It is the handling of the manner of it all that gives the second embassy the look of a conventionalized comic routine: the wonderfully simple, unreflective Americans in Paris. Strether is of course displaced, his official function at an end, and he becomes a bit actor on the margins, not even allowed the mediating role for which he has prepared himself. His efforts at interpretation are rejected with contempt by Sarah and there are certain senses in which his identity seems to fade. He procrastinates in the face of the interpretative task, becomes a low-key conversational guide to the pleasures of the city, an ancillary to their version of the grand tour. The grand confrontation with the spirit of Woollett is postponed, its view made subject to oblique enquiry, diffused and casual contact, until it is finally revealed in all its majesty in the interview at the hotel. Again the theatrical handling of Sarah's crushing presence is done with an overbearing farce that makes it a mixture of violent and ridiculous.

Strether's tentative explanations and defensive gestures have a dignified vulnerability that is close to pathos.

If Strether shrinks before the moral conviction of the Pocock embassy it is partly because of his habitual politeness. Is it also because the law of Woollett is written in his heart? If so, the language of that law no longer is. Yet what power may the law have whose language, and hence, whose rationale, have faded away, except for the palpably stupid and bigoted for whom rationale would have no meaning? In the ensuing conversation with Chad he distances himself: they could not understand him and he cannot quarrel. Yet the exchange also follows a long meditation – waiting again – on Chad's balcony, in which he tries to recapture the voice with which his new experience spoke to him three months before:

> All voices had grown thicker and meant more things; they crowded on him as he moved about – it was the way they sounded together that wouldn't let him be still. He felt, strangely, as sad as if he had come for some wrong, and yet as excited as if he had come for some freedom. But the freedom was what was most in the place and the hour; it was the freedom that most brought him around again to the youth of his own that he had long ago missed. (p. 426)

And this concrete sense of loss is put with an intensity and immediacy wholly alien to the world of Woollett; the substance of his loss becomes 'to a degree it had never been, an affair of the senses'.

> That was what it became for him at this singular time, the youth he had long ago missed – a queer concrete presence, full of mystery, yet full of reality, which he could handle, taste, smell, the deep breathing of which he could positively hear. It was in the outside air as well as within; it was in the long watch, from the balcony, in the summer night, of the wide late life of Paris. (p. 426)

In the palpability of the past in the present we are reminded of *The Sense of the Past* and of 'The Jolly Corner'. Yet there is something evanescent in this rebirth, and it will be important to ask about the possibilities and limits of this powerful sense of freedom. But its precarious quality is marked by the acceptance of a parasitic ground. With the entry of Chad he is aware that: 'It was in truth essentially by bringing down his personal life to a function all subsidiary to the young man's own that he held together' (p. 427). So the self that seems to be rediscovered is wholly dependent on another, a real being living in the present. But what gain is there in the freedom of a vicarious existence? Does this perilous contingency qualify any substantial transformation that might come out of Strether's embassy and limit for him, almost invisibly, any consequence of his 'wonderful impressions'? Is there any irony in the thought that these impressions are pure moments of consumption, have no value or importance beyond being consumed, rest in the isolated self as intransitive mental states? Would such a view imply that, just as the transformation of Chad is dubious in the end, so it is with Strether?

The man from Woollett has glanced out of the window and seen the all too alluring world in which a venture of his own will never take place. Yet Strether must remain loyal to the old order while abandoning it. It is not that the transformation of Strether will be seen as ultimately illusory but that a vast space will open between the world he has come to understand and the one he must inhabit, and where impressions of the other will no doubt be strictly his own. This intransitivity of freedom, this discovery of limits, must affect our sense of the whole – whether we can touch bottom or not.

Chapter 7

Strether's Reasons

Much that we have seen of Strether's 'reconstructive' process has been made possible by his two female interlocutors, Maria and Marie. A large proportion of the newly found confidence, the enlarged sense of himself comes from those voices that buoy him up and underline his personal importance in the unfolding and consequences of his embassy. First of all, the underlying diffidence of the man who has never made much of a mark in the world is turned to advantage. Confidence is built on the slightest observation. Maria, out of the whimsical circumstances of Waymarsh going shopping, assures Strether that Waymarsh is stupid compared to himself, and that his own failure in life is a form of distinction: 'Thank goodness you're a failure – it's why I so distinguish you! Anything else today is too hideous. Look about you – look at the successes. Would you *be* one, on your honour?' (p. 84) This little scene imposes a revaluation which may have its ironic touch, but is perfectly consonant with James's growing disquiet about America and the nature of success in American life. But the man of failure is invested with a number of unspecified powers with respect to others: he is to save Chad and at a later point to save Marie.

These powers are largely the creation of women: from the plenipotentiary role derived from Mrs Newsome to the strategic arrangements of Maria and Marie. Chad too, for obvious reasons, flatters the ambassador and magnifies his role. Marie, in their first interview, even if some of the touches here may go awry, puts herself in the position of soliciting approval, seeks to enter his confidence and indeed to persuade him to save her. No one seems to doubt that he can persuade Mrs Newsome of the beauty of the current state of affairs, or to see that in varying the terms of his involvement his borrowed powers are likely to be transitory. And the putative capacity to make some fundamental difference to Chad's position creates Strether's importance among Chad's acquaintance. As the embassy continues, the scope of its role increases. Attributed powers take on a semblance of reality.

There is of course a change of his affective commitments. The feeling for Chad moves from fastidious distaste to delighted surprise to the magical moment of identification in Gloriani's garden. The relation with Marie is essential to the growth of awareness, the model of old-world civility. A certain modest satisfaction pervades it all, but he is 'conscious of everything but of what would have served him.' (p. 155) The growth of self is selfless. A creation of others, a servant of others, he cannot establish and preserve an identity without the curious mixture of trust and expectation that flows into him from others. Even the *ficelle*, who from the beginning sees herself as a continuous mediator between 'the huge load of our national consciousness' (p. 66) and those possibilities of the civilizing power that is Europe, has a clearer sense of an innerly-shaped identity that provides a sharply focused point of view – and this in spite of James's avowed intention to use her as a mere device. But even she, here proper to the role in which James has cast her, has an existence ancillary to the lives of others. It is largely in the bloodstream of the Newsomes – the absent mother, the hidden Chad and the terrifying Sarah – that we have a sense of the will directed to the ends of the self. Only in Marie de Vionnet is there that simple longing – shared as Strether notes with such as chambermaids – in which we see any marked indication of desire.

Certainly, insofar as desire is a form of presence in the self, it is wholly absent in Strether. Only in the selfless regard for others does such a force manifest itself in the final pages, simply in the desire for the appropriately satisfying conclusion to the action. But one must ask whether the element of shyness, the reticence which is a mark of good manners also marks the void over which one would have to step for any substantive engagement with what he himself has called 'life'.

Of course there is a large literature of such enigmatic distancing, which is far from Jamesian, from the grand Russian tradition of 'superfluous men' through Musil, Rilke, Sartre and so many modernists. But with James this hint of the void is placed in the most active and fully collaborative social exchange. The only alienation Strether suffers is within, in a space that the endless round of visits cannot fill. There are curious aspects of this: a *Bildungsroman* where the registers of new awareness and understanding are so vividly and systematically evoked and yet where something in the still centre is unmoved, and a sentimental education without sentimental engagements or the kind of desire that could bring them into being. The 'charm of it', as James puts it, is to some extent affected by what we think of the ending, under the spell of the closely choreographed ritual of withdrawal.

This ending implies the working out of several conditions, and one of them relates directly to the narrative form. For if James had considered (a most improbable thought) an alternative ending, he would have known that he was writing another sort of novel altogether, in which the resolution that saved Strether from Woollett for golden years by the Seine would have cast light back over the whole. Leaving aside any of the highly improbable personal connections that might have evolved, it is impossible to imagine how one would see the whole from such a perspective. It would somehow fail to ring true even though in the evolution of Strether's character it is as reasonable as not – and though the choice of somehow remaining in Paris flashes through Strether's mind. And this failure relates to our sense of the sort of novel it is, with an artistic integrity that is more than contingently tied to its outcome. The choice of any alternative destiny would change the meaning of everything else. The deeply memorable – and consciously marked to become memory – episode in Gloriani's garden would lose its revelatory character and be subsumed into a continuing form of Parisian life. After all, one could go to Gloriani's on any Sunday. The extraordinary vision would become routine rather than emblematic, as Gloriani's profile is to Strether. Instead of a profound revelation of life, it would become simply – life.

The narrative control of expectation has further remorseless effects, imposing a necessary rigour which it would be fatal to violate. Consider *La Princesse de Clèves*. There is no reason, after the death of her husband, why the princess should not accept the approaches of the Duc de Nemours. She is attracted to him, did not love her husband and accepting Nemours would violate no sentimental or social code. But with the slightest crack in her resistance, a study of austerity and pride would become a vulgar romance. And Jamesian fastidiousness could, surely, never accept the reduction of his wry and ironic comedy to any such lower form of satisfaction.

But Strether's final refusal, against the grain of indicated advantages, does not make him a hero of the absurd, however much he acts against his interest and understanding, indeed, against the value of all that he has discovered in the course of his great enquiry. For the load of American consciousness – to paraphrase Maria – has a deeply determinate form in the Puritan version. If the law of Woollett has been seen through, criticized, weighed in the balance and found wanting, utterly dismissed, its grip of steel still represents some Eumenidean truth, a truth for which we must find psychological and social forms.

One version of this representation lies in the moral value of disinterest and of the self-denying conduct which is its implementation. Strether's evolving reflections are not related to ends, but only to understanding. This perspective is built in to the comedy of discovery, the abolition or effacement of moral categories. Nussbaum sees value in the implicit power 'to confront reigning models of political and economic rationality with the consciousness of Strether'[6] – a value both of perception and as moral property. But as we have observed, it is part of Strether's gradual attuning of sensibility to discover that these assumptions cannot, above all, be expressed in moral terms without a crassness that in some way falsifies. Context destroys the 'reigning models'.

So if any paradigm or alternative model can be found through the operation of awareness, of understanding itself, it seems to be James's very point that this is not easily resolved into moral expressions, codes, categories. Its very nature is to see their divisiveness and their limits. But we are dangerously close to using the term 'moral' in two quite different senses. One is in reference to a set of rules by which our social and personal obligations are determined. The other is as the indicator of what the best possible form of life might be. Some of the discrepancies involved will be examined further in *The Golden Bowl*. But if we wish to conceive of a 'morality' of awareness, of understanding for its own sake, the implication is a form of distancing which seems a necessary part of Strether's positioning of himself and of his decision-making process.

By distance, I do not mean alienation. The greatest passion is involved in the identification with Chad and the fulsome sympathy with Marie. The sight of Jeanne at Gloriani's is the magical moment that gives Strether a new and glittering sense of the possible beauty of the world, the lyrical invitation it extends to him. In these imaginative senses the engagement is powerful and unqualified. And yet upon reflection, there is that tiny gap, the curious 'inner distance' between experience and its register. There is something paradoxical in the sense of so close and yet so far, so deeply involved but with a necessary small corner of reservation.

Is the particular price to be paid for a morality of awareness, of perception, precisely the inability to act in any substantive way? Strether does of course act, or presumes that he is doing so, although that action may well be no more than creating for others the space for reflection – a space which may be illusory. For some (Chad and Marie) it is not needed, while for the spirit of Woollett it is totally wasted. And if his action for others is perhaps less decisive than he has wished, action for himself is impossible. One feature of this is not entirely clear. Has this inability been coded into Strether from the start? Or is it part of the 'sentimental education' that he has discovered the practical effect of this inner distance, a deep resistance to the operation of the self?

A totally disinterested morality would be no morality at all. If observation, perception, reflection do not lead to some form of choice that is consummated in some course of action, it is strangely empty of the responsibility which we normally attach to moral reasoning. We must look both at the abstract implications of detaching reasons from actions, and at the full sense of what Strether's experience has brought him, to see how we understand him as the vehicle of this larger concern.

'To be right' is the final rationale that Strether gives for his return – for which the necessary condition is: 'Not, out of the whole affair, to have got anything for myself.' (p. 512) We can hardly universalize a morality of such selflessness for it is in a sense concerned only with the self, and expresses a profound egoism. Strether for one thing fails to note the value he has come to have for others and hence, that his disappearance will be a loss. No social or moral order in which our obligations to each other are reasonably expressed can be derived from this. The effect is limited to the single context of 'the whole affair'. And to an unanalysable choice of a principle which need apply only to himself. One might even say that there is no *moral* reason for Strether's selflessness, only that to do otherwise would simply be inappropriate, unworthy of him as he sees himself.

But does he see himself as he always did? For if a certain ambiguity hangs over the transformation of Chad from provincial oaf to charming *boulevardier* – real, apparent, or Strether's illusion – an even greater ambiguity hangs over Strether. When he pronounces the judgment and the decisions he finds necessary, is he the same man from Woollett or is he the transformed Strether who has undergone the greatest, most consequential educational experience of his life? The turbulent mixture of 'wrong' and 'freedom' we saw earlier almost suggests an immovable set of opposites, with the evocation of his youth a quasi-Proustian reflection that has a value in the present only as perception, only as a contemplative moment which is almost outside of time.

But that will not be the case, and the most difficult assessment is to relate the process of Strether's thinking to its self-denying conclusion. If the process has involved the gradual sifting which has broken down the rigid terms of moral categories; if it has connected past with present in a fashion that gives a new wholeness to Strether's life; if it has involved the receptiveness to sensation and the quiet assessment of the civilizing effect of *ambiance*, of that feel of the singular value of the accumulated past and its palpable presence – then how do these aspects of the process we have been watching evolve into the complication of consciousness with which Strether may contemplate his return to Woollett? We may of course regard this consciousness as a thing-in-itself, the end towards which every train of thought and pattern of reflection is devoted. The mental state would have its perfect and selfcontained existence. This would represent a teleology which excluded such peripheral things as personal choices, circumstances, affinities, affective involvements, or anything beyond the value of that mental state itself. Yet one can think of nothing in James which elevates the pure mental state to an utmost value at the cost of the larger tissue of human connections. Value in James has usually enough of such tissue for there to be a certain uncharacteristic bleakness in isolating the inner consciousness.

Chapter 8

Values in Collision

We have reached a point where the pain of discontinuity will be covered by the perfect assurance with which James manages his closing pages. The *ficelle* ties it all together in a package of her own, for the sense of her final sigh indeed contains 'all comically, all tragically'. The high consciousness of James's art was to bring these opposites into perfect balance in the most natural and unportentous way, treating them perhaps with the spirit of elegant fatalism. Yes, it could not have been otherwise, no matter how many and how alluring the exit lines. But do we end with the dismissive effect of a wry and tidy formula, or does James imply that in some ways these opposites can be managed in ways that perhaps Strether has failed: that comedy and tragedy may have their reciprocity, their equilibrium, but one which does not imply an equivalence? The comic mode of *The Ambassadors* may match the finality of tragic effect but have a quite different place in our perception of the whole. The Muses, as we know too well, are quite different, and the image of Garrick torn between them precisely presents the claims of opposites which are irreconcilable.

The sense of comedy as a tissue of verbal games and tones has given its distinct colouration to large stretches and important aspects of *The Ambassadors* and this is surely part of Maria's meaning, that we conclude on that touch of absurdity which is really something of a joke. James substitutes this dimension of comedy for the other that is more normally the counterweight to tragedy, the form of dramatic solution by which we regard with satisfaction the happy outcome of an action. The opposites may be fused by what seems the highest artifice, but the skill is partly in that substitution by which we might almost take one sense of comedy for another, and accept a symmetry which I think eludes us. 'All tragically' has the train of consequence which 'all comically' does not.

If tragedy represents sacrifice and loss there is no doubt of the full effect of Strether's final choice in his obedience to an inner law. Perhaps some principle of formal closure should lead us to accept this slightly deceptive and asymmetric balance for the wry wonder that it is. Yet the train of consequences, however implicit, is surely part of the story. If we only ask what has been sacrificed for what, interpretations of this ending force themselves upon us. Have we a case of what Isaiah Berlin would call a collision of values in which the 'all tragically' represents the incompatibility of real values? One type of example he gives, from the *Antigone*, is that of the conflict of two principles within a particular culture and where both principles have their validity and force. But the tragic effect also lies in the collision of different forms of life where there is a profound but incompatible value in both. 'What is clear is that values can clash – that is why civilisations are incompatible.'[7] Such collisions may express our deepest convictions and commitments and of course this touches the heart of the Jamesian enterprise, the exploration of characters with precise regard to their values: true, false, half-false, in fragments or otherwise, etc.

Our problem is, how deep is the conflict represented by Strether's choice in all of its cultural and personal implications? Earlier I played down the 'international theme' on the ground that an expatriate's world is not exactly Europe. But there is no doubt that the world to which Strether returns is very different from the one which he abandons. Looked at closely the values may be hard to define. Unlike those of the *Antigone*, the particular loyalties that the action evokes are unclear and diffuse. The rule of law by which a Creon might act or the piety of Antigone be defined have their solid and distinct cultural force. That there should be a choice of Woollett – even if *contre coeur* – or a choice of a Parisian existence, or a principle by which Strether is determined to be right, is to look at what is difficult to state or encompass, where all is qualified by complex, contingent circumstance, the mystery of personal affinities, attachments, purposes, loyalties or even distastes of which any individual's life is so heterogeneously composed.

There are examples in James of the conflicts of values that occur within the more restricted scope of a particular society, where the rules of play are more akin to the Antigone case, if less monstrously consequential, in that they involve alternative rules of the game within the same system. In *The Tragic Muse* a young man's choice between the active political life and the life of art, and a young woman's choice between her theatrical career and a distinguished marriage, are given an allegorical tidiness as in earlier philosophical debates between the claims of the active and the contemplative life. That these choices involve differing forms of life within a society has some solidly presented consequences. In *The Ambassadors*, the consequences are deferred and masked by a suitable obscurity. It is as if the distance between things were too incalculable to measure and the imagination retires before the receding space.

Yet while Woollett as a final destination is allowed to fade, its features receding into an indefinite distance, its parodic forms leap forward in the vulgarity of Jim and the mindless severities of Sarah. They produce a sense of shock because of the absence of context, and yet, of course, it is the shock of the expected. The mediation of Mamie is not quite the bridge that anyone can cross and she alone, in almost imperceptibly distancing herself from Chad, produces the unexpected. The plans made in Woollett will not necessarily have their foregone consummation. But the power is there to terminate Strether's embassy and to awaken the latent businessman in Chad that Paris had apparently displaced.

It is through the second embassy that the 'international theme' resurfaces, not in terms of the understanding of Europe, but of the opposite. Rather than the interplay of conflicting cultural ideals, there is simply total absence of connexion. The ships pass in the night and far out of sight of each other. The little world of the expatriate community may be accepted as the basis of an evening's chatter without noticing what anyone is like. The rather gushing effort to please on the part of Marie de Vionnet results only in her dismissal as hardly 'an apology for a decent woman'. And we have noted the word 'hideous' applied to Chad's 'transformation'. Is James indicating a cultural gulf too vast to entrain us in any plausible dialogue, one that is beyond the scope of Berlinian discourse?

Certainly there is more than one version of parallel tracks. The little world of expatriates, established in Paris for whatever escapist reasons of their own, seems to feel no sense of conflict. They can even face the lugubrious charms of Waymarsh without revulsion. And they are perhaps more alienated in their Parisian refuge than they quite understand. The margins of an easy cosmopolitanism are hardly stretched. Perhaps it is partly the unacknowledged awareness that it would be an adaptation that he could not make that stirs in Strether the overwhelming authority of the 'right'.

Except for the professional mediator in Miss Gostrey who makes interpretation a way of life, only Strether works at the terms of dialogue, at the possibility that the great cultural exchange can have its immense and beneficent power. But he recognizes the lure and danger of the alien. In one of his bursts of matchmaking when he is trying to interest Bilham in the matrimonial possibilities of Mamie he almost embodies in that effort, including leaving his worldly goods to Bilham, the possibility of the beneficent bridge. 'I've been sacrificing so to strange gods that I feel I want to put on record, somehow, my fidelity – fundamentally unchanged after all – to our own. I feel as if my hands were embrued with the blood of monstrous alien altars – of another faith altogether. There it is – it's done.' (p. 393) The underlying strategy, which Bilham's common sense sees through, is rather jejune. But the 'strange gods' become fixtures of the mind.

But which gods are our own? Strether's commitment dangles in the air as if possessed of something profound whose existence is assumed but which might vanish if overtly named. We perhaps touch on a 'clash of civilizations', but through Strether's kindly and innocent manner see it reduced to the personal, to the desire to build that elusive cultural bridge through the marriage of Bilham and Mamie. But then, would they not, of necessity, adhere to 'our own' gods? In any case the legitimation of marriage, blessed by Strether's own patrimony, would create that area of safety for those children of promise which would still leave Chad and Marie, whose cause will be in the end the most impassioned commitment of all, beyond the moral and cultural claims of those gods of our own.

Strether has called his wish 'expiatory' yet there is an essential vagueness to his transgression which neither specifies a moral principle nor one of cultural loyalty. There is no allusion to the shadowy presence of Mrs Newsome. The moral and cultural seem fused in their sacred role. And here James seems to indicate the irreducible core of his perception of America, at least of that New England America which denied, even defied explanation. The power of Mrs Newsome is not fully articulated, and perhaps could not be, but remains emblematic in its obscurity. It is partly a spirit of resistance, of refusal of the other, of finding what Berlin might call a 'great good' in that innermost nugget of a self that refuses desire, which cannot be seduced or bought, which cannot accommodate to whatever appeal or inducement might move that bitter nodule of authenticity. We have a touch of this in some of William James's letters to Henry when he fears a loss of his real sense of America. And there is the famous comment of Clover Hooper Adams – whose Washington salon was as close to the cosmopolitan as the New World might allow – that Henry James should go and 'run a hog ranch' in deepest America to recapture the authenticity he was losing.[8]

This hostility to the anglicized James was to increase in his later years, and to attach itself to the complications of what has been called the 'final manner'. But the deepest American perception is represented by a depth of blunt severity which comes through Strether's final refusal of Parisian temptation. If, however, the price of 'being right' is to embrace exactly nothing, we can see that his mind is moving close to rejection for its own sake. If Woollett's presiding genius is in the obscurity of power, and if its very product has become the unnameable, we come close to an implicit nihilism for which no possible articulation is provided, but which is foreshadowed in the closing sections with an increasing intensity.

The process of withdrawal begins long before the final revelation on the riverbank. Strether's powers begin to fade before the new wave of ambassadors and he finds from the morning of their arrival that his marginalization is under way. The act of entering the carriage with Jim sets him on the path to relegation. I have mentioned this shrinkage on Strether's part but we must see it as part of a larger process. For one thing, Woollett's new cast will make its own assessment. The consciousness which was shaped by subtle stages of understanding will be brutally dismissed in a moment's encounter. But its irrelevance to others has already been marked by the desultory and diminished character of his involvement. The friendship with Maria, the mediator between America and Europe, also weakens; there is, as is often the case with teaching, a diminishing return. They are less important to each other because interpretation itself has lost its importance. The one great revelation that remains will require no explanation; and in any case, everyone understands except Strether.

This gradual diminishing is of course partly the result of *force majeur*. In a sense, the great cultural incommensurability slips beyond him. It is not to be managed, for the agents in control are quite indifferent to any version of matters beyond their own. It is as if the subject matter of the novel, so meticulously evolved, is brushed aside. The unnameable object reigns in all of its economic glory. If, however, the point of it all is to display the unvarnished effect of the dominance of wealth, of the mixture of brute force and debasing magnetism, the effect may be seen but never recognized. A certain propriety covers the exchanges of the second embassy, even if the conventionalized images of the American in Paris are played for a mixture of comedy and banality. Only the crisp dismissal scene with Sarah in the hotel has any directness. Otherwise people go through the motions of being where they are, reducing the Parisian *ambiance* to routinized tourism.

Such a Paris is of course alien but poses no problems, for it is simply taken in Woollett's terms. One will next be off to Switzerland to look at some mountains. Could Mamie possibly have some perception that goes beyond the tourist's passing scene? We will not know. The tourists' impressions will be wholly unlike Strether's, but impressions all the same. For him the incommensurability will have been noted, measured perhaps, but found an unacceptable distance to travel in more than his perceptions. The warm air of a walk by the Seine, the dazzling moment in Gloriani's garden, the elegant world of Mme de Vionnet, are objects of understanding and sympathetic involvement, but not to be internalized as part of an operative world of his own.

Does this mean that incommensurability is never mastered, and even that such mastery is never attempted? Certainly those passages that bear most directly on any transformation of himself place such a possibility, in the recapturing of that elusive youth which James has sketched so lightly as to leave us pondering its real existence. To follow this would be to see all the mental activity directed to the past. And this is a past that can hardly be used in the present and is never realized for us beyond the quite secondary sentimental reflection – secondary, that is, to all of the immediate demands and ramifications of his embassy. But if this recapturing of the past should be a conscious design, James never tries to embody it sufficiently to persuade us of its substantial importance. To this extent a minimal justification of Leavis's demand for the 'adequately realized' is possible.

But there is never the slightest doubt that the recreation of his awareness is a matter of present involvement and challenge. Even Waymarsh notes the degree to which the strange gods have come to inhabit Strether's changing outlook – and notes the importance, to the extent that it is worthy of betrayal. But any direct question about what has happened to the old American loyalties is turned aside. In some senses their own original form eludes us. Does Woollett stand for a general quality of American life? Or is it precisely designed to give a sense of narrowness and oppressiveness in its most benighted purity? There is no doubt that it is conceived to heighten and intensify contrast. The anti-hedonistic aspect is so clearly drawn, and its symbolic opposition so precisely flagged. James takes a similar but more radical step in *The Golden Bowl*, in the conception of American City which is the totally empty image of American darkness.

The point is put to Strether rather straightly by Mme de Vionnet: 'Where is your "home" moreover now – what has become of it?' (p. 480) But this question is quickly turned to the matter of her own responsibilities in Strether's life, and the query about 'home' vanishes without response. Yet the pressure on Strether in this final interview marks out quite powerfully the degree of his withdrawal, and the inner necessity for it. 'You'd do everything for us but be mixed up with us.' (p. 484) She has marked the distance decisively. Strether did not come to Paris to involve himself, but to act in the interests of others. His experience may have changed his view of those interests, and of his sense of himself, in quite radical ways; but that does not allow a direct involvement with the objects of his embassy. A line has fastidiously been drawn; and Marie has identified the essential apartness of the man himself. But again the directness of the query leads away from Strether himself, and towards the involvement with Chad which was the point of departure of the story.

One must look in the end at 'us'. Whom would one join, and to what community would one commit oneself? No doubt Marie means a private world centred on Chad and herself. Yet one has just seen what a perilous dependence a connection with Chad would imply. One sees the centrifugal forces which radiate through it all. Could the presence of Strether, Maria and those few friends who share a small collection of personal ties shore up a common world? There is no particular reason that the little circle of cultured expatriates should not have a rewarding reciprocity. And yet there is a flaw in every link.

To look at the component parts of any such community is to feel the fragility of the artifice. Paris is a happy place, but none but Marie will ever be Parisian.

will go back to, he replies 'I don't know. There will be something.' This something will include neither Mrs Newsome, nor what James's scenario calls the 'poor fatuous Review'.[10] But the representation requires no very concrete image. The miasmal and indistinct close over Strether as, in *The Golden Bowl*, they do over Charlotte and Mr Verver.

It is almost as if only through Europe, or by way of it, is definition possible, the focal distinctness that has put in question an area of greyish obscurity where representation falters and even breaks off. *Nothing* of any interest or significance will happen to Strether. There is something empty at the centre of this world which Strether accepts in a mature awareness that it is right for him. Emptiness and appropriateness are conjoined in self-knowledge. But there is 'rightness' in this as well. It is not merely that gaining nothing is exactly what he has chosen as the necessary condition of his own form of life, it is that his values could not be realized through anything other than the negation which refusal embodies – an austerity that sets the self aside from the world of pleasure and of 'gain'.

Not that we can attribute this to Woollett, for Woollett has no doubt its own forms of pleasure, although they are not exactly specified, and is certainly committed to gain. Its rather unscrupulous past with respect to gain in the earlier days of the family business, before it was obscured by the moral glory of Mrs Newsome, is confessed quite evasively by Strether. James portrays fully, if largely by implication, the banal, philistine character of a commercial society whose grasp of the 'tremendous things' or of that shining world of art and taste will never be more than décor.

Strether is the mental prisoner of a law of Woollett that is not his law. There is no need to mark the difference explicitly. The inner crisis of Strether bears no relation to the way in which the moral law of Woollett is concerned to exercise itself, with whatever cultural apparatus it surrounds itself. In a sense the commercial society is as alien to him as the Parisian. It just happens to be his. Can we therefore see a version of cultural difference internalized as the personal sense of 'difference' to which one returns? Is it that in the end civilization is simply frozen? Whatever the dimensions of our social being, there is nothing we really can value beyond the capacity to give shape to experience, to create a form that in ways we cannot wholly justify satisfies our desire to see the world as a harmonious whole.

Strether's decision once taken, each connection must be fully articulated and the consequences drawn. This in effect falls into two distinct modes. One is the dealing with Chad, in which the moral sense of the action must be fully spelled out. Whether it is really a practical matter, something which might affect the course of future action and determine Chad's loyalties and choices, is not as clear as is the nature of Strether's own inner necessity. He must affirm what is really his final discovery and final commitment, the overwhelming value he sees in the relation with Marie. 'You'll be a brute, you know – you'll be guilty of the last infamy – if you ever forsake her.' (p. 499)

It would be in such a relationship too, that one might, at least Chad might, cross the cultural divide and affix himself in the civilized world that Strether knows he must himself forsake. Beneath the appeal is the thought that Chad could love her. (This value, too, is vicariously embraced.) But the terrible presage is suddenly upon him. Chad's mind has turned to the practical concerns of his business: to Strether's uncomprehending astonishment there is talk about advertising and the sale of products. The original aim of the embassy will come true and the whole effect of all that he has learned and undertaken will be lost. No precise moment has been fixed, but the mental bent has declared itself and all of the civilizing process, the 'improvements' will enter into the great commercial game – for which they will merely exist as amiable façade. There might even be a more cheerful aspect to Woollett when the young exploiter of scientific advertising takes the helm, and a less morally mundane atmosphere. But the cultural mission of Adam Verver is unlikely to flow from Gloriani's garden. The world of making things, selling things, of bustle and profits has its notional vitality and Chad's cultural veneer may be of use in the boardroom or at dinner with his clients, although its tonalities may gradually adapt to Sarah's more forthright taste.

Where then is 'improvement'? If in the end the totality of connections, interests, obligations – the whole fabric of one's social being – takes precedence over the personal passions, Strether in this matter takes his stand. The value of the unique and personal is asserted frequently enough. But behind it is the realization that the order of things will have its way, in that complex, diffuse mixture of demands, direct and indirect, which always constitutes the way of the world. And this Marie understands better than anyone.

The concern has been with manners, with the invention of manners in the case of Chad, and if in the end we shall find his to be mere veneer, manners will nevertheless sustain the necessary loss with which the novel closes. If the episode with Chad is an ironic manipulation, the ceremonial of departure will make the nothingness of Woollett a part of the world of language, of consideration, of the agreed courtesy on which civilization depends. Manners too will be the embodiment of the understanding which has come to Strether by way of the cumulative sensations, the reflections in Nôtre Dame, the long process of finding his way through the tutelage of the *ficelle* and the conversation of Marie de Vionnet.

It has come partly through the gradual realization of the indirectness necessary to real awareness, which began to show in Gloriani's garden as the moment of hesitation, the recognition of that small chasm between the object of attention and his perception of it. And it lies in the tiny but profound gap between sensation and the register of consciousness. This is expressed to some degree through the value implied in the touch of shyness, of a proper diffidence in the face of the unknown or uncertain. And there is the terror.

In an idle moment of conversation about Waymarsh, Maria jokingly remarks 'You're in terror of him.' And Strether picks up and extends the idea: 'You did put your finger on it a few minutes ago. It's general, but it avails itself of particular occasions. That's what it's doing for me now. I'm always considering something else; something else, I mean, than the thing of the moment. The obsession of the other thing is the terror.' (pp. 66–67) This is a description of an inner distancing which comes between Strether and whatever quality of experience. The excited moment of identification with Chad broke through it, for an instant. But even the most highly charged moments of contemplation are fraught with self-conscious reflexiveness. And the sudden awareness of this – is it the first time that Strether has fully acknowledged it? – has slipped a tiny abyss into the comedy of his unfolding quest. But the shyness has a value, a touch of discreet good manners in the face of others. At one point he attaches it to the charm of Marie: 'he was struck by her tact, the taste of her vagueness'. (p. 275) In her, this disarming aspect, the blurring of precise intentions and expectations, may be exactly what one might expect from the civilized Parisian world. Such indirections are the necessary opposite to the crassness of Waymarsh or the brutal mindlessness of the second embassy. But it remains a social mixture, a form of the agreeable, while in Strether his double awareness is an epistemological trap, a special form of the self-awareness that will grip him forever in his isolation. But it is through these gaps and hesitations that sensibility evolves, above all in the gradual understanding that others require the slow process of appreciation to grasp what is essential to difference, both in meaning and in substance.

'Difference' of course, does not enter into the language of Woollett, and each perception of it involves a degree of rupture. But it is through the longer effect of this process that perspective evolves, and in a sense it is a perspective one can never lose. Maria has paced the process, protecting him from such a direct access of difference that might 'be an arrest of his independence and a change in his attitude – in other words a revulsion in favour of the principles of Woollett'. (p. 490) But once understood, there is something about the awareness of difference that is irreversible. There is a kind of knowledge which cannot be undone, even if the field of using it will be withdrawn.

The irony of returning to Woollett will be that he will bring the result of a reflective process that will be ruthlessly alienating. Yet this is also the way to transcend the nothingness, for it is part of that tissue of human discriminations that Woollett has refused. In some metaphysical sense Strether must accept a nihilism that only the effect of reflection can keep at bay, and the inner decorum which gives one not the crassness of Woollett's certainties, but the mixture of generosity and *finesse* that, for James, makes civilization an absolute value.

Two things no doubt require explanation: nothingness and value. Yet we cannot try to give them the sorts of explanation that would so destroy the sense of their Jamesian context as to nullify their critical utility. The notion of nihilism may be far-reaching but have restrictions on its use. I certainly do not refer to anything that resembles an ideology, a general set of conceptual beliefs which can be extensively generalized. Perhaps in 'The Beast in the Jungle' one sees the private construction of a fantasy self, dramatically reduced to nothingness. But that is one of the rare James works which evolves with almost no sense of social context and is hinged on the hypothesis of a single relation, and a love which is never realized. Strether's own rule of negation – nothing for oneself – is not a moral principle in that it does not concern itself with others in any way; still less is it ideological. That Strether's private decorum embraces nothingness is no more than another 'complex fate'. In James, 'nihilism' is simply the shown absence of those great goods that might illuminate an individual life and which by good fortune one might find embodied in a living social form.

Certainly those great goods have only a contingent and hazardous existence. They are not founded in religion or metaphysics, or in positive moral codes with external foundations of any kind. Eliot's view of James's 'baffling escape from Ideas; a mastery and an escape which are perhaps the last test of a superior intelligence' correctly places that work of intelligence in the subtle interplay of persons in a social entity where the real substance is relational, and the chemistry of these subtle substances defies explanation. And, 'there is something terrible, as disconcerting as quicksand, in this discovery'.[11] But in the subtle interplay those great goods may, in their elusive and transitory way, be found, as indeed is the impact of their absence.

That interplay of course demands the place, the moment, and the interactive other. Without them, we are lost, as the retreating Strether will be lost. The contingent structure, in which sensation, personal rediscovery, vivid human exchange and understanding seemed to transform one's life, vanishes. With that interplay lost there is only memory. If Eliot found the disconcerting quicksand especially vivid in such special cases as *The Turn of the Screw* it is more subtly and pervasively there in two of the final masterpieces, *The Ambassadors* and *The Golden Bowl*. Both of them end in the abandonment of a 'great good place' where the subtle interplay of life has its highest rewards, for an exile in which all of those goods will be lost and where the form of life itself lies beyond imagining.

To this sense of loss there is one remedy which the civilized world can propose, decorum. If civilization itself is the subtle interplay, marked at its best by personal, intellectual and aesthetic relations, its line of defence, in the face of the barbarous and crass, or indeed the merely shallow and empty, is that decorum which its code of manners will embody. Form, in this long perspective, is largely the harmonious rules of arrangements, and the due order of courtesy. They do not deal with perfection, with ideal worlds or with those great surpassing passions that drive us to extreme courses, but it is through these social and artistic forms that our experience is interpretable, that we make that sense and that shape, however provisional, that distinguish a civilized being. Look back at the encounter in Nôtre Dame. We have a personal experience in the frame of one of civilization's greatest monuments. There is a double track in time as the American positive present reaches back through a romantic reading to the age of faith, while Strether's private experience of the present takes on these colourations to shape his own adventure. Each perception, the evocative power of the misty light in the dim nave, comes laden with associative values, the vast spin-off of the centuries that the cathedral has put so powerfully together. And even the mysterious figure – who turns out to be Marie de Vionnet – is discerned as the 'heroine of an old story, something he had heard, read, something that, had he had a hand for drama, he might himself have written'. (p. 273) It is the maker of form within us that responds to our cultural surroundings and gives us the necessary means of reshaping and control.

We shall look at this again in terms of *The Golden Bowl*. For Strether it is enacted through those ceremonial features of departure which go beyond the firm moral injunction which he has left with Chad. It is one's duty to go, and to tell others with that mixture of firmness and consideration that will close the door upon his embassy with suitable dignity. I have noted that in his commitment to the self-denying principle he seems not to consider the others who have shared his moments of discovery in their company. A certain blindness must therefore be masked.

One might ask whether or not this blindness indicated a moral weakness in the face of the Parisian world, and whether decorum conceals a fear of facing the freedom he once so passionately sought. Such fears may be connected in obvious ways with the revelation he has received, the recognition that the senses may take one beyond a walk by the Seine and that a certain carnality is part of the form of life he has discovered. However one might wish to take such a speculation, the consequences remain hidden and Strether's departure is again a recognition of limits, even if the matter of them should be hidden from himself. Any form of hedonism, as with anything gained for himself, would in the end be indecorous. The laws of decorum are restrictive as well as considerate. They constitute that mode of being oneself which expresses both an inner necessity and an outer commitment to form.

For James such order is so deeply subsumed as to be unspoken. A certain calculated naturalness is one of its marks. The touch of ease which Strether was beginning to find, and which brought him up against the severities of Waymarsh, was a variant on the strictures of Woollett which might in certain circumstances have bent the code beyond recognition. Is he on the edge of this in his ecstatic moments on the river bank? One of Strether's problems from the start is to discover the latitude possible to him, by which he may expand in the direction of one code while remaining safely within another.

Of course, this is to act as if the Paris/Woollett division provides the sharp outline of two alien cultures. That there is a profound degree of alienness within is the necessary foundation of our story. We cannot speak merely of 'form' but of 'forms' and it is clear that the representations of Woollett and Paris as forms of life have a substantial and highly consequential difference, without as we have noted being all that distinctive in themselves. But Woollett is not the Puritan community of the New England divines (it is perhaps Strether who is 'the last Puritan') but a provincial commercial centre with its proper share of moral narrowness, while the Paris of *The Ambassadors* is hardly the great cultural and political centre but an alluring playground for the American expatriate. Aspects of their representations may be sharp and clear, but to try to distil the difference, to establish some firm sets of values, would be to step into diffuse distinctions. Perhaps the inner contrast would be between Gloriani, the embodiment both of creative power and of personal magnetism, and the melancholy Review with its stern and pallid confrontation with the great issues of the time. If two forms of life are in collision it is paradoxically that one is in flight from the other and sees its freedom in evasion.

But it is the degree to which social customs are shared that allows the effect of formal manners to obscure the distinction. Strether's good manners, shared, no doubt, by both Americans and Europeans of a certain level of education and affluence, have a levelling effect. The change in Chad's manners, on the other hand seem to indicate the effect of having been to some kind of 'charm school'. Does James have a flicker of sympathy with Sarah's judgment of 'hideous'? For all her crassness and brutality there is not exactly an indication that she 'doesn't know how to behave'. Perhaps it is intentional that some kind of mystery hangs over the changes that have made Chad an acceptable member of Mme de Vionnet's circle. What he might really be like is thus bracketed off as mysterious, and perhaps in the end insignificant. The hints at the very end, as Strether glimpses the bright young businessman blooming at the end of the 'civilizing' road, will be sufficient.

If form is the method by which novelists reconcile opposites, it is also the means through which we can control the wayward and untidy aspects of the self. Central to decorum is simply manners. As social anthropologists – Norbert Elias or Claude Lévi-Strauss – tell us in a vast array of contexts, manners ritualize the functional in ways that may systematize but do so as extended artifice. Our table manners, arrangements in family life, body decoration, modes of social exchange, may fit an infinite variety of models, but it is the comprehensiveness of the artifice and formal commitment to it that create a working social order. In the Jamesian meta-morality, the coherence of our world – filled by conflicting objectives and values as it is – is created by artifice, by such subtle and intricate social devices as manners, and by the literary means that make us see that the necessity of loss is properly contained. We may see this as tragic in Isaiah Berlin's sense, or as the wry and ironic series of accommodations that James handles with such discretion: the representations of the cross-purposes that are irresolvable, that curious space in the heart of things that one must simply accept.

If Strether changes, it is entirely in terms of sensibility and reflection. Externally he is the same, and the mixture of amiability with the somewhat uptight code of Woollett is a constant. But this constancy is also a link, and one of the many features that gives the book its perfect sense of formal control. For the art of making us see and accept 'all tragically' as the outcome of a wry deployment of comic means has a natural ease. Just as we see quite calmly the shadow of Mrs Newsome presiding over the commercial enterprise which is the growing monstrosity of American life. The destruction is there, but out of sight. We do not see a representation of Woollett, we see its effect. We sense its presence in the flight of the expatriates; we hear its representative voices in the second embassy; we feel the crushing impact on individual sensibility or moral difference. It is perhaps in this model of energizing force that the deepest level of the conflict lies – which intensifies the paradox that the heroic failure, the man of detachment and sensibility, should sense that he belongs in Woollett. It is as if a proper self-denying destruction is the key to the authentic truth, to his own identity. If Strether's moral vocabulary is put in question, his moral assurance, his seriousness of resolve, are not. While there may be a crypto-nihilist somewhere in James, it is not reached through the destructive effects of comedy on the possibility of value, but has a darker tone altogether.

But why should this fusion of power and emptiness co-exist in the great republic of enlightenment and opportunity? James will explore this implicitly in the image of American City, more closely in *The Ivory Tower*, more closely again, as we have observed, in *The American Scene*. These are representations of a totally different order. Each shows a new form of contextualizing, of readjustment of the image, of an experimental reordering of the contours of the quicksands of truth.

Notes to Part Two

1. Henry James, *The Ambassadors*, Penguin Classics reprinting of the New York edition, London 1986, p. 9. Further quotations will be indicated by a page number in the text.
2. This theme was developed in William Righter, 'Strether's reasons', a paper delivered as part of a symposium with Martha Nussbaum at the Centre for Philosophy and Literature, University of Warwick, May 15, 1996.
3. Leavis's strictures are cited by Harry Levin in his introduction to the 1986 Penguin edition (p. 7). But James's own notebooks suggest that he was less dazzled by Paris as a location than Leavis imagines – rather the reverse, in fact. 'I don't altogether like the *banal* side of the revelation of Paris. It's so obvious, so unusual, to make Paris the vision that opens his eyes, makes him feel his mistake. It might be London – it might be Italy – it might be the general impression of a summer in Europe – abroad. Also, it *may* be Paris.' James, 1955, *Notebooks*, p. 226.
4. Krook, 1967, *Ordeal of Consciousness,* p. 8.
5. Martha Nussbaum, in conversation.
6. Nussbaum, 1990, *Love's Knowledge,* p. 193.
7. Berlin, 1990, *Crooked Timber,* pp. 12–13.
8. Diary entry by Mrs Henry Adams in the spring of 1880, cited by Gore Vidal in his introduction to the Penguin English Classics edition of *The Golden Bowl*, London, Penguin, 1985, p.7. It is not a form of American 'authenticity' which one imagines Clover contemplating for herself.
9. James, 1955, *Notebooks*, p. 412.
10. *Ibid.*, p. 417.
11. Kermode (ed.), 1975, *T.S. Eliot*, pp. 151–152.

PART THREE

Amerigo in an American Nowhere

10.   Characters in a Void
11.   The Shaping of the Prince
12.   Anomalies of Place and Time

Solomon J. Solomon, *A Conversation Piece*. © Leighton House Museum, Royal Borough of Kensington and Chelsea.

Chapter 10

Characters in a Void

Few critical works have the marvellous and compelling intellectual power that James gave to the preface to *The Golden Bowl*. The exploration of his method, the reflections on the character and value of the novel form, on the powers of language and the 'sovereign truth' of the artist, constitute an intellectual enterprise with a life of its own. If through some freakish circumstance the novel itself had vanished and the preface alone remained, we could follow its speculations and imagine the scope and richness of the missing masterpiece. And one effect of this grandeur is the authority which certain claims have had over the reading of *The Golden Bowl* itself.

One of those claims sets terms of astonishing rigour. 'We see very few persons in *The Golden Bowl*, but the scheme of the book, to make up for that, is that we shall really see about as much of them as a coherent literary form permits.'[1] Such are the terms of the *gageure*, the supremely difficult task that he set himself in the self-imposed limitation. This world is as enclosed as that of a Greek tragedy: four principals and a chorus of two. Their lives are played out in splendid isolation, without the clutter of social connections or quotidian activities interfering with the delightful and remorseless concentration on themselves. Do these selves press upon the limits of form? Certainly the fullness with which consciousness is invested might so far exceed the norms of human exchange as to demand in this novel a concentration that stretches our attentive powers. But so it is intended.

Nevertheless, the representation of the four principals is far from exhaustive. And one reflection on *The Golden Bowl* that a moment's perspective may insist upon is the immensity of what it omits. Does the claim of 'as much as' sacrifice too much to form, or even act as camouflage for what is concealed? If not 'concealed', at least omitted with a breathtaking ease. For the assertion that the novel works from two points of view – first the Prince and then the Princess – puts the other two main characters in shadow. This is the more startling as James had as an earlier title 'Charlotte', which suggests the development of another point of view.[2] Martha Nussbaum's fascination with Charlotte[3] indicates how powerfully another point of observation, another consciousness, another potential structure of understanding, calls for articulation. But Charlotte's emergence as a centre of consciousness is only fragmentary and episodic. As for

Adam Verver, Gore Vidal confesses to not having noticed him at a first reading.[4] The extended portrait of him at Fawns that opens the second book is clearly a necessary part of the structural background, but is far from being an entry to an angle from which the whole action is viewed. An important intention may lie behind this, for there are critical moments in the second part where we do not know what Verver may or may not know. This hidden and secretive nature may have its considerable role, but we are very far from 'as far as'.

So a paradox arises from our sense of unease, of simply looking over our shoulders and asking where the others may be. And this somewhat puts in question at least one aspect of James's strongest conviction that this was 'the most *done* of my productions – the most composed and constructed and completed' of his fictions.[5] What kind of completeness is it which propels us towards the filling out of substantial empty spaces? There may well be a sense of 'completeness' which expressed the degree of formal order necessary to the carrying out of James's artistic intention, an aesthetic completeness, if one will. But even such a principle cannot deny us the intellectual curiosity which arises from the opacity of Adam Verver or from that blankness with which Charlotte assesses the defeat she must treat as triumph. In the most anguished of the novel's critical moments, much is seen only from the outside, through the appearances which are interpreted by others. So, might we conclude that this 'solidest' of works is a fragment, and that the completeness of seeing is an illusion sacrificed to those ruthlessly restricted angles of vision that the Master has chosen for us?

This sense of limitation and direction becomes steadily stronger through the second volume where we are drawn into Maggie's self-knowledge and the growing sense of her own purposes and powers, so that all of the possible courses of action begin to fall away before the force that will make a single line of consequences ineluctable. A clarity is created through exclusion. And James in drawing us towards this proper resolution consigns to oblivion the alternative assessments, the complementary voices, the unfulfilled perspectives.

Who could wish otherwise, for a single word changed, or any shift in that intense, delicate balance? We submit naturally to that fusion of conviction and restraint which constitutes a deep form of persuasion. If the perfection has been bought at a price, it is one which we are all willing to pay. Our awareness of the stripped away, the suppressed or absent elements is the awareness of shadow novels that will never be. But it is also that realm of shadows which marks the edges of what 'a coherent literary form permits'. Does coherence travel on too narrow a gauge? For the speculation which lies on the other side of James's set of determinate and winnowing manoeuvres can be concerned less with the alternatives that the imagination might demand of us, than with the understanding of where formal limits must necessarily fall.

Or is there simply a moral unease when we feel that the formal effect has implied a moral closure by which someone has been deprived of a voice – a voice which in some ways is essential to the other voices? Maggie's own authenticity, to that degree, depends upon the authenticity of others – implied or otherwise. Yet the principle of artistic economy is obvious enough, and too full a representation of other voices could pull the novel apart, or force upon it an even more comprehensive model of coherence, which one could hardly dare to imagine.

Nevertheless, we cannot deny our awareness of what we do not know. And the very tightening and controlling process that so concentrates the focus as to exclude all others suggests in itself the shadowy surrounding matter through which Maggie's perspective is cut. But this matter can only exist as hypothesis. While we know how much we do not know, of course we do not know what it is. And it will remain a tissue of suggestions about the matter of the novel that we will never verify.

One natural complement to this may lie in what James himself does not know. The gradual surrender of authorial authority in the late novels – manipulated and illusory though it may often be – involves a sense of limit. James speaks in his preface of shaking off the 'muffled majesty of authorship' and 'disavowing the pretence of it while I get down into the arena and do my best to live and breathe and rub shoulders and converse with the persons engaged in the struggle that provides for the others in the circling tiers the entertainment of the great game'. (p. 20) The figures of theatre, life and art are so superimposed that the representation has taken on a life of its own. And by placing himself within that representation James insists on the shared world of his characters limiting his own perspective. James may therefore imply that he knows no more than we, or indeed Maggie, about the relationship between Verver and Charlotte. The hints are inconclusive, and beautifully terse. Yet such an obscure, off-stage matter is of the deepest importance; and this James knows. But he can accept the opacities (above all in Verver), the grey areas, the blind corners. The notebooks effectively show the acceptance in the creative process of the working of what he calls his 'law of successive aspects' as both a strategic and a limiting principle. More marked in the late works, it is perhaps at its most extreme in the scenario for *The Ivory Tower*, where the tentative touches of characterization seem to be right for the final product – a product which of course never materialized. The full realization of those separate aspects never took place, leaving us to speculate as to whether the necessary coherence of a work of art could have been maintained. One effect of the 'law' is to move towards a descriptive impressionism in which the signs are intended to be only partly readable.

A concurrent effect is seen in the visual presentation of Charlotte as *The Golden Bowl* moves towards its conclusion. Consciousness is almost wholly invested in Maggie, yet the images of Charlotte are rendered more and more intensely through description. Does this vividness belong in the eyes of Maggie alone, where beauty, grandeur and sexual danger might seem at moments to be a personal, untranslatable obsession, or is it a thing shared through the easing of indirect discourse? Certainly it stretches Maggie's 'point of view' and the effect is to point to what lies beyond both her knowledge and ours, and to put in question those relations that a focal consciousness can only unevenly transmit.

The areas of qualified, uncertain, or missing clues, those fragments of knowledge on which one would like to depend but cannot, reflect the novel's pervasive obsession with the problem of knowledge itself. Who knows what about whom? Indeed the book is full of the sort of mysteries that could be carefully planted or simple open spaces that the author has left with abandon. Where did the money really come from? Why do they hate Verver in American City? Over such questions something larger seems to hang than the matter of what they make at Woollett. The missing level of explanation adds to the area of darkness around these figures, who sometimes seem to loom out of the void as if they had no possible context, or one in which the reader is for some reason not invited to share. And this runs counter to the great 'example' in James's master, Balzac. In Balzac characters are situated, they come from somewhere. (Although one must make an exception for Vautrin, or the occasional figure whose very importance is in the mysterious.) The Balzac world is a tissue of causes and explanations – social, economic, psychological – which is the basis of a solid knowledge. The difficulties and cross-purposes relate to that knowledge and do not efface it.

In *The Golden Bowl* there are few details and almost no context. Charlotte's past is conveyed in a paragraph (p. 78), with the merest cryptic pointer towards explanation. The Prince has a hypothetical background – which we will shortly examine – without a trace of realistic consequence following from it. And the Ververs are as we have seen. It is as if most of the presuppositions of realism had been abandoned. No relationships matter but those fundamental things for which context is superfluous: father, daughter, husband, wife. It is a fable reduced to its mythic core.

The first person to notice this hermetic isolation was probably Edith Wharton, who put the question: ' "What was your idea in suspending the four principal characters of *The Golden Bowl* in the void? What sort of life did they lead when they were not watching each other, and fencing with each other? Why have you stripped them of all the *human fringes* we necessarily trail after us through life?" James had answered in a disturbed voice "My dear – I didn't know I had!"' '[6] Here is the great gulf which indicates how little Wharton had understood. As a true novelist of manners she would have been concerned with the 'human fringes'. To James their elimination was the essential condition of the experiment, the isolation of his characters being the ground of that special intensity of affection and conflict. *The Golden Bowl* is not in the usual sense a novel of manners. Manners enter in only as the existential part of a civilized order.

I want to look at the stripping down process in relation to the Prince, as he is supposedly one of the vehicles of the novel's consciousness. But it is also worth noting how far, beyond a preliminary hypothesis, this attenuated context, this foreshortening to mythical components, abolished the 'international theme'. Ostensibly, of course, this is the simplest, most classical version of that traditional tale: American heiress, European nobleman. But looking more closely, as Edith Wharton might have looked, such a scene dissolves. We are even physically nowhere. Of course the place names indicate: Portland Place, Eaton Square, Gloucester, and so on. But to the names nothing is attached, nothing of England belongs to them. Perhaps the sketch of Fawns suggests a page from *Country Life*, but these are atmospherics that have almost nothing to do with an English or European way of life.

The Prince is as *déraciné* as the Ververs. They know nobody – Lady Castledean, 'a new joke' (p. 501), is mere plot device. And the Assinghams are necessary to the Ververs, but no one is interested in them. What Fanny does, even in the breaking of the bowl, is in terms of Maggie. Fanny is a necessary appurtenance, like a Racinean *confidante*, who enables us to follow the growing understanding Maggie has of herself, and whose corrections and amplifications for the rather obtuse colonel furnish a line of interpretation that the narrative requires. What we see of her indicates no particular features of American and European difference. Perhaps the colonel alone, as pure caricature, has a touch of native authenticity. Manners are supremely important, but in a sense that is more a part of all civilized communities than the product of one or another of them.

Hence nations lose their identity – except by distant implication. If America and Europe are present it is in some remote aspect of their aura. It is in a far-off call that is not exercised through social discrimination, or differing forms of life, that we might possibly see in action. They are present as some mysterious paradigm which has a distant appeal, a mystical voice with an echo in men's hearts. 'America' is Ariadne's thread, which leads to the distant centre, but probably can never lead out; 'England' is a convenient *mise en scène*; and the 'Italy' of the Prince a hypothesis which, once mentioned, is consistently forgotten, or resurfaces (p. 156) as a piece of amusing décor which is suitably far away.

Chapter 11

The Shaping of the Prince

The evanescent Italy of the Prince is introduced almost by apology. He is first seen in Bond Street, surrounded by the goods of the world, meditating on *imperium*. A touch of the *flâneur* is revealed as he glances at shops and passers-by, while waiting for an appointment. His thought is largely undirected, but we are aware that he finds himself in that truer *imperium* which is to be found by London Bridge or Hyde Park Corner than by the Colosseum or the Palatine. Another *imperium* lying in wait is slowly unfolded. If Gore Vidal finds the Prince the most sympathetic of the characters, and others find him irritating or off-putting, it is a tribute to James's extraordinary power in creating conviction out of such improbable elements.

Consider the primary circumstance. A European aristocrat marries an American heiress whose fortune is to pay off his debts and mortgages, reface his crumbling pilasters and maintain him in a form of life which would otherwise sink him further into debt. Such a story has many versions, but there is a *prima facie* improbability in this one: it is difficult to conceive of such a person totally abandoning his own form of life for the quite alien world of two reclusive Americans. Would he not normally assimilate his wife to a form of life of his own? And would not such a form of life be extensively peopled, especially by miscellaneous relations? And would there not be an official mistress, the occasional connection in the *corps de ballet*, horses, dogs, *la caccia*, pals, evenings over cards at the *circolo*, and a demanding round of social obligations for his bride? The tedious father-in-law would be suitably distanced to, say, a villa in Fiesole, where he could pass the time chatting with such as Messrs Horne and Berenson about his collection. One can also see the necessity of a grand Roman wedding, at which the raised eyebrows of assorted *principesse* would coolly imply 'she's a mousy little thing, but Amerigo has done well out of it'.

Here, of course, is a social *imperium*, an *imperium* lost, or more properly, abandoned. I articulate it because it is abandoned so lightly as to leave no trace. But it is not simply the abolition of the 'human fringes', but a step through a closing door that is the isolating condition of all that follows. James therefore wishes us to believe in something remarkable and strange, to take as a simple given, the thought that the Prince should wish to enter such a world, and to submit totally to its own rules of play. And it seems to go far beyond any motive of giving good value in selling himself. Attracted as he is to Maggie he is not passionately in love, but has simply hit upon a good thing. Of course he needs the Verver fortune, but it would be reasonable and indeed conventional to have a due share of it on terms more recognizably his own. Yet he undertakes to make an alien object of himself, to submit to a process of accommodation with a curious plasticity. He wishes to learn – to learn so as to submit more fully and effectively. All edges are to be smoothed to the fit, and the Ververs note approvingly that the Prince has not proved 'angular' (p. 136).

James clearly understands the reader's problem at the surface level of presentation, so that a rationale in terms of conscious decision is evolved. There are gestures at psychological grounding: something in the Prince seems to have turned away from his grandeur; there is an intelligence which warns against greed and a humility which reflects a degree of disgust at his family's wasteful past. (pp. 51–52) It prepares him for that moment of standstill which comes in contemplating the expectations of others. A strange forgetfulness fuses easily with a passive self-interest. When he thinks of his previous existence he recognizes that it 'had more poetry . . . yet as he looked back on it now it seemed to hang in the air of more iridescent horizons, to have been loose and vague and thin', with 'large langorous unaccountable blanks. The present order, as it spread about him, had somehow the ground under its feet . . . and a bottomless bag of shining British sovereigns – which was much to the point – in its hand.' (p. 273)

The insolidity of self and solidity of circumstance suggest a crassness that much else in James belies. We have imagination and charm and a truth of awareness that sees the crack in a golden bowl. The ideal of the *galantuomo* shines both in his appraisal of Mr Verver and in aspiration for himself. It is the *galantuomo* – man of integrity and honour – who does not 'lie, dissemble or deceive'. (p. 51) James seems to wish to fuse this honour with the pervasive growth of bad faith in a wholly seamless representation. For he wishes both of these aspects fully registered without cancelling each other out. We simply swallow the paradox. It may press somewhat on the temptation to disbelief, but that we must, in the first instance, resist. James seems to suggest powerfully that the complexity of human nature is such that one can be a man of true distinction, honour and integrity, yet violate what are normally taken as the deepest of human commitments. Such a paradox is difficult to avoid and there is no doubt that James intends to force it upon us. I shall return to it in a later section, asking how far this takes us into questioning the value of the moral terms and categories employed in *The Golden Bowl*. But in considering the construction of the Prince it is clear that James has posed for us a problem of belief which demands of him the utmost precision in tact and balance, a persuasion that works through the angles of vision we bring to the work, as well as those formally proposed.

For one of the means of making the improbable seem familiar lies in the skilful violation of one of those most important claims made in the Preface (p. 20) about James's method. In proposing to abandon authorial omniscience, in accepting what Nussbaum calls his 'finitude' he has fixed the point of view of the two volumes in the consciousness of first, the Prince and then, the Princess. Yet if the second book is devoted to Maggie's growth of awareness, of consciousness in her powers, the focus of the first is more varied and uneven. For one thing the use of Mrs Assingham as narrative guide, 'perhaps all too officiously' as James suggests (p. 21), pre-empts a substantial part of the point of view. And from the beginning of the second book, with the portrait of Adam Verver at Fawns, through the discussions with Fanny and Charlotte that lead to the marriage of Adam and Charlotte, the Prince is largely excluded. And many of the episodes of the third book, in which he does substantially participate, do not show him as a registering consciousness, but as a presence in the flow of dialogue. So the metaphor of the opening door – 'It is the Prince who opens the door to half our light on Maggie, just as it is she who opens it to half our light on himself' (p. 21) – is effectively more assymetrical than James would quite allow. There are wonderful passages which record his apprehension and assessment, his process of learning. These constitute special and important sections within the narrative, but they are far from controlling it. Indeed they could not, for the needs of the narrative dictate that there are so many necessary sources about which he must be ignorant. The light from the Prince's point of view is markedly incomplete. The representing of it 'in his interest' is not quite the same.

Also there is much that the Prince does know but which must be held back from the narrative, and only partially and at length revealed: the extent, terms and inner feeling of his relationship with Charlotte, the development of whatever internal conflict on the renewal of their affair, indeed exactly what happened at Matcham and Gloucester. James's discretion in these matters is perfect. The Prince knows about them, but we have little or nothing to measure their impact or their depth. All of this is seen from the outside.

Most important is the manner in which consciousness is revealed. We have certain passages in which the thought process of the Prince is quite fully represented: the reverie in Bond Street, or the meditation that follows the renewal with Charlotte in which he sees the Ververs as innocents who had no need for knowledge, as 'the good children'. (pp. 269–275) And these constitute a powerful, if sometimes unconsciously ironic, commentary on the action. Yet they have the effect of set pieces, of moments when we must stop and see the Prince's sensibility and reflective process plain. They are far from any synthesis of a general understanding through which the action is filtered. Rather than seeing by means of a sensibility, it is itself the demonstration that represents a carefully posed picture. Yes, the Prince is like that.

But the asymmetry is deeper still. If much of *The Golden Bowl* is the story of a shift in powers brought about by understanding and ruthless skill, this story belongs to Maggie alone. The Prince's progress is unevenly defined, and lacks that developed unifying consciousness. Perhaps there is something alien in the model of Roman prince which was less approachable than James believed. And one wonders – as at moments with Mme de Vionnet – whether 'the European' poses a difficulty as a fully developed vehicle of consciousness that he did not recognize. Hence, with the Prince, the steady pull away from hypothetical consciousness to object of study, to ambiguous symbol. The puzzling fragments, however brilliantly assembled, convey the strong sense of artifice.

A further problem arises, seemingly even for the Ververs themselves, in the fullness of his very project of accommodation. He is meant to 'ring true' like an authentic object of art or uncracked crystal. Yet the more vividly he might realize his project of identifying with the Verver world, the more he would have to abandon his role of *morceau de musée*, to become ordinary in his lack of angularity, hence to fail them in ceasing to be the perfect thing they set out to purchase. The very learning process would itself undermine identity. Rather than having the unflawed beauty of simply being himself, the plasticity of his accommodation implies a flaw. The 'Amerigo' without a surname sends a contradictory amalgam of symbolic messages. Neither we nor the Ververs will, again, 'touch bottom'.

In the author's proposal to abandon omniscience, in accepting 'finitude', we see posed in a variety of ways the problem of what we need to know. That so much of the Prince may be obscure to us may excite, amuse or irritate, but it is consonant with our normal understanding of others, and surely acceptable that, except for some unresolved puzzles, there is a character palpable enough. James seems to tread delicately through dangers which he keeps at sufficient distance. Some balance between the fullness of treatment that will 'see us through' and those great absences that are necessary to selectivity must be found. But it is far from a constant. Strangely fragmentary as we have found him, the Prince is a monumental articulation compared with Charlotte and Verver. Him we know somewhat, Maggie quite fully, Charlotte in fragments and Verver not at all. The play of knowledge and ignorance across the half-lit spaces exerts a powerful pull on the imagination. Hence our attraction to Nussbaum's *Charlotte Stant*; and perhaps the piquant thought of a lost volume called *Adam Verver* among the works of Gore Vidal would have an appeal. But this appeal is the outflow of curiosity, the imagination's outer edge.

This problem of knowledge will follow us in various ways. But the question of what James knows but does not tell is only intermittently part of his controlling power. *Some* finitude is real. The saga of American City is posited but not seen. But there are matters in this vast omission which are closer to us, simply because there are points where interpretation bears down on us. Or is it part of James's artistic economy to drop into the void the elements, however relevant we might find them, that do not add to the crushing force of resolution which will come in the end?

This may suggest the simultaneous evolution of two techniques, one of them acknowledged, indeed claimed, and the other which has developed in its margin but is necessary to it. The claimed technique is that of saturation, of knowing as much as is consonant with the unity of a work of fiction. The other is its discontinuous shadow, in which some full understanding is indicated by touches and fragments. Inference trumps representation; we see not so much the opening of a door, but the possible chink of light under the second door on the left, down a corridor which we know is there but which we have not traversed. The inner dimensions are not amplified or given that remorseless fullness which the more demanding model of knowledge would require. The difference is marked by the degrees of internal interpretation that the four principals undertake. For the massive internal development which gives the book its shape and character is in the articulation of the second part, in which Maggie's understanding, both of others and of herself, is a grandiose and totalizing act of interpretation.

The Prince too interprets, as he is indeed supposed to do, but rather *grosso modo*. He poses large-scale general questions about the sources of his changed circumstances. What are these curious creatures, Americans, really like? How can one 'learn the language'? – all as if an anthropological enquiry were under way. But this seems taken without any very great depth of curiosity, as if the general question would contain all of the possible answers in some global sense. He talks to Maggie as if playing a delightful game. The appropriate language for the Ververs is a civil *badinage*. There is the feel of inverted commas around much of his utterance, as if an unspoken, indeed unspeakable language game must be marked out, which implies a certain alienation in every participative act. But once such a language game is launched, it cuts off the possibility of interpretation by the closing off that it performs. Having decided about a mode or style and given it the suitable characterization, the intellectual curiosity which initiated it is satisfied.

The thought of interpreting Maggie in a continuous and revisionary way does not occur to him as a necessary part of their *modus vivendi*. His necessary adaptation has found the appropriate mental set which will accommodate both passivity and alienation. For if at the beginning 'he felt his own boat move upon some such mystery' as the American character (p. 56), or if he turns to Fanny Assingham for the kind of commentary that will help him fix his coordinates, he seems to gradually replace this need with a stylized quiescence. One is indeed in the 'boat' which is Mr Verver's boat (p. 228) and which is 'a good deal tied up at the dock, or anchored, if you like, out in the stream'. (p. 230) If there is any consequent restiveness, a need for the occasional swim, the image of the motionless boat, comfortable and claustrophobic, suggests the enclosed world of the Ververs, somehow divorced from *terra firma*, insulated from place and time. One accepts its totality, its peculiar global identity, which may be something rare and strange, but which when once grasped and chosen leaves further examination in abeyance, allowing the 'good children' to bask quietly in the condescending affection that acceptance bestows. (pp. 274–275) Only in a totally new circumstance, when Maggie's own consciousness has assimilated the whole action and the breaking of the bowl cuts across all established understanding, does the challenge to 'find out' force a return to interpretation. But the challenge is, at least from what we can see openly, simply and tacitly refused. The Prince merely retreats into an opacity which will accede to the transformed circumstances without the necessity of reinterpretation – or at least without the need to articulate it.

Verver seems not to interpret. Or at least not more than once, when in the decisive moment of announcing his return to America he reads the necessity which Maggie has prepared for him. (p. 512) The one occasion of exposure to his inner world, as he stands on the threshold of the billiard room at Fawns, is an authorial *tour d'horizon* which describes and explains. We are given the working understanding we must have of this strange and elusive figure, without Verver himself much intruding in the matter. James to some degree anticipates the difficulty that we will have with this fusion of passivity and power, the uncanny simplicity and childlike innocence. Vivid as it is, there is clearly something in this extended description that is deceptive. 'The spark of fire, the point of light, [which] sat somewhere in his inner vagueness as a lamp before a shrine twinkles in the dark perspective of a church' (p. 130) is far from any sense of Verver's voice or any representation of his own awareness of himself. But James gives us only the most exiguous touches of that voice, suitably reticent and low key as befits a man who 'had fatally stamped himself – it was his own fault – a man who could be interrupted with impunity' (p. 130), who has no 'form' (p. 45) but the 'marked peculiarity of seeming on no occasion to *have* an attitude' and whose short and simple sentences occasionally sport a colloquial 'ain't'.

But in this long descriptive passage there is a grand air of the scope of his undertaking in the museum of American City. For James has posed himself a more perversely difficult task than creating conviction from the curious aspects of the Prince. Insofar as he has intended a passably recognizable portrait, there is the enormous improbability that so great a tycoon could limit his world in Verver fashion. This economic titan – James is quite clear about the scale of it – this peer of Vanderbilt or of J. P. Morgan, is so simple, mild and withdrawn as to suggest a hopeless organizer for a small-town study group. Yet we cannot conceive him as other than operating at the highest level of economic power, and certainly, knowing how to use that power.

Think of the world of Jay Gould,[7] of mergers, of fearless men manipulating capital and converting vast fortunes into power, and ask where is Adam Verver. The image of gold recurs insistently. But James has eliminated any understanding of its ambience or its source. Just as he may not know what is made at Woollett, he does not see the sources or shape of Verver's power. Again, as with the case of Wharton's 'human fringes' everything is sacrificed to the formula that the foursome demands. Meanwhile the figure of Verver slips slowly away from us to disappear in obscurity, 'a small spare slightly stale man, deprived of the general prerogative of presence'. (p. 160) Yet he remains a pivot for the action of others, a shadowy efficient cause. Do we need to know more? It depends on what we conceive as the scope of our understanding. I shall argue in Part Four that these dimensions do matter, that this very blanking out, partly in the name of artistic economy, contains a kinetic force from which James has deliberately turned away – as Brydon does from the ravaged face in 'The Jolly Corner'.

Nor does Charlotte interpret, for all that she was at one point the imagined protagonist. We are given passages of intelligent and penetrating comment, but they are not so much interpretation as direct involvement with the interplay which will in turn be understood in another perspective. The sharp perception is all presence – the very opposite of standing back for a reflective view. The conversational immediacy lacks the distancing of innerness, something the Nussbaum project might have to create. But the effect is to create a character more seen than seeing, an object of contemplation for the consciousness of others. Or does she suggest an element of ultimate incoherence: a consciousness that must exist but which cannot be revealed without releasing a destructive force on the necessary shape of the whole?

This restriction bears with it two important concomitants. Charlotte is by far the strongest physical presence in the book. The other characters have their modest features: the Prince and his moustache, Verver's duck waistcoat and check trousers or Maggie's straight flat hair and nun-like appearance. But these vanish beyond their introductory tagging. Only Charlotte is *seen*: a physical presence at the head of a staircase, or on the terrace at Matcham, or above the entrance at Portland Place, even 'throned' at the final tea party where the ceremony of farewell is enacted. But the power of presence has its own ambiguity when she looms out of the darkness in the card room at Fawns and becomes a dangerous 'splendid, shining, supple creature that has escaped its cage'. (pp. 488–490) The animal imagery reinforces the physicality, a suggested mingling of the visual and sexual that is both alien and 'splendid'.

The physical image is surrounded by a repertoire of adjectives in the repeated assertion of some distinctive quality which does not have a determinate character. Charlotte is not only 'splendid' but 'wonderful', 'wonderful and beautiful' (p. 564) implying a grandeur which has no distinctive features beyond the impression it creates. Her 'greatness', as opposed to the mousy Ververs, has also another quality: it is hers by virtue of nature alone. There is no apparatus, no basis in wealth, power or ancient title. She is the only character who is no one but herself. James's thumbnail sketch almost shrinks as it plants the essential clues: the mixture of tongues, corrupt parentage, abandoned childhood. (p. 78) We see the adventuress with her mongrelized cosmopolitanism typecast. And somehow her name itself, 'Stant', is not reassuring, being uncomfortably close to that of Lady Castledean's downmarket lover, Mr Blint. She is neither American nor European, but a free-floating agent. Yet her past has as marked an outline as that of the authentically American Ververs. They, indeed, come from nowhere. Yet it is an American nowhere that carries its cultural configuration with it, sufficiently to be noted by the Prince as something to be 'read'.

Even free-floating agents must themselves in the end be 'read', but only when they violate the rules of play which govern their unwritten contract, the contract that affixes them in their role, which to the Ververs is expressed in terms of function. The Prince, *morceau de musée*, is to fulfil the static requirements of the great collector, while Charlotte can be seen quite straightly in terms of 'what we got her for' (p. 390), and so much of that is summed up in the 'splendid' physical presence. The reductive effects of such a functionalism can be simply and unthinkingly accepted until some small crack appears, the system reveals a flaw. Once a challenge appears to the ordered relation, then the image begins to have a possible life, a set of consequences of its own – and danger: for then the splendid animal must be caged.

This is a construction more exiguous even than that of the Prince. With him, even if he is not the type he is claimed to be, we can attempt to read the interstices. Reduction may also bend the quality of the Prince to the smooth non-angular fit that his function requires. But he may still mistake his place, and above all his powers in the working out of the Verver world and its great game.

Chapter 12

Anomalies of Place and Time

The dislocations which create the internal tensions of James's major fictions have certain classic forms. In certain fundamental ways the inherited coordinates of life have vanished, receded into background. A normal circle of family and friends is replaced by an alien world – as we have seen with the Prince – which involves understanding both of that world and of the self. The sequence of errors and understandings, adjustments, shifts of perspective and of focus provides a vast repertoire from which the words and tales draw in permutations whose variables are proof against formulaic repetition. For the slightest change in the 'combination' produces the unpredicted complication of the 'affective interest' in the 'attaching case'.

One has seen how many of these disproportionate elements have been brought together in what is so often called 'the international theme'. It is traceable from the stories of the early 1870s, growing both in complexity and in the sense of its implications. For however cased, the very notion of what it was to be American seemed to demand a placement in terms of one's civilization as a whole. Such a placement could only be established contrastively, by a critical analysis – or certainly portrayal – of the many degrees of affinity and difference which would bring the distinctiveness of both Americans and Europeans into a view of what kind of creatures they really are. The famous letter to Norton that sets the terms for 'the complex fate [of] being American' sets it against, indeed 'entails ... fighting against a superstitious valuation of Europe'.[8] The valuation will undergo its metamorphosis, the complex fate remains.

Time, of course, complicates the question of what people really are with the possibility of what they may become. *The Sense of the Past* poses that open possibility, alas all too briefly and cryptically. But are we to view those transformed Americans of the late James, Spencer Brydon or Graham Fieldes, as supplanting an older form of American with a new one which perhaps has naturalized a European culture into American character without losing some essential integrity? Their plight has become their salvation. Yet at what cost? And how then to assess the durable alienation which seems to afflict Charlotte?

But if we try to look at *The Golden Bowl* in terms of 'the international theme', or, for that matter, any of the other displacements of time or place that might engage its actions, we see a difficulty implicit in the earlier remarks about the construction of the Prince. While profoundly concerned with manners and social values at a certain degree of distance, it is not a novel of manners in the usual sense of implying the distinctions involved in two (or more) competing social orders. For what has been sketched has further consequences. The Prince is not a European, the Ververs come from nowhere – a never-never land called America – and Charlotte is an international tramp whose deracination is total. The Ververs' America exists largely in the Prince's hypothetical construction. They are very peculiar and somehow one must account for that. Italy does not exist. England is merely a pleasant and anodyne place whose representation through the weekend party at Matcham is no more than a cartoon. If in the distance lies American City, it only slowly begins to assert its featureless and terrifying presence. In any identifiable version the 'international theme' has vanished. And if not entirely dead in terms of the formal plot structure, it has been totally emptied of content.

There is of course the Prince's desire to learn. But what he learns has little or nothing to do with America. And his very willingness to accommodate in the understanding of others makes him the true American of the novel. The Ververs have only their project, and the palatial settings with which their wealth can furnish them. There are ways in which the Prince's learning will be part of this *cercle*, not of the world which has produced it. And insofar as he has entertained the American design of reforming himself in a suitable mode, this is devoted not to a complex inner transformation but to making things work. For there is no innerness to transform, just as there is nothing about the Ververs to learn.

Perhaps one of the difficulties of the intense hermeticism of *The Golden Bowl* lies in this very extreme form of its delimitation. This may create a temptation to treat it as if it were a quite different novel, with proper affinities with the related works in the James canon. As if perhaps the world were closely analogous to that of *The Ambassadors*. But the awareness of Strether is one which is prepared for a real transformation, and that change is exactly the most far-reaching use of the 'international theme'. A consciousness shaped by the cultural boundaries of Woollett becomes increasingly responsive to another world, larger and richer both imaginatively and in terms of personal freedom. The disillusionment concerning a 'virtuous attachment' is modified, partly through Little Bilham, by a revised sense of the meaning and possibility of virtue. Learning and transformations abound. Even the superficial transformation of Chad has its value at the level of manners. The full sense of the relation of a culture to the kind of person that might live in it has its meticulous if ironic working out. And the rich comedy of social forms, with the incongruities of roles in conflict, gives a vivacity wholly uncharacteristic of *The Golden Bowl*.

It is this very absence of the sense of process, excepting the deeply inner transformation of Maggie herself, that heightens the feeling of hermeticism in *The Golden Bowl.* We have some short and charming passages of introduction in which the obsessive themes are handled as if in play. The lightest touch however contains the greatest consequence, and the badinage between the Prince and Maggie (pp. 45–51) contains – an often sinister – promissory note in every line, as if the end is all too precisely contained in the beginning. All touches are those of a total and final picture, of a self-contained world working according to its own laws and where the essential features are determinate. Perhaps this accounts for certain of the aspects of being 'done', of 'completeness' that the parts seem to reveal so much of the whole, and a strong sense of the whole is contained in miniature in the most apparently casual or unassuming aside. And part of the beauty of the formal construction may lie in the tensions between that sense of what is not there which I have described, and the equally powerful sense of a determinate totality. It gives the double pressure of wanting to know more, in the recognition that our knowledge is fragmentary, and knowing all too well how the force of determinacy in a necessary totality holds us firmly in place.

One consequence of this is to keep us from believing that an open-ended process is going on. I do not mean, of course, that we see the whole working out of the plot from its opening stages. It is rather that we do not feel that internal change, that process of realization leading to possibilities that affect the shape of their 'form of life' as a whole. We see Maggie's gathering realization, the moment of connection, and the shaping of her admirably controlled 'arrangements'. And the challenge of 'what do others know', leading to 'what will they know' and 'what might they do if they did know', suggests possibilities of a vertiginous and brinkish kind. But this is quite different from the presupposition of open-endedness with which the 'international theme' proceeds. We are somehow aware that inwardly no one will change and that Maggie has a vested interest in a single alteration which will mark not the opening of anything but a formidable closure. In this no doubt there is some degree of analogy to *The Wings of the Dove* where the crisis of illness forces a gradual closure in which discovery and transformation – such as they are – are transferred from the American innocent to the English manipulators. Is there some thread of a sequence that leads from Strether's changed awareness, which nevertheless refuses a further transformation of his life, through the transference of awareness in the *Dove* to a world where awareness is limited by the formal terms of the inner foursome in the *Bowl*? For Maggie's growth of awareness relates to one thing only, and that is a single 'fact' in her domestic circumstance.

One can see the transformations in *The Ambassadors*, which affect several of the characters, as related to place, the qualities of a different culture with different social codes, and those rather narrower changes in *The Wings of the Dove* as the gradual understanding consequent on the failure of a design. In this, the terms of play of the 'international theme' seem already abandoned while its structure remains intact. And in *The Golden Bowl* this is simply more extreme. Again the American innocents, but enclosed in their hermetically sealed vessel. Lawrence Holland writes of the 'crisis of transformation' but this is simply the transformation of the terms of play within the foursome, 'the old community'. What transformation there will be is simply in its destruction, and in the measure of the consequences, a measure that will be revealed in all that horror from which the participants carefully hide, masking it with their talk of value and of splendour.

A further effect of this hermeticism is to make us feel not only the isolation from all aspects of the outer world which would inform personal change in any cultural sense – Europe and America do not meet since neither of them has any substantive presence – but also that the possibility of process and change is in important ways so qualified as to leave time itself a marginal feature. As we are in an unreal place, so we are in a strangely attenuated temporal zone. We have, of course, seen two marriages, the appearance of the Principino, and one or two occurrences. This is not merely the paucity of action, the feeling that no other events have intruded. Of course there have been endless long afternoons when Maggie and her father have exchanged quiet nothings over tea, and Mr Verver has doted on his grandson. Perhaps the Prince has slipped down to his club. About Charlotte we know little. But the figures are suspended in amber and time has had its stop. Except for a single moment of implied action followed by one moment of 'discovery', the only movement in time will be the gathering for the ceremony of farewell.

There can be no temptation to imaginative meddling with this perfect opacity. We can feel no call for further action, or the gradual alterations that might affect our sense that something has, however quietly, moved on. But the gathering for the departure indicates an even more timeless world beyond it.

Yes, Strether will go back to Woollett, where there will be some small change in his circumstances, but the world of Portland Place suggests a stasis which no doubt is intended as a paradigm. The romance to be consummated there is like that of fairy-tale castles. Nothing can *happen* there. Just as the distant world of American City seems to place human feeling and consequence behind it – to create some circle beyond Limbo where one is fixed, as Fanny observes, forever. This has implications which we shall explore further, in looking at the relation of life to art, at the content of the allegory of American City.

But if one posits a world in which process has stopped, and in which significant action has come to an end, this may also reflect back on the characteristic qualities of a method where a carefully deployed *chiaroscuro* obscures the precise nature of what has or has not happened, and where what is not said is such an overwhelming part of the 'action'. We must accept as a condition of our own understanding the vast areas that are not to be revealed, and the slow consequence of a single shaft of ambiguous light. One feature of this is the stillness and the power with which silence speaks. Except for the running commentary of the Assinghams, which resembles a continuous post-mortem at the end of the great occasion which for some reason or another we have largely missed. But this talk is largely interpretation – the meta-dialogue which substitutes for an action. And when Fanny *has* acted, at the crucial moment when the bowl itself is broken, the world of interpretation, with its chain of causal explanation and tissues of connective hypotheses, enters that of the unspoken. Yet what this moment will effect is the further course of action which is also conducted under the rule of silence – and where that silence is not merely a constitutive feature but the guiding principle: that knowledge shall be withheld, and the absence of knowledge will determine all further development.

Hence the insertion of an interpreted world into one which refuses interpretation, and in which the resolution of its conflicts can only be achieved by such a refusal, since interpretation would render only contradiction. The novelist must outflank the interpretative impasse by silencing this voice, or rather by showing that it must be subsumed into covert means.

The second substitution lies in figure. I have mentioned the animal imagery which attaches to Charlotte. But the most powerful image is that of gold, perhaps at moments somewhat obsessively omnipresent. On the surface one might feel that a rather obvious form of pressure is being applied to a descriptive aspect of the Verver world. Certainly a rather light-hearted form of persiflage about realms of gold is a thematic accompaniment of the Ververs. But the aura, the golden shadow that they bring with them, is more cryptic than revealing. Perhaps those light touches are meant to make us feel at ease with dimensions of the story that, we well might feel, are more disturbing than sits easily with 'the good children'. One effect is a mingling of allure with alarm. Yes, that golden glow like a Claude sunset sheds a wholly pleasing and civilized light over the private world of personal affection where the grand scale of life has yet a modesty in its manner, a quiet consideration on the part of gentle and retiring people, where the suffusion of gold has no discernible active principle: no aggression; no vulgarity. Yet in a deeply passive, understated way, the measure of what gold can do to others looms like the threatening sky that may presage a storm. There will of course never be a storm; the bare hint of darkening will be quite sufficient for the quiet application of the force of an intent, often so barely stated as to require a careful reading to shape the appropriate form of acquiescence.

This more alarming aspect may at some points seem to be part of the unspoken conditionality of the narrative, that some scale of appropriateness is operative by which the Ververs are entitled to a monopoly of purpose, and this in turn is part of our awareness that they are the focal point, the axle, the centre about which all other actions or considerations revolve. This centrality may sometimes seem hidden or effectively masked – as it should be in much of the first volume – but the operative principle is there even through the representations of the Prince's consciousness. The subordination of will is evident in his reading of that of others, in the continual movement of assessment and interpretation which positions him with respect to their world. And it is shown in a decisive way with Fanny Assingham. Like the proper matchmaker that she is, there is the clear aim that all parties should roughly speaking get what they want – or at least what they ought to want. The carefully elaborated explanations by which she leads the colonel into the depths of the story may spell out what the Prince and Charlotte may have been and, at later stages, what they may possibly have done; but the assumption is always made not only that it is what the Ververs know, think and feel that are the essential determinants, but that their off-stage mental world is the very thing for which the action exists.

It is what 'they' think.

At one or two points the predominance of purpose is recognized by the two principals themselves, most devastatingly in respect to Charlotte: 'Whenever one corners Charlotte', Verver says, 'one finds that she only wants to know what *we* want. Which is what we got her for!' (p. 390) To which Maggie replies: 'What we got her for – exactly!' Yet the chapter ends with the brooding thought of 'how the pair would be at work' (p. 393), as if slowly it had grown on Maggie that there might be purposes other than her own. Although in the context ' "More company" at Fawns would be effectually enough the key in which her husband and her step-mother were at work' (p. 391), the implication that they might have other intentions is seen as disturbing. Even though Verver recalls that '*that*, originally, was what we were to get her for' – to extend their social life. Yet the desideratum seems gradually to suggest threat, as if it could contain possibilities, which might become alternative intentions, even a 'design'. There is a certain crassness to this scene, as if a window were suddenly opened, and the controlling power of the Ververs' intentions were revealed as the natural state of things. But James doesn't dream of elaborating on what it is to have 'got' somebody. The sense of power is keyed low, and except for the odd comment of Fanny – 'One beautiful woman – and one beautiful fortune' (p. 414) – or one or two of the meditations of the Prince on his own dependency, the source of that power is only tacitly registered. It is rendered in the ambiguous figure of the omnipresent gold. Yet the golden presence is not analysable, or indeed representable in any way. In effect, one does not understand or interpret Verver by way of gold.

The opacity of Verver, the blankness, the uninterpretability is simply matched by his figurative substitute. And the presence, shadow, allure, magic, threat of gold will never be tied to any of these dimensions but will operate its own *chiaroscuro* without the necessity of spelling out. It is this reticence which will allow Verver's nothingness to survive the cursory inspection which is all that the reader is permitted. What we have seen earlier was a problem of narrative method, of finding the proper ways to present the necessary figure to whom no internal development is allowed. Yet one can see clearly that the problem is not one of finding a mode of representation for something which is known. It is rather that he is simply not known. Rather than having those distinctive features which we can consider, examine, value, rather than assimilating to a type that has the necessary attaching explanations, there is a strangeness that goes beyond the problem of convincing the reader that there is such a sort of person. Here the strategy of avoidances I have mentioned may be either the acceptance of the unknown or the mask of some figure which one cannot see or face directly. Like the mutilated ghost which appears as the substantial if missing truth in 'The Jolly Corner', there is something hidden which could not have been predicted. The exact tension of that story is to produce the apparition without it being the obvious explanatory device either for Spencer Brydon or for the reader. The surprise of the encounter lies in knowing that there is 'something', but not knowing what it is. Brydon stalks it in the name of a knowledge which is necessary to him, and knowledge of the creature he has not become is necessary to the completion of the self he is.

Of course Mr Verver is not a protagonist in the same sense. James conceives no interest in him for his own sake. He is simply taken at face value – except that he is the wholly faceless man. Where at first glance there seems to be an exception, it proves the rule, for when attention is drawn (p. 161) to the 'deeply and changeably blue' eyes set in his 'neat, colourless face', what is emphasized is 'their ambiguity of your scarce knowing if they most carried their possessor's vision out or most opened themselves to your own'. We almost never *see* him. The face value is simply gold.

Again we have abandoned representation in the manner that is normally the procedure of the novel. James has not tried to create a reasonable image, a plausible context, a causal chain, an intelligible pattern of explanation. In his whole character and moral being he is simply 'as good as gold'. The 'good', 'dear', man as Maggie says, or 'dear sweet man' as Fanny has him, exhausts the possible attribution of qualities in a few simple and wholly indefinite adjectives. There is nothing more to be said. In a book which is so much about knowledge, where knowledge 'was a fascination as well as a fear' as Maggie reflects (p. 422), Verver lies beyond knowing. Yet perhaps not entirely beyond fear, as 'the realms of gold' will produce their own silent terror. Is this terror related to the good, dear man? In the strange nothingness of wealth and power installed in an allegory of innocence – an allegory that contains the application of power in the name of a higher good, the source and nature of which must remain unquestioned? There will be certain limits to knowledge. Yet we will feel a need which pushes beyond these limits to find the necessary resonance of the allegory. Its very simplification will draw us through the way in which a higher good can work its will. Through the normal acquisitive spirit in which abstract wealth is converted into objects, these then become part of the allegorical scheme which will create the Museum of American City.

Of course the vehicle of power, insofar as it is exercised in front of us, will be Maggie and not Verver. There may be some magical process of transformation by which Verver in effect *becomes* Maggie, as the wingless and crawling thing emerges through the chrysalis and becomes the butterfly. And would there be some vague if simplistic historical message in such a process, a part measure of the way in which the forces in a culture can – as with Mlle de Saint-Loup, the '*étoile*' or crossroads in a forest – concentrate their varied and far distant resources in the beauty and distinction of a single person? Then, even more than the Prince, that *morceau de musée* (p. 49), she would be a cultural paradigm, communicating the fairy tale in the perfect union. If this is the object of the inner transformation we can see the necessary grandeur.

The further transformation is by way of the object, the visible presence of civilization's process, something as capable as the gold which passes from hand to hand of entering into both commerce and allegory. To grasp the use of the object we must see it as a means, both to the metamorphosis of gold and to the creation of that civilization which will be the product of its contemplation. And this in turn should suggest the dissemination, the quiet distancing and appraisal, the slow growth of the finer senses, of the rule of decorum, of the nuances and sensibilities which should compose the civilized community.

So, *The Golden Bowl* would thus be a double allegory of reciprocal transformations, of inner and outer resolutions. One fairy tale may contain another, and whatever we may see of loss or of sacrifice may be the condition of two forms of greater good, of visions of the beautiful life.

Notes to Part Three

1. Henry James: *Preface to The Golden Bowl*, the Penguin English Library edition, 1985, p. 22. Further quotations will be indicated by a page number in the text.
2. Edel, 1972, *Henry James: a Life*, vol. V, p. 574.
3. Nussbaum, 1983, 'Flawed Crystals', pp. 25–50.
4. Vidal, 1985, p. 12.
5. Edel, 1987, *Henry James: a Life* (abridged), p. 585.
6. Edel, 1972, *Life*, vol. V, p. 364.
7. Powerful American railroad executive, and financial manipulator whose speculation in gold caused the panic of 'Black Friday' on 24 September 1869.
8. Edel, 1985, *Henry James: a Life*, p. 88.

PART FOUR

A Dark Fable of Love and Power

13. The Perilous Equilibrium
14. The Triumph of the Will
15. A Map of Incommensurability
16. Fictive Resolutions

Alvin Langdon Coburn, *Portland Place, London*, 1906.
Courtesy George Eastman House

Chapter 13

The Perilous Equilibrium

The power of substitution has turned life into art, and indeed into the cultural artefacts which are to embellish American City. Thus the triumph of life also points the way to the triumph of death. For death itself is subject to arrangement and codification, its shadow present from the earliest moment of *The Golden Bowl*, as when Maggie suggests to the Prince, ever so lightly, the equation of burial and American City. So too the victory of 'love' tears the word from the context in which it poses a danger, reshaping the patterns of desire. These transformations run in double harness until at the end they pull apart, in a terrifying sense of consequence.

Perfection, or assumptions about the perfect life, consciously pursued and carefully enacted, and put aside from the great scheme of common existence, define the community of *The Golden Bowl*. Are there external coordinates, or is this sealed vessel set apart from history and time? One has noted how incidental is the faint background presence of London, or of the life of the country house. If the Ververs[1] have a 'history', it lies somewhere behind them in the shadow world of American City, where that overwhelming reality of wealth and power has its indistinct essence. I shall look again at the historicity of the Ververs when considering their life as collectors, as despoilers of the Golden Isles. But it is hard not to feel the powerful effect of withdrawal, of creating one's own rules of play for their private life, this perfection of fulfilment which is to be found in the harmonious world of father and daughter, of husbands and wives.

It is through selected and restricted angles that we view them. There is so much that James does not tell us. On the one hand, we are drawn in to contemplate the 'attaching case' almost as if a Jamesian version of laboratory conditions had been created, where the conflict of incompatibles could be given its purest and truest demonstration. Yet the link of process to principle is sometimes obscure, almost always resistant to open statement. The order of things is transformed in a manner that avoids conflict, maintains appearances and conjoins an inner violence with utmost decorum. There is an uncanny mixture of plenitude and emptiness; the vast work can seem a parsimonious fragment.

A measure of Jamesian indirection is that one effect of this incompleteness could be seen as indications of completeness of another kind – a filling out of possibilities implicit in the original community of *The Golden Bowl*, but a filling out which is also a narrowing, and which works by progressive shifts of awareness not unmixed with surprise. The ground for something quite improbable must be slowly prepared. And it must come about at the expense of something which James has been at great pains to suggest, the notional equilibrium within the community of four protagonists. For the series of carefully constructed relationships depends on a feeling of symmetry. Charlotte owes her very presence in the community to the conscious choice based on the principle that symmetry should be established. And the self-enclosed world of the Ververs calls for such an extension, a promise of the self-sufficient, encapsulated foursome where an implied equilibrium is created. We must believe in it in order to believe in its destruction.

Of course disequilibrium is the stuff of plots and of the changes essential to the 'interest' of it all. But James has powerfully suggested the balance to be undone by the action of the Prince and Charlotte and more fully by Maggie's evolution from passive participant into controller and remaker of all. It is this process, so gradual and so overwhelming, so concentrated in a single awareness, that creates the marvellous tension of the ensuing action. But we cannot fail to believe that the foursome in its original equilibrium represents to its creators, the Ververs, a form of timeless perfection, a perfect arrangement suitable to their sense of having created themselves and a 'form of life' distinguished by its beauty and completeness.

This perfection is not easily described, and James conveys a sense of felicity without suggesting any substantial context for the perfect life. Father and daughter spend their time together, although an evolved conversation between them is not easy to conceive. The best years of a constructed form of life are passed over in silence. The Prince seems to be on the committee of his club. Only later when the harmony is broken do we find him turning over the pages of newspapers – especially *Le Figaro*. Charlotte may be about town on one project or another. None of this needs to be invented. Not exactly that all happy families are the same, but that perfect happiness has no content and needs no narrative.

There are of course those hints that such perfection cannot last, and growing indications of those asymmetries within the community that will lead to the Fall. Are they fully contained in the suppressed past? James keeps his protagonists largely clear of such awkward fissures and we are left to the partly hypothetical commentary of Fanny Assingham. She and the Colonel have complementary forms of community. As matchmaker she has a glimpse into the past, although we are never certain how much she knows and how much authority her explanations have. Of course she is, as in a Racinean tragedy, a necessary interlocutor for the conversations that ground our placing of the action. To such a *confidante* of three, although increasingly of Maggie, is granted a certain access, and certain clues. To such a *confidante* the Colonel acts as chorus. Like the Argive elders or the men of Colonus he asks for plain explanation and translates suggestions into either/or. His touches of obtuseness mask his importance, for it is the very literalism of his reductive cast of mind that provides James with the pivot for Fanny's further hypotheses and refinements of speculation. He is used also as a measure of the futility or irrelevance of such literalism.

Where do we touch bottom? It is not in the simplicity of representable action or in getting the facts of the matter straight. If the Theban chorus must uncover such a truth as 'who is Oedipus', no such discovery in *The Golden Bowl* can have a role without refraction, interpretation, reassessment or the relations it might imply. His distance from the action is a necessary constant as the second volume draws Fanny further in, and in the end makes her a crucial actor in the breaking of the bowl – a necessary substitution, for there must be no blood on Maggie's hands, or even broken glass.

However, even at the most hermetic period which follows Verver's marriage we are deeply aware of an asymmetry which makes its own part of the equilibrium. Charlotte notes (p. 243) the ambiguity of the notions of doing. What are she and the Prince to do? 'Isn't it the immense, the really quite matchless beauty of our position that we have to "do" nothing in life at all? ... There has been plenty of "doing", and there will doubtless be plenty still; but it's all theirs, every inch of it; it's all a matter of what they've done to us.' The perception is closely joined in narrative to the renewed liaison, although separable by a substantial time, and used to place a warning about the danger. But the problem is omnipresent as the essential condition of life. A clear judgment is lodged. 'Nothing stranger surely had ever happened to a conscientious, a well-meaning, a perfectly passive pair.' (p. 249) While the mixture of passivity and dangerous propinquity will have its effect, in that there will be one thing which one can 'do', the acceptance of the passivity points to a feature of the unspoken contracts which underlie the community. But of course one must ask if there is a reasonable 'form of life' sustainable in such 'perfect' passivity. Does the acceptance touch upon the contract, or is this an acceptance – including as it does the offloading of one's own capacity for action – that cannot be made?

The Prince responds to this remark with a characteristic silence. But he has his own capacity to analyse the nature of the contract, which is conceived as a sequence of negative surprises, of realizations that nothing or very little is required (pp. 245–246). It is a slow dawning that everything is taken care of – in relation to Maggie as in everything else. This is partly expressed in terms of the heaviness of time, and he paces the floor in facing the 'dreary little crisis' of not finding Maggie in for tea. There is a terse little demonstration of the *anomie* at the heart of this smartly managed world, in which the fusion of personal and financial describes a perfect 'community of interest'. Of course James is preparing the moment of erotic revolt which will put that community in question, when the appearance of Charlotte at the door, rather than Maggie at tea, produces the devastating turn. The perfect harmony of arrangement suddenly becomes artificial. Does James wish us to understand it as a thing of beauty, with a most singular perfection which is struck by the violence of something brutal and animal? Or does he wish us to take that 'nothing stranger' at its face value, to admit that the arranged world of the Ververs where everything is done for everybody is fatally flawed? The badinage between the Prince and Charlotte suggests both the impromptu and the inevitable, but we can always read this scene in terms of their interpretation of the rules of the game, or even of how easily might surface an agenda which they have hidden from themselves.

Such 'hiddenness' can be a correlative of the passivity which is a necessary condition of the way in which the community operates. And Charlotte's cry of despair falls short of measuring the incommensurables that the community contains, but clearly indicates one of its fault lines. For it is difficult to conceive of the community as having a perfect equilibrium, when it implies that agency is reserved to certain of its members but not to others. The Hegelian postulate of slave mentality as part of the natural order could hardly apply, even if it were coherent in the first place. For the whole point of the community is the equal value of its four components. And the question is whether or not the value can be sustained if agency has an assigned place, if there is a built-in asymmetry to the operation of the will.

The terms of the tacit contract by which the community was created cannot be fully spelled out without a conflict between value and agency presenting an intolerable strain. But in certain cultural settings, perhaps in the not too distant past, the terms of 'love, honour and obey' sanctioned the asymmetry in such a wholly conventional way that a cultural mist might soften the outlines of any such conflict. A natural order of things might well contain such imbalances. But in James's own context such a doubleness would reveal a system of unequal values which would deprive *The Golden Bowl* of its marvellous tension, of its carefully wrought equilibrium. The whole effect requires the Prince and Charlotte to have equal value with the Ververs, in effect, equal rights. And in any case it would be difficult to assimilate this particular set of relations to any widely observable social code.

While the passivity of Oblomov may simply be accepted as a fact of his nature and the negative spring of whatever is connected with him, we cannot doubt that the passivity of the Prince and Charlotte is intrinsic to the contract. (That we can conceive a passive element for all forms of idle or useless lives – or interesting or alluring or decorative ones – does not enter into the matter.) The status of the contract remains an obstacle to our further understanding. A superficial Kantian might find that the asymmetry violated the requirement to see all men as equal in themselves, which would surely invalidate the original commitment. But surely not in such conditions of bad faith. On the other hand, its terms are persuasive, and part of an order of arrangement which the world normally finds plausible. Of course people marry for money, and their behaviour is expected to conform, to accept a role which has its built-in version of decorum. And if this is accepted as indeed the normal condition, how not equally so when the usual social roles are reversed?

For James has produced, in the shaping of his community of four, conditions that combine with extraordinary ingenuity the force of decorum and the tension of extreme circumstances. The mixture of past and present relations, of special intensity of feeling between father and daughter, of social isolation and inward looking both strengthens the role of decorum and exacerbates the peril. What can such a community include; and what must civility exclude? We see these masters of supreme courtesy dallying, as it appears, without effort or attention on the high wire, all awareness of the abyss seemingly banished. And without the offstage presence of an outrageous carnality so it might be forever, an Eden in which lust and time are kept at bay.

Yet the counterpoint to Charlotte's despair about 'doing' is the self-sufficiency of Verver and Maggie. When the marvellous equilibrium is drifting towards its crisis, Maggie's unspoken truth of how the Ververs 'use' Charlotte is subordinated to that reciprocity in their own relations – implying another sense of 'use' between them. To the Prince, she feels like crying out 'we use her ever so differently and separately – not at all in the same way or degree. There's nobody we really use together but ourselves, don't you see? – by which I mean that where our interests are the same I can so beautifully, so exquisitely serve you for everything, and you can so beautifully, so exquisitely serve me. The only person either of us needs is the other of us.' (pp. 377–378) The difficulty of 'the *note*' of jealousy that would have been struck, had she uttered the words, does not undermine its truth. And James positions so strong a statement to sharpen the awareness of the consequences of those cracks that have crept towards the surface of the sublime structure – awareness that such an 'asymmetry' underlay that tightly strung order.

We began with an image of symmetry, and it is argued quite openly that the introduction of Charlotte is to provide exactly that. And yet we cannot escape the conclusion that it is both a carefully devised plan and that the notion of an inner symmetry is to a large degree illusory. But how are we to see this illusion in evaluating the action that follows? Has James at this point put it so fully to use for purely dramatic purpose? Or is the flaw in that equilibrium a revelation of its moral failing? This would matter profoundly to the argument of Hilary Putnam that the violations of symmetry by the Prince and Charlotte – in treating the Ververs as they would not be treated – is the essential moral violation.[2] Insofar as the asymmetry is a failure of reciprocity, how is one to measure it against a clear sense that the original community is asymmetrical, even founded on the denial of reciprocity in the all-important sense of giving to the Ververs a monopoly, not only of what has been identified as agency, but of the right to action, the right to choose and to will?

Of course, Putnam appears to be right that Verver and Maggie operate with an openness that is impossible to the Prince and Charlotte once the liaison is established. But even this requires, as Maggie's thought about the perfection with which she and the Prince serve each other would indicate, some qualification. Such thoughts, inexpressible even to Adam, are the reflection of a reserved area, just as there is a private world of father and daughter which the others cannot enter and whose existence they can only dimly ascertain. Asymmetries abound. But some of them seem to be part of the tissue of tacit arrangements by which the community is ordered. Shall we value this equilibrium or shall we find in its oddities an unacceptable model of community? Certainly one's instinctive response is to find it too bizarre to be generalized in any way. Rather than an acceptable version of a moral order, or a patent violation of any normative conception of one, it seems merely an oddity, a series of finely-tuned arrangements that are *sui generis*, unrepeatable, and only by an extension of effort credible. The adjustments are too special altogether.

We could of course invoke a principle of loyalty to that very establishment, conceived in terms of a caring benefaction, of an overwhelming concern for the perfect ease, the effortless wellbeing of its members. Such loyalty to the smooth progress of the little boat would mean accepting the cost of the necessary terms. And the cost is difficult to assess because the tightness of the circle, like a Black Hole, draws the light into it. Has the Prince never sought to establish with Maggie such a relation as to qualify the Ververs' intensity of rapport? And has Charlotte undertaken to create out of her marriage anything that might be special to Adam and her? The rays of light retreat. The failure to produce a playmate for the Principino receives one substantial (p. 256) and several passing references (pp. 342, 420) but nothing illuminates what we might see of Verver. Impotence, or a depth of decorum which excludes sexuality? – it is possible that according to the law of 'successive aspects', James doesn't know.

But Charlotte's comment that 'it's as strange as you like, but we're immensely alone' (p. 256), seems to indicate anyone outside the father and daughter 'in concert'. The thought of acting on one's own seems the only possible consequence and the very conceiving of it is the end of the equilibrium. For it is an assertion of the will which the finely tuned world excluded.

The startling thing is the rigour in which the alienness of sexuality is placed, cut off as by a Great Wall of China from a protected order within of the civilized and humane. The very animality – and we are at the edge of a long sequence of animal images – belongs to another order of being. The incommensurability is absolute. And the presence of the Will is felt as a brute form of animal instinct, the blind Schopenhauerean force. But can such a force exist within a community, or is its very nature hostile to a civilized order of any kind? Its form is sexuality, and of course the Jamesian distancing of sexuality is pervasive. But if Charlotte incarnates the animal will in all of its splendour as a threat and destructive force, what are we to make of the Prince who combines a disturbing passivity with a disruptive sexual allure? Does Charlotte embody the Schopenhauerean will in the active form of desire while the Prince as desired object – again, if differently, *morceau de musée* - is somehow untainted by its darker aspects? Then the 'conscientious, well married and ... passive pair' is Charlotte's assessment, a picture of that arranged world of the Ververs which is constitutively threatened by the possibility of action. And the 'pair' also contains its own asymmetry in Charlotte's animal force, and the Prince's equanimous capacity to respond – and also to withdraw.

The assessment shifts as the Prince takes in the physical picture of Charlotte by the fireplace (p. 249) which works an almost Proustian effect of connecting past and present. Perhaps it is possible that the past could be accommodated in the community, if reduced to pure recollection. Through the Proustian presence of physical detail, 'particular links and gaps had at the end of a few minutes found themselves renewed and bridged'. James balances the disturbing physical presence, the consequentiality of the connection, with the 'moral intention' of the dull dress and hat which has nevertheless a 'positive picturesqueness'. Does even an avowedly moral presentation so contain the devastating effect? So that the revival of 'the sense of the past' interlocks with the present and meets the future in a striking physicality – 'as in a long embrace of arms and lips'. (p. 244)

The perilous and delicate balance of this scene comes from James's necessity to convince us of at least three things. The intentions of both parties are good, and they aim to stick by the unspoken terms of the community. The Prince notes the discipline which is so implied: 'It's precisely boring one's self without relief that takes courage.' (p. 252) The somewhat unnatural tensions of that contract must also be seen as intolerable to the restless energy that has driven Charlotte like a demented tourist through the city. That energy is a sign of the animal force, of the blind drive that will recognize, acknowledge, accept and submit to the community's requirements – and yet cannot. We must be convinced that what destroys total acquiescence is a great natural power and authenticity. And finally we must be aware that difference within the community may be perceived, that they – Maggie and Verver – are 'extraordinarily happy' (p. 258), happy in their own terms, which are to some degree mysterious. Both Charlotte and the Prince admit to failures: partly of understanding, partly of identification. They have joined, but not to belong, and part of the consequent action lies in this recognition. In some way they cannot penetrate the heart of it. They are excluded and find common hope in each other. Yet in doing so their aim is to preserve rather than destroy, to make out of difference the working awareness that will keep equilibrium possible.

Is this good faith or bad? Of course the conventional answer is clear. But have the rules of play within the community such a mixture of strangeness and indeterminacy that a 'reading' of it, so to speak, can be based on the implied and unstated differences? The scene includes a series of recognitions, with a consequent awareness of the 'case' (p. 257) of the others, and of trust between themselves. This clearly is the moment, not merely of a personal choice, but of abrogating the power of action to themselves, action which can only be covertly effective, a strategy which implies the realignment of the community's powers without a change in its forms. And one might also speculate that the notional force of the Schopenhauerean Will could not be domesticated, given its carefully balanced mixture of expression and control.

No doubt Putnam[3] is right that such a covert strategy would treat the Ververs as they would not be treated and introduces an asymmetry into the community. It is as we have seen, not the first, but it is different in not being operable openly and in treating the Ververs as the 'good children' Amerigo has decided, and with some reason, that they are. Their tenderness towards the others is 'founded on one's idea of their difference' says Charlotte (p. 259). Some ideas of difference clearly do not require the same level of consent. But is this particular asymmetry different in kind from the asymmetry with respect to the will that is already built into the community structure? Certainly it embodies a violation of conventional morality that the other does not. The power of crypto-purchase built into great wealth is simply one of the ways of the world. And insofar as the power of the will is ultimately exercised, it is inseparable from this social and economic fact.

How does this affect our sense of the value of the community of four? Loyalty to that community is undoubtedly conceived as something of value in itself – although not all communities depend on the same reciprocities. Putnam is certainly correct to regard it as the object of Maggie's famous lie to Charlotte, when she denies that she suspects her, that the community should be preserved. And the strategy of the Prince and Charlotte is to maintain it. Yet it must also be destroyed, destroyed in a deliberate and decorous fashion by the moral determination of Maggie. Was the faultline in the first asymmetry of abrogating all agency to oneself, or in the second asymmetry of carrying out a hidden policy based on the acceptance of difference? And how should we measure the cost of the destruction?

I shall come to the latter problem in the chapters that follow. But it is not idle to consider alternative ways in which the community could either preserve itself or end in alternative arrangements which made another use of sacrifice. Suppose we think of the methods by which this community could prolong its life. It would of course involve change consequent on Maggie's awareness. One can imagine a stand-off in which the affair is silently broken off and the tensions surrounding it gradually recede. Maggie might then have exclusive possession of her husband without the triumph over her rival. Stiff upper lips and utter discretion could cover all. Tea would be served as usual. The world would remain as it was with a challenge to its inner character contained and defeated. Or we could conceive of an accommodation on the part of Maggie to her 'discovery'. In fact she really hasn't much evidence of anything, and what she has might be carefully neutralized by skilful management – 'care' – on the part of the Prince. There might be some ambiguity, the equilibrium between deception and acquiescence might shift from time to time. The methods might vary from the banal to the ingenious.

We can think of various versions in which the perfect façade could be maintained and the community retain what one could call its perfect integrity of decorum, which will contain its mixture of moral uncertainty and asymmetry in whatever form. One can also conceive of rather un-Jamesian conclusions in which the Prince and Charlotte decide that the compact is broken and the cash is simply not worth it. But here we would be in a different sort of novel altogether. Even if one could imagine a sinister irony, it would touch a certain truth in destruction. And the sacrifice would be of another order.

One reason for thinking about the alternative stories, alternative resolutions of a curious and tightly wrought conundrum, is simply that they will involve quite different moral principles, and forms of moral reasoning, differing ways of placing the essential problem in acceptable longer perspectives. Acceptable, that is, provided the novelist so persuades us. And alternatives may point to other versions of how resolutions might employ quite different forms of life. But here I only wish to look at the ways in which the community may be valued or otherwise. Its carefully constructed 'symmetry' can surely only be lost at a price. Throughout Maggie's gradual discovery of her self and its powers runs an infinitely delicate series of movements of will, of the recognition of a necessary discipline. Nothing is to be acknowledged and nothing changed.

Except of course that everything is changed. And the destruction of the community seems to be viewed less in terms of its loss than in the processes of that loss. The open acknowledgement of the hidden violation which would lead to conflict and recrimination would be brutal and uncivilized. It is the maintenance of appearances that counts. Instead of roughly broken, through Charlotte's impulsiveness, or a momentary failure of Maggie's discipline, it is to be carefully dismantled, with the fiction preserved that in some imperative way it remains intact. Nothing is decided beyond the desirability of a journey. And its rationale is hardly more than hinted at. An oblique suggestion produces a commitment to action, with only the sketchiest version fully articulated to hint that there might be reasons for such an action. Why should Verver and Charlotte go back to American City? The momentous conversation in which the determination is made (pp. 509–512) moves with an elegant evasiveness around the possibility of there being real reasons. That Verver should offer himself as a sacrifice is recognition of some unspoken stratum. The fatal utterance of names is avoided. Verver's working out of the implications of his marriage is handed back to him as his own responsibility, as if the original project of the community has been discontinued. The implied breaking of the connection of his marriage to hers is however more performed than explained. In a book so often prolix in working out the most exact sense possible of the rationale of an action, the cause and circumstance of a feeling, the understanding of the relations a word or gesture might imply, here no understanding is thought necessary. We have stripped everything away for the realization of the single and wholly determinate factor. They will return to American City because Maggie wants it. The dynamics of all the relations, the strategy of 'case' and the artifice of community will vanish. And all in response to an act of will that not only need not justify itself but of course cannot.

The fatal words must be avoided, for the community must seem to exist in the moment of its dismantling. And it is not Maggie who names Charlotte, but Verver, and simply by conjoining her with American City. So, 'then it was that the cup of her conviction, full to the brim, overflowed at a touch! *There* was his idea, the clearness of which for an instant almost dazzled her. It was a blur of light in the midst of which she saw Charlotte like some object marked by contrast in blackness, saw her waver in the field of vision, saw her removed, transported, doomed'. (p. 512) *His* idea, then; we are to make nothing of its possible origin in Maggie's remark, only moments before, that her father surely didn't claim 'that my natural course, once you had set up for yourself, would have been to ship you back to American City?' (p. 511)

But by then the fatal bowl has long since been broken and the mixture of assertion and damage limitation since that moment has been the fine product of Maggie's art. A nostalgic moralizing is in the end made to cover it all when Maggie holds that 'they're the ones who are saved ... We're the ones who are lost'. (p. 555) That father and daughter are the sacrificed while the others 'deserve' their moral salvation creates another asymmetry.

Chapter 14

The Triumph of the Will

The extraordinary pattern of discovery, self-discovery and self-assertion by which Maggie's consciousness develops in the second half of the book is clearly its most powerful and authentic representation. If there are reasons why the Prince is a doubtful artifice, if Verver is shadowy and Charlotte a fragmentary presence, the revelation of Maggie is the heart of it all and gives to *The Golden Bowl* its character of *Bildungsroman* and of sentimental education. The shape of a classical novel form emerges through the obliquity. The transfer of consciousness – or the evolution of its independence – is drawn with a gradualness that carries its perfect conviction. And the movement from awareness through self-awareness to policy and decision marks the transformation of the self in terms of the growth and use of its powers.

It is in effect the growth of the will, what we shall be tempted to call the moral will in contrast to the blind Schopenhauerean force which has, if momentarily, yet at decisive moments, marked the character of Charlotte. The latter is the antithesis of the ethical, while the will that evolves in Maggie is to be seen as its incarnation. And this is the product of language, of reflection, of the many touches of conscious decision as to what one is to do about one's life as a whole and one's obligations to the others that share it. It is the richness of detail in the portraying of this process that gives us our only fully realized portrait, and gives cumulative strength to the power of the conclusion.

Yet it is well before this process gets under way, or the occasion for it is even suggested, that we have had Charlotte's remark to the effect that 'they' *do* while she and the Prince are done to. This monopoly of agency seems the expression of the will in some important sense, even if largely unrelated to the ethical will which is to follow. Our portrait of Maggie begins in a sweetness and innocence which has a colourless low-key quality. Her appearance is likened to a hen's. Yet the passivity must in some way be deceptive. We have after all seen the Prince, and from what we have seen of Verver it is unlikely that he took a very forward role in such an operation, although the buying of a prince is made to seem, for such as he, somewhat routine. We know little or nothing about the part that either of the Ververs has played in this, but it is made clear that it is consonant with their life's work as collectors. Charlotte too, though less of a museum piece, is clearly an object for the collection. And here it is clear that the initiative came from Maggie. So the innovation of the symmetrical community is hers.

Beyond this she seems to lapse into masterly inactivity – 'masterly' because the sense of doing is not that of doing anything, but of the exercise of power in doing nothing. This is one aspect no doubt of the world of affluence, but inaction can be as powerful a determinant as action. The 'case' administered by the Prince and Charlotte – through the arrogation of the power of action to which they will find themselves ultimately unentitled – is indistinguishable from their daily routine of attending upon others, waiting to attend upon others, or not attending upon others, but not being free to do anything on their own because there might be something that others might desire. The release of sexual energy on the part of the Prince and Charlotte transforms the denial of the will into an assertion of it, yet in a form which is identical to that denial. And it is the sense of this difference that Maggie grasps, and expresses in the slightly paranoid form of perceived 'designs' upon her. For if one quite casually accepts that what one got Charlotte 'for' is the anticipation of one's own desires and total acquiescence in them, it of course becomes a totally different matter if that acquiescence is the mask of another agenda. It is not only a desideratum but an absolute necessity that the Prince and Charlotte will not only behave as if they had no will of their own, but literally be totally without one.

Now this is a curious conception of others to be held by 'good children'. In the scene that ends chapter 5 of Part II, James has shown Maggie's perception that 'more company' at Fawns would be an act of submission to Charlotte, an indication of the way 'her husband and stepmother were at work'. But linking the very thought of the possibility of such an agenda with the bluntness of a claim to possession seems to open a window on the most reductive view of person as object, and the most casual acceptance of one's exercise of power. How much does James wish us to understand from this? It is oddly placed in a larger sequence which shows precisely the beginnings of what will become the moral will in Maggie's 'new uneasiness'. If James intends an equilibrium of effect, in which that growth and transformation of the self is also marked by the causal operation of power, it is difficult to see it as other than a qualification, a recognition of the raw force of that power.

And it would be easy to attribute this to the world of enormous wealth. As rich men have many goods, chattels and services at their command, so they employ proper subordination in domestic arrangements, one realized so silently that there is no sharp awareness except in a sudden self-searching moment of assessment. Is this an aspect of an innocence which shows its dark side? Perhaps the innocence of a girl who seeks a perfect life and the sweetness and kindness of a 'dear little man' cannot be wholly free from such a passive use of power. What is at the least indicated is the emanation of a form of will which antedates the passage to self-discovery, a form which is simply accepted and assumed.

So we can distinguish at least three aspects of the will: one is the Schopenhauerean, animal, irrational, and infused with desire. The second is the creation of moral reflection and is the will as embodiment of this process, the authentic version of a Kantian moral will. And finally there is something more passive and mysterious than the others and more difficult to give a name – one might call it some form of residual will to which is attached some quiet and deeply felt identity, that combines the innocence of good children with depth of assurance in their own self-sufficiency. It cannot quite be expressed in social terms as it is almost hostile to any form of social activity – more company at Fawns or going to Matcham. But its private world rests upon certain presuppositions about the secondary nature of others, that the priority established in one's private rapport has an ontological precedence, and from its terms all other matters, at whatever distance, proceed. This residual will lies at the beginning of all policy as a condition of what follows, as a causal principle of what 'we want' which it would never occur to one to question, this setting of conditions for the world and for others passing almost unnoticed.

But with the beginning of Maggie's reflective process what happens to this other residual aspect of the way in which the Ververs work? Is this presence part of the transformation process, subsumed into the new moral being? It is tempting to see both this primal sense of certainty in oneself, with the world ineluctably an oyster, and the more active operation of an instinctive drive, akin to that of Charlotte herself, as subsumed into a moral category. We can certainly see the presence of this instinct, which resembles the growth of desire, in the final moment of the novel which brings us to the very point of physical possession. Is the growth of something like physical passion an accompaniment to the shaping of that moral will which controls the second half of the novel? Certainly most critics have seen the transformation of Maggie as the growth of an immature girl into the adult woman. Certainly too, the learning process that the complex tactics of the second part force upon Maggie creates a series of operations, of ways of putting together, and suggests a radical departure from the unexamined world of the beginning. The small details of manoeuvring others convey a breathless mixture of desperation and purpose in the making and pursuit of a design. 'I live in the midst of miracles of arrangement, half of which I admit are my own; I go about as before, I watch for every sound, I feel every breath, and yet I try all the time to seem as smooth as old satin dyed rose-colour.' (p. 401) The world of calm unthinking possession has begun to recede; the agitated moments of perception are the early stages of preparing another kind of mastery. James is of course dramatizing the vulnerability that leads to calculation, to understanding, to the operation of power, to the creation of a moral code which will alter or supersede the unthinking one.

We might also ask how far the residual will of the early parts and the Schopenhauerean drive we can gradually identify are consonant with each other. And here the division opens which corresponds – in part at least – to Schopenhauer's own, for clearly that residual will expresses the form of order which gives the whole tissue of relations their original shape, which creates the life-project of the Ververs, the original community, every aspect of their established form of life. And even if its formal relations must be altered we are quite aware that the essential spirit, the Verver ethos and project, will remain. Therefore this aspect of will, ruthless in possession though it may be, is a will-to-order, to enable the establishment of a civilized mode of existence, while Charlotte's represents the destructive force, the chaotic *id* – however urbanely it may express itself. To assume that any such elements enter into Maggie's evolved self supposes that not merely a transformation, but a synthesis, a putting together of opposites is somehow possible.

But we can consider the hypothesis of such a synthesis, one which releases that primal principle of order from the challenge of an alien and destructive element. In a sense it has survived easily, for its latent powers are enormous. It expresses the governing laws of the community partly in terms of the wealth that sustains it, partly in the body of shared interest and culture – to some extent no doubt already derived from that wealth. The instinctive will is almost a discovery, something that has not been part of Maggie's comfortable existence but which is called into being by that most banal of stimulants, through the jealousy that another's sexual presence arouses, and a discovery which implies its own transformation. If this is an essential part of the *Bildung*, it is as a spring to action that it is first seen, and as romantic consummation that it ends. But it does not enter into Maggie's consciousness in a way that allows any part in her deliberative process, and indeed couldn't. As a form of the inadmissible it provides an unacknowledged force; and in any case, whatever attempt there might be to make use of it would lie outside Maggie's vocabulary. But its presence is important because in some of its aspects at least, *The Golden Bowl* is a romance, and in the working out of the action, in its concluding pages, James has chosen to focus on that particular note.

What shapes and dominates the action is of course the moral awareness, and insofar as there is a synthesis of these forms of will it is tempting to see this as its determining element. There are important scenes in which this is necessarily true. The very stages of growing awareness are the means of articulation, the recording of progress, and of shaping determination. It is the tissue of conscious reflection and allusion that compose the civilized self. And we must be more explicit about the ways in which this moral will and intellectual development can relate to the operation of power which may proceed from a more primal source. For it is the combination of power and the growing consciousness to direct it, with the moral being that develops with that consciousness, that constitutes our deepest uneasiness with the development of *The Golden Bowl*. We see the operation of power for moral purpose. We are put in a position to applaud, to feel a satisfaction in such a resolution, however uneasy we may feel about the concomitant sacrifice.

But is the question of power and its use inseparable from the evolution of the moral will? We are to rearrange a world which was carefully designed but is deeply flawed. Weighed in the balance and found wanting – and we are given the weighing process in all of its intricacy. But is it the growth of moral awareness that shapes the conclusion and all its consequences, or is it simply the recognition of power, a power made palatable by the subtlety of its application? In saying inseparable, one must remember that a substantial critical response has chosen not to see them in that fashion. The creation of the moral will has seemed the perfect vehicle for the triumph of love, or rather that the unity of power and love is not, in terms of the ultimate resolution of *The Golden Bowl*, in any way problematic. The equation of power, the moral and love (cf. Dorothea Krook)[4] places that moral will in the ascendance, and puts its operation beyond any possible qualification. The transcendence of lesser values in 'the surpassing dignity, power and beauty of the moral' could hardly admit of any flaws, or any limit to 'the plenitude of peace, power and joy that flows for Maggie from her vision'. Such a notion of transcendence reduces an element of pain or conflict or sacrifice to insignificance.

So visionary a sense of the conclusion might seem to assimilate everything to the single and higher principle – and one problem that seems put in an excessively abstract and un-Jamesian manner is this almost mystical evocation of an apotheosis of the moral. And yet it does correspond to a certain movement of abstraction in Maggie's own mind in the great revelation scene with Fanny Assingham (pp. 395–408) where the nervous and uncertain opening of a Pandora's Box of suspicion leads to the assumption of the ability to bear anything for the sake of 'love' (pp. 404–405). This is neither love of Amerigo nor of Adam but something pure and universal, like the recognition of some sublime and transcendental principle.

Yet the path to this is both by way of the confession of torment and an equal confession of the manipulative use of power – in the devious strategy of making the Prince and Charlotte go to Matcham together when they would rather not have gone, simply to see if they would. 'They've been afraid not to.' For their awareness of her awareness has become her means of taking the initiative where she has had no part at all, and exploiting the slightest awareness of false positions to create a certainty of false position. 'They move at any rate among the dangers I speak of – between that of their doing too much and that of their not having any longer the confidence or the nerve, or whatever you may call it, to do enough ... And that's how I make them do what I like.' (p. 404)

The Assingham response, 'You're terrible', mingles with the sequence of emphatic judgments that has punctuated the scene. Maggie is 'absolutely good and sweet and beautiful' (p. 401); has 'a little golden personal nature' (p. 402). Now it is difficult to conceive of the recognition of these qualities as not setting up a counterpoint in which alternative recognitions are loaded with the tension in which lover and love are joined. There is no sense that James wanted us to perceive a seamless fusion; we are to recognize that something quite unexpected is happening. The very combination of hysteria with the discipline of 'mildness' is startling enough. Something is shown of Maggie which is paradoxical and disturbing. One is that love is abstract and pure, without focus or object, while power is contextual and detailed, present in all of the calculations that go into its operation. It is as if love must be taken on trust while power can not only be described, but defines the relationships into which the community is now to enter. A process is under way and the steps will be shown to us. But through it Maggie will preserve an innocence – 'Is that what I wanted?' she asks when it is clear that her total victory is leading to the departure of Adam and Charlotte. To which Fanny Assingham replies: 'Oh it wasn't for you to say. That was *his* affair.' (pp. 534–535) And this operation of the will is to be subtly camouflaged by the degree to which both Adam and Charlotte present the decision for departure as their own. But this is part of the exercise of discipline by which the moral will is to avoid the worst consequences of its action – and almost to place its awareness of itself outside that action, as if the perfection that one sought for one's life could have no part in desiring it so.

Such perfection is not perceived in terms of desire, or of agency, but rather as the magical artefact – either the famous pagoda, marvellous but without an entry, 'visible and admirable' but in some way failing to answer, as the bowl itself 'without a crack'. These emblems of flawed perfection nevertheless convey the imaginative claim of something which lies beyond the world of process and change. Are such worlds themselves flawed, dangerously distanced from the passions and commitments implicit in the moral will? The relationship of persons and objects, of process and assent will keep its uneven movement to the end.

But the belief in perfection, as a goal, as a moral aim, infuses the relation. And the image of a life without a flaw is the point of departure for Martha Nussbaum, in 'the assiduous aspiration to perfection, especially moral perfection'.[5] However it is worth noting that this perfection is unlike that of archaic ethics; it does not embody the picture of a total self like the *kalos k'agathos* but locates its perfection in doing the right thing, in precisely the moral dimension of one's being which nevertheless animates the whole. If 'Maggie had never in her life been wrong for more than three minutes' (p. 206), her sense of rightness fuses a moral authority with a simple and direct understanding – an innocence which rings true with a kind of wholeness that knows no parts. When the Prince observes that the Ververs have no use for knowledge, that must imply for grasping what is new, alien, for understanding other persons and things. But there is another form of understanding which lies in uncorrupted moral sense, in which one's primary intuitions are deep and true and require no further 'knowledge'. Nussbaum is therefore somewhat misleading in suggesting that one will seek a perfect life one does not possess. The heart within is as pure as the little silver cross blessed by the Holy Father, and nothing, not even the prudential lie to Charlotte, is meant to indicate otherwise. The transformation by the moral will is to embody that purity. The activating principle of one's life is pervasive yet must also be translated into an operative will to accomplish a necessary transformation of what is external to oneself. The inner life and the community or other version of one's private world must be brought into accord, an accord only possible through that operation of the will.

In one of his last interviews[6] Michel Foucault remarked on the relation of any search for a perfect existence to the source of those forms of obligation which paradoxically make it possible, and hence on the variable shapes of the interdependence of the beauty of life with the moral understanding by which we accept the nature of our obligations. He sees this in terms of the way these obligations establish themselves, by recognition and submission, by what he calls the 'mode of subjection' (*mode d'assujettissement*), that is, the way in which people are invited or incited to recognize their moral obligations. Is it, for instance, divine law, which has been revealed in a text? Is it a natural law, a cosmological order, in each case the same for every living being? Is it a rational rule? Is it the attempt to give your existence the most beautiful form possible? If we wish to do something like finding the most beautiful form of life, we face problems of moral calculation, we must formulate principles of choice, and above all learn to make our submission to the necessity such principles may imply. 'What is the *mode d'assujettissement*?' Foucault asks:

> It is that we have to build our existence as a beautiful existence; it is an aesthetic mode. You see, what I have tried to show is that nobody is obliged in classical ethics to behave in such a way as to be truthful to their wives, not to touch boys and so on. But if they want to have a beautiful existence, if they want to have a good reputation, if they want to be able to rule others, they have to do that. So they accept those obligations in a conscious way for the beauty or glory of existence. The choice, the aesthetic or political choice, for which they decide to accept this kind of existence – that's the *mode d'assujettissement*. It's a choice, a personal choice.

At some levels this choice looks quite simply like a calculative sacrifice of the lesser thing for the greater. But an important element of the incommensurate enters into the choice. The beauty, the glory of the thing far surpasses the small normative commitments one undertakes for its sake, both in degree and in belonging to another and superior order. The beautiful form of existence is separated by some enormous gulf from those social and human arrangements that must be submitted to it. Yet one is aware of basing the beauty of life on these lesser forms of obligation. Many things may be subjected, as one sees in *The Golden Bowl*, to the greater principle, where almost anything may be sacrificed as long as the beauty of that principle is in view.

But how do we assess this disproportion and see the propriety of subjection established? For subjection could come to serve many principles, and in *The Golden Bowl* we observe the studied operation of subjection in a world where principles are continuously and meticulously examined or re-examined. The Foucaultian conjunction of obligation and the 'glory of existence' touches the heart of a work where the fascination with the incommensurate moves uneasily between alternative versions of that glory. What is the overriding principle that underwrites and legitimates such an existence? James's involvement with such a 'particular attaching case' seems to proceed from the fullest sense of the difficulty, from the fullest rendering of incompatible versions of that existence, brought into the closest and tightest formal bond.[7]

Chapter 15

A Map of Incommensurability

All of our comments have relied on those indications of the closeness of the formal bond, but the necessity of subjection and the finality of sacrifice also accept the incongruity of what has been bonded together. The crack within the crystal has been there from the start. To create the pure and ideal world of Maggie's moral imagining that imperfection must be uncovered and transcended. There is no doubt that in *The Golden Bowl* this will involve the pain of sacrifice, a sacrifice that both destroys the carefully controlled community, and destroys much in the characters themselves. We must face this loss for the sake of a higher good if we are to believe in the triumph of the moral will. Such triumph is impossible without a recognition of its cost. But the final effect must hold these opposites in a newly evolved equilibrium, in which the incongruity of pain and triumph is made whole.

In formal terms one can see the overlay of two plot structures, and the literature on *The Golden Bowl* largely acknowledges this. The book has been seen as a tragedy where the fatal error of the protagonists has led to suffering and loss; or as a triumphant journey through error to self-knowledge and the perfect consummation of romantic conclusion. Of course most accounts recognize the duality and it is impossible to deny in terms of the first description that Maggie gets what she wants, or to doubt under the second the degree of suffering inflicted, and inflicted as a finality rather than as a transition to some more desirable state. To attempt a characterization of the plot structure in such generic terms as Northrop Frye's would lead to contradiction or at least to the confusion of many qualifications. Of course, one can claim, and this seems the message of much of James's own writing about the novel, that the special character of the form is precisely its comprehensiveness – that, as it's put at the end of his preface to *The Ambassadors*, 'the Novel remains still, under the right persuasion, the most independent, most elastic, most prodigious of literary forms'. The very limits of this elasticity may well be what this 'particular attaching case' puts to us, and the prodigiousness of the novel glows in the accomplishment of such a finely balanced duality of claim. The response to that duality may involve another asymmetry of a subjective kind – the hearts that glow at Maggie's redemptive love and those that have an irritated feeling that Charlotte has been sold short by too careful a stacking of the cards may well not be the same. And yet that they also may at least make their demands powerfully is part of that duality, of that perfectly arranged conflict of genres that the novel's capaciousness allows it to maintain.

Hence the 'most prodigious' form is employed to create a tense structure of incommensurates. How can we put the divergent and conflicting elements of our world together, set a course out of opposition, create intelligibility out of chaos? The novel does not of course 'solve' the particular conflict, but it provides the vehicle for seeing it resolved in the most comprehensive arrangement. If in an ideal world there would be no conflict between the components of the *summum bonum*, the very existence of the novel is linked to such conflicts, as a record either of their destructive effect or of their successful restructuring.

However, a dimension of this balance is brought out in the shifting of tone. As we move towards the romantic climax, the air darkens, and the final scene unfolds in a ritualized crepuscule. I shall return to the effects of this ritualization when looking at James's method of transcending or at least arranging the incommensurate. But the discrepancy creates its tensions to the very end. The act of parting is in a sense the ultimate breaking of the bowl, now prolonged for 130 or so pages. The formal implications, the art of the necessary arrangement, will be considered in Part Five. But there can be no doubt of the double movement of the action. As the triumph of the Will is to be consummated, the glory is real enough. But it is equally clear that it is attained at terrible cost.

As the imagery becomes more menacing, the hunted and captured animal is secured, there is an overwhelming sense of conflict between the satisfying triumph, the main conclusion of a romance, and the momentous aura of sacrificial fatality. There is the 'silken halter' around the victim's neck (p. 523), the 'wordless smile' of Verver's which Maggie translates as: 'you see – I lead her now by the neck, I lead her to her doom, and she doesn't so much as know what it is, though she has a fear in her heart.' (p. 524) The insistent repetition of the gathering awareness of 'dream' (pp. 524, 540, 541, and so on). Charlotte is seen as 'at bay', far off, 'pale in her silence and taking in her fate' (p. 535) and Fanny Assingham assesses that fate with awe: 'I see the long miles of ocean and the dreadful great country, State after State – which has never seemed to me so big or so terrible. I see *them* at last, day by day and step by step, at the far end – and I see them never coming back. But *never* – simply.' (p. 535) And, 'she'll be – yes – what she'll *have* to be. And it will be – won't it? – for ever and ever.'

Glory and *assujettissement*, with a sacrifice in finality and terror. We have, certainly, the course of that glory, partly as the full operative sense of the will, partly as the legitimation of sacrifice. But for all of the warmth of the final embrace it has a certain pallor. And a sense of detailed calculation that derives

from a close identity with Maggie's own consciousness, with her determination and thought processes. She must see it 'through'. The establishment
of her own being demands the sacrifice of another. The necessary move, the
complex rationalizations are carried out in the light of day as Charlotte recedes
into obscurity. How are we to regard this strange duality if not as one where the
conflict of values is articulated through the use of two languages, one fully
developed in the foreground, the other indirect and symbolized, distanced
through accumulation of tones and figures.

   How far does this double movement create a tension, even a sense of
unresolved conflict indicating sufficient contradiction that the romance model
of the basic plot is fatally qualified? Certainly there are two sacrifices:
Charlotte is doomed and Maggie and Adam accept the loss of each other. The
Prince of course loses Charlotte but seems to indicate that the transformation
of Maggie will efface any sense of that loss. The mutual sacrifice of the
Ververs is effected largely *sotto voce* and an appropriate stoicism masks any
unsuitable outbreak of emotion. They will no doubt make the sacrifice because
it is right, according to a kind of inner law. And they will do so without
questioning the ground. They will also do so in accordance with a higher law
that transcends the right: one which establishes the ensemble of right and good
actions within a tissue of relationships that constitute a civilized life.

   It is tempting to see in the conflict and the sacrifice it entails a profound
colliding of values, an incommensurability that we can formulate in terms of
the grand principles which the protagonists embody. Maggie's almost mystical
commitment to the power of love, as disembodied almost as that we might find
in the Great Garbo, assumes a legitimation which excludes its profane *alter
ego*, without any reflective process. The social code marks the difference,
although this is merely assumed and seldom referred to. One wouldn't, would
one? But a deeper reason than the social code lies in the appropriation of
consciousness, the assumption of the overriding importance of a personal
perspective, as we have seen. If this consciousness not only makes the widest
and most unquestioning assumptions about the shape of love, indeed of all
values, but is directed by her own moral centrality and may be read as the
usurpation of the moral agency of others, there is no doubt as to its authority.
But this full and elaborate articulation belongs largely to the working out of
means, addressed in the precise and clear language of an increasingly
accomplished tactician. Are we therefore meant to see this burgeoning of
mastery as effacing the figure retreating into the shadows? Such a reductive and
Manichean reading would be alien, in the most elementary sense of making
assujettissement totally efface the interest of the struggle, of the interplay of
persons who are valued, rather than of the conflicting values themselves.

Insofar as the Great Good of a perfect life was conceived in terms of the harmony of the community of four, that ideal is fatally compromised and the sense of loss, of the pain that accompanies Maggie's triumph, cannot be entirely smoothed away in the glory of her victory. But what further does the sacrifice imply, beyond the pain of parting? Isaiah Berlin speaks of those conflicts of values, those 'collisions', which are intrinsic to the human condition. The classical examples of conflicting principles, Antigone or Orestes, are the subject of a tragic literature where sacrifice is necessity and follows ineluctably from the terms of the conflict. And Berlin argues that this tragic view of life is simply a feature of the human condition. The 'notion of the perfect whole' is 'conceptually incoherent'. 'Some among the Great Goods cannot live together. That is a conceptual truth. We are doomed to choose, and every choice may entail an irreparable loss.'[8]

Certainly we have a story of irreparable loss. Although it is based, for James, not in a conceptual truth but in a contingent one. Or is the romance element so strong that the narrative necessity is overwhelming? One must, among other things, feel one's 'way' through the conflict of romantic and tragic forms, or perceptions, or views that are intermingled. Perhaps there are two conflicting senses of what the truth of the novel may be. For the great principles which might engender these tragic collisions are absent in their conceptual form, but live obliquely in the commitments to a form of life. Has James allowed the hubris of an imagined perfection, a private and encapsulated version of the Great Good, something doomed by the incommensurables of a pure and a carnal love? The notebooks make clear that James was setting himself the most intractable of problems with the very purpose of feeling and working out the deepest conflict of loyalties, the most disturbing and poignant division in affection. It is extracting the moral from such division by pitching the stakes at the highest level that the intensely worked equilibrium of the novel is intended to maintain. The golden bowl is to be broken, the ideal world of the Ververs destroyed, and the result rendered as triumph. Yet the effect is to establish the dual movement that we have already identified as the novelist's language: the precise surface clarity of Maggie's calculation and arrangement and the metaphoric darkness which, like the beast in the jungle, captures and destroys. And the equilibrium between these languages is also a form of arrangement. It is this equilibrium which ensures that suffering occurs but is not seen to occur, that sacrifice is made yet is not accepted as made. The prodigious form will not only contain the presence of triumph and sacrifice, regulate the pressure of opposites but play the metaphorical game of adjusting one's awareness of the falsehood that it embodies, to place the triumph of possession in a golden glow.

We can of course plot the axes of interpretation in ways that bring the moral dimension to the foreground, as much critical writing has done. But there may also be a sense in which the 'prodigious form' acts precisely to avoid the reductions of moral judgment, to tell us that, in the *chiaroscuro*, loss is gain. A 'perfect' world, a 'perfect' equilibrium, has proved imperfect and will be replaced by a perfect life, which, as in a romance formula, is the life *à deux* excluding all others. Does the romance formula then suggest a narrowing of the prodigious form? One cannot deny the perfect harmony of the romance form with the conventional social moral code that this particular romance embodies. (In a substantial romance literature the tragic conflict is through the collision of erotic power with social order – a transgression. Here a transference or displacement moves from the disturbance of eros to its domestication.)

On one axis of modification, the moral code, which operates – if not entirely – as Maggie's code, can in certain ways be made fully comprehensive. Everyone can be seen in terms of a moral triumph. For the Prince and Charlotte are 'saved' and while Maggie and her father are 'lost' to each other, the moral triumph of their own vision is complete. Even the ambiguities in the moral code itself are so subsumed; 'they have done it to *him*, to him, to him!' mingles the deontological horror of 'it' with the positional value of Verver's authority, the legitimizing power for the community, which has become part of the triumph of a totalized morality in which victors and victims participate. This may efface some of the impact of sacrifice for it is the representation of the greatest good.

Hence in an ironic sense the compact of the Prince and Charlotte, which seals both their affair and their servitude, has the fulfilment of a rigorous duty as its final consummation.

Such servitude of course invokes that alternate axis of interpretation in the pervasive presence of Mr Verver's power, something embodied in 'him' and yet ruthlessly effaced by James to create an image and atmosphere of total innocence and benevolence. We have looked at the nature of the contract which that power employed, the quick, even unspoken areas of acquiescence which are only obliquely and playfully acknowledged, above all in the disappearance of any of the harsh or conventional features of that power. Think by contrast of the direct corruption of Brydon's ghost, or the savage old men in their houses in Newport in *The Ivory Tower*. In *The Golden Bowl* the sublimation of power not only casts a certain glow over its almost invisible source, but so diffuses the effect of power as to convey loyally the ease of agreement. Participation is so elegantly achieved and the presence so evanescent. It is the dominion of a self-effacing passivity. The power is mediated, even modulated through another prevailing code, that of manners, and it will be through manners in the strong, highly formalized, social sense that the final accommodation of the book will be enacted.

But one parenthetical consideration about the nature of power should be noted. I have mentioned the degree to which the Ververs monopolize the possibility of agency, indeed of the right to agency. Maggie's move to exercise the latent and camouflaged power inherent in the asymmetry comes when she fears that others may exercise power over her – for one thing in recognizing a certain inscrutability in Charlotte's thought. (pp. 334–35). It is not that Charlotte has expressed anything that is new or remarkable, or that there has been any change in her behaviour, but a certain necessity of interpretation arises invisibly, creates a fear and requires a narrative, an account. The very sense that there might be closed rooms leads to the fear that there are such, and that in them there might materialize the slightest thought that had not been predicted. And from this it is a few short steps to the fear that she is being manipulated, that an agenda exists somewhere which she did not originate and in which she is a passive element. She and her father may fall into Charlotte's 'plan' (p. 387), and the awareness of this seems to originate only with that full and restless consciousness doubling back upon itself in search of a cause, a reflection that creates its own object and goes on to respond to it.

What is mapped in this response is a sublime intricacy of working out, of developing and refining the reflective process, from an indeterminate awareness to the elaborate and conscious powers of the final pages. This is marked not by deductive steps or any destructive mode of enquiry – in fact a number of conclusions are based on rather flimsy evidence, and one moves from primary unease to passionate conviction through a mixture of guesses, uncertain inference and wholly fortuitous circumstance. But the process very acutely relates perception to behaviour and to consequence. So the careful strategy of mastery works more by small and fragmentary realizations, directed by the awareness that all change must seem a way of staying the same and that any policy of Maggie's must seem to be that of another. Maggie will in the end be seen to follow the Prince in the placing of Charlotte when he makes his own choices clear. (p. 565) And of course the decision to return to American City will be Verver's (p. 512), to be embraced by Charlotte as the mixture of cultural mission (p. 535) and above all by the constructed passion to place her husband first, 'to *keep* the man I've married'. (p. 542) The elegant series of disingenuous verbal manoeuvres that leads to Maggie mustering 'the signs of an impression that might pass for an impression of defeat' produces Charlotte's assertive 'I want really to possess him'. (p. 543) All of the operations of power have been displaced in the mental processes of others, have surfaced in the motives and policies of others to give the semblance of the shaping of action. The art of Maggie's suggestion, direction, control passes unnoticed in her careful self-effacement, except perhaps in an awareness that the Prince is never in a position to articulate. James has in effect created the intricate process with every aspect and nuance displayed for us while keeping it wholly concealed from the other principals. The privileged Fanny of course provides the occasions for oblique and partial understandings, for mediating judgments – half grasping it all and providing the ground of further explanation, her commentary marked in limits which are not imposed upon us, but which we can nonetheless use.

However the aim of this sublime indirection is to underwrite the nature of civility itself, even of what we must call the overriding rule of civilization in the supremacy of manners. The mark of an acceptable order of things is to make all relevant parties feel that they themselves have willed it so. And the art of doing so is in putting nothing directly, creating no recognition of the possibility of conflict, covering the pain of sacrifice or loss, smoothing the twists and turns of life with a semblance of harmonious arrangement. Civilization's rule is that of decorum, not in the narrow sense of correctness – it would be a distortion and cheapening of James to see this as a mere keeping up of appearances – but in the sense of order pervading all behaviour, all relations with others, expressed with such an ease that the effect, even if noticed, can hardly be mentioned.

Utmost decorum is maintained; any aspect of the struggle that surfaces is modified and refracted so that its terms are deceptive. Charlotte's defeat is made to appear victory, a victory necessary to the very self-esteem which is her undoing. That manners reign supreme is compatible with the radical transformation in which knowledge and self-awareness become weapons. The Ververs may have no use for knowledge, but the single moment of awareness suffices for a ruthless instrumentality. Out of diffidence has come a terror, and beyond it a new *episteme* for our Foucaultian heroine. The alien world of sexuality must be mastered and in the end legitimized. But it is through the application of a repressive code that the terror of 'it' is to become the triumph of 'love', and the operation of this code consists precisely in the knowledge of when to say nothing. The strategy of power is avoidance, and its tacitly recognized necessity.[9]

Above all, the avoidance of the kind of word from which there could be no return, which would create an open division. The community is to be broken yet maintained, its operation abandoned but its myth continued. The temptation to do otherwise must be faced and articulated, most dramatically in the moment of Maggie's observing through the window the community that she can destroy (pp. 488–489) and in the famous lie which denies to Charlotte any possibility of destruction. The former is handled with a reflective distancing, a synoptic sense of the relationships involved, and the destructive effect of allowing her moral righteousness to find its voice. Patrick Gardner's excellent comments on this scene[10] emphasize the 'aesthetic "distancing"', and certainly the standing back to see the pattern of life as a whole is its striking feature. But it is not exactly an aesthetic whole that Maggie would destroy. Unless one wishes to describe the complex tissue of civilized behaviour as aesthetic. That would be an over-reading of the aesthetic dimension of Maggie whose few remarks in this vein, seeing people as objects of art, seem a conventionalizing *façon de parler*, a mode of presenting her and her father's supposed outlook. (I shall later give reasons for not regarding the Ververs as aesthetes at all. They have, rather, chosen a high-minded hobby, which is directed to the civilizing and improving of their fellow-countrymen.) It is within the terms of the code of manners that later the Prince will be accessible to Charlotte – 'for high decency'. (p. 551) Crude confrontation would be to abandon all of those principles of courage, measure, decorum, decency that have governed their lives.

Yet the ensuing scene with Charlotte (pp. 496ff.) is contorted and turbulent, set in the context of Maggie's reflection on the awareness of 'horror' – 'the horror of finding evil seated all at its ease where she had only dreamed of good'. (p. 489) From the 'distanced' vision to the lie there is a crescendo of moral fury which is superbly rendered in the forbearance by which 'the right' is established in its improbable way: 'the right, the right – yes, it took this extraordinary form of humbugging, as she had called it, to the end'. (p. 498) An awareness has quickly shaped into a moral discipline.

This predominance of moral quality however contrasts with another aspect of this conflict which concerns the question of the greatest good. For insofar as there is a sacrifice and some goods are indicated as greater than others, it is not clear that those goods are different in kind, or involve different principles in their construction. We may aim at a perfect form of life, but the expectation of happiness in that form of life is not marked by any disagreement among the four principals. It rather involves only questions of persons and means. The ideal of love as Maggie expresses it looks as if it is stripped of consequence, and we have seen it as an abstract and transcendental principle; but it does not announce another order of values. For what is the 'case' that the Prince and Charlotte have taken as a life commitment, their mutual affection and Verver's 'all-embracing' benevolence, if not forms of 'love'? The sort of general issue which would arise from the clash of incommensurate values does not arise in the dramatic form of showing the conflict of principles. The principles are shared. It is only in their perceptions and application that they differ. After all, part of the transformation of Maggie herself is into the carnal possession in which Charlotte has preceded her, a possession legitimated through the further moral ambiguity of the fact of purchase and the automatic attribution of rights which is part of both the marriage and community contracts.

One concomitant feature of James's method is that the overt use of moral language takes on a disturbing indeterminacy in the contexts within which it is used. *The Golden Bowl* is so rich in general speculation that it is the very plenitude of moral reflections, or of toying with general principles or possible laws, that may complicate and even confuse. Issues concerning freedom and commitment, the nature of personal identity, moral responsibility, community and obligation, aesthetic form and forms of life arise, qualify, and replace each other kaleidoscopically. They are raised in general ways which a philosopher could recognize as putting an arguable case, sometimes in indirect discourse, sometimes in interior monologue, sometimes in direct exchange between characters. They may be seen to change their force as the changing awareness within a scene represents them in an altered light, may be balanced by alternative formulas, and qualified or contradicted. So they are harder to hold on to than the similar remarks of other novelists. They are more equivocal as 'touchstones' – and partly because they are so numerous.

We are used to thinking seriously about those passages in novels where the general formula stands out and seems to have a revealing centrality. Consider 'only connect', Forster's key to the crises of divided worlds in Edwardian England, or 'to the destructive element submit yourself', that cryptic reflection in *Lord Jim* on the relations of intelligence to the instinctive life of man. We can see these as pointing in some larger direction, and indicating a sense of the whole. But when the Prince says '[e]verything's terrible, cara – in the heart of man' (p. 566), the ground slides beneath us. Its sense in context is only part of its force, and the Prince's use of it contains much that lies beyond that context. But understanding his meaning is problematic. Does it apply to them all, reflect the Prince's deeper understanding of himself, or is it merely a facile throwaway by which the Prince converts an awkward moment into a defusing generality? Yet any claim to generality is caught up in the law of 'successive aspects', as James forces us to see the language of the novel from an angle internal to it. And this makes the sense of context itself uncertain as the circles radiate out from the stone dropped in the pool. Which circle makes the real interest? Here we are almost balanced between generality as a form of truth, and generalization as a social tactic.

And the Jamesian atmosphere is always one of moral saturation, so that every act, however aesthetically directed, is morally significant, even if that significance may possibly 'turn' if we shift our perspective. But it is impossible to conceive an act as wholly idle, as morally casual, or as totally crass like an evening at the Crazy Horse or a one-night stand. Perhaps the closest we get is in Strether's purchasing 70 volumes of Victor Hugo, and then wondering if it is the one thing that may be 'the fruit of his mission'. (*Ambassadors*, p. 274) There is no Jamesian space for the socially casual or morally inconsequential.

The essential distancing, which is partly the product of the law of 'successive aspects', subordinates conviction to an intellectual curiosity. The many general observations are set in the special brackets of a context where they are not so much ironized in the name of a subversive intent, but ironized through the manner in which another view or perspective is taken. It asks implicitly: 'Can one reasonably talk like this?' 'Is this really innocence?' 'Have we chosen the right word?' and so on. What matters is the examination of the successive features of the 'attaching case' that work through the possible permutations it may have. Except that unlike linguistic philosophy, what is examined is not the conceptual aspects of the language which this discourse employs, but the circumstances which might fill out the successive features and give them meaning. How are goodness and innocence connected, knowledge and responsibility? Though the characters may examine the terms themselves, the effect is not a conceptual analysis, but a phenomenology of their use. They are fitted and refitted to alternative versions of circumstance: a reshaping of conditionality in such a way as to resemble an experimental method. We may try to discover the nature of the right thing, but as we enter further and further into the complexities of the particular case our moral certainties waver, dissolve, re-form – and in doing so reveal a world subject to a radical sense of contingency where fallibility is intrinsic to the project of understanding.[11]

One effect of the use of the 'successive aspects' is the modification of the authorial voice: of his authority both with respect to his knowledge – as in what is unknown about Mr Verver – and with respect to the operation of his moral judgment. If an author accepts his finitude, accepts that his point of view is limited and partial in the assessment of what he has created, it also qualifies the general force of whatever the book might tell us. The indirection itself suggests that there are certain conclusions that would be inappropriate, certain assertions of one's knowledge and control which would be beyond the artist's conception of his powers. Where James assumes the character of moral philosopher, it is as one who stands back before the generality of moral rules, who sees relativity and limitation not as a *desideratum*, but as the conditionality of 'the degree to which his [the artist's] impulse and passion are general and comprehensive'. (p. 30)

To that extent *The Golden Bowl* is not an example of the mode of generality of the moral philosopher, except insofar as the artist has subsumed such reasoning into a vision which is relational and qualified. In at least one sense of moral philosophy, the formulation and use of general principles and their conversion into working rules of conduct, this is not the embodiment of moral philosophy but its destruction. What could we do with the categorical imperative in *The Golden Bowl*? It could give only the shakiest guidance. What James tells us is that we cannot use rules seriously. And that is because we would not know what to do with them. They would come apart in the attempt to work them out, or fade away as instances of mere banality.

For the strange mixture of the arbitrary and the necessary in *The Golden Bowl* suggests no real form of exemplarity. The novel does not enact the idea, but absorbs it and turns it into the fabric of its own internal laws. There are no 'examples of' or 'allegories of', out to show a general truth by way of the fable. Rather, in *The Golden Bowl* the language of morality has been examined, picked up, turned over, taken to pieces. But this very process has in the end indicated its unsuitability as an ultimate explanatory scheme. The fable has resisted it as a language of interpretation. At the same time it has used it. One effect of this may seem to be a moral scepticism that is more a fatality than a choice, where the arguing through of moral aspects has left us with incompatibilities that must be resolved by other means, where the balance of different kinds of ethical and aesthetic claims has brought measure, exhilaration, and terror to the final ceremony of departure. A resolution has been created, or imposed.

Insofar as we can use Nussbaum's 'very simple Aristotelian idea that ethics is the search for a specification of the good life for a human being',[12] we find that our deepest problems lie in specification. If our most comprehensive values are so universally shared, how are we to arrange our conflict over their working out, contain the conflicts which fury or pain might possibly turn to destructive ends, if not through the painstaking operation of restraint, manners – and deceit?

The openly acknowledged area of consent is to the rule of decorum itself. Consent to Maggie's rule will take place, but the general criteria that govern that consent cannot be given. James has placed difficulties in the path of formulating such general criteria. One is that finally the story is more intelligible than the 'explanation'. The presentation of the coexistence of irresolvable conflicts in values 'makes sense' in narrative that it would not make in abstract schematism. Equally, in the narrative form, incompatible concepts may show us ways of relating or of entering into an understanding that the form of argument would not accommodate. Rich as the novel is in moral concepts and reasonings, it is the narrative that works out their relative values and establishes, perhaps ambiguously, their ultimate relations. Putnam argues that 'the work of fiction must not be confused with the "commentary"', and it is the commentary that is (or can be) a work of moral philosophy'. On the other hand I think James poses the possibility that the description of his most complex and controversial conflicts adds up to a total story which is intelligible beyond the possibilities of a conceptual sorting out. Putnam also speaks of a 'great philosophical picture'[13] as if philosophy too were a kind of description. If so, one version of this might be a Foucaultian phenomenology of moral choice, an examination of how and under what conditions the necessary subjections can produce a much-sought glory of existence. Such uses would suggest that philosophy and narrative were complementary modes of description which are not always perfectly separable from each other.[14]

However, if the smoothing of conflict has been undertaken through the submission to civilization's practice, this does not resolve the conflict which we have noticed between the bright and clear triumphalism with which Maggie and the Prince face their future and the lowering darkness which hangs over the departure for American City. The intermediate period of danger is the subject of reflection. The transition will pass without incident: Charlotte will not 'get at' the Prince, nor will any feature of the established accommodation be distorted. Yet one waits upon the moment of departure with a suppressed emotion which must be converted into form. They await the separation in the deep conviction that confidence and strength are expressed in the art of doing nothing. And from inaction the few necessary 'decencies' are turned into ceremony.

The final book is by far the shortest of the six. Except for three or four moments of verbal accommodation, the essential conflicts of *The Golden Bowl* have been resolved. The illumination of Maggie and the stages of her awareness have occupied the centre of the narrative, followed by the understanding of the restraint which is necessary to her strategy. The final lines of Book V are the completion of that strategy with the cry of 'failure' which will be the necessary gesture to Charlotte's ego, the deception which is essential to the rationale of parting, which will allow Charlotte's pain and humiliation a thin veneer of pride. The final book will sketch a few consequences, note the odd significant thread, make the arrangements for departure, arrangements which amount to a ritualized system of controls.

We will learn that to Maggie's strategy has been added Amerigo's masterful sense of tactics. Any shift in his complicity from lover to wife has been accomplished so smoothly as to be almost imperceptible. And the problem of Charlotte is to be met in doing and, effectively, saying nothing. 'Therefore as we're doing nothing we're doing it in the most aggravated way' says Maggie. (p. 550) The absence of any speech or significant action must set the tone of the formal departure. Absence, avoidance, silence, and every proper attention. The delicate conversation with Maggie about what Charlotte knows, that leads to the question of Amerigo's acceptance of Maggie's own knowledge, ends with the superb finessing by the Prince ('richly though ambiguously' (p. 567)) which enables the anguish of reconciliation to slip quietly past the heart of any deep differences. Maggie's own pride will feel the mixture of verbal tact and 'chemistry', as our own crass age might describe it, 'with a terror of her endless power of surrender'. (p. 568) She saves herself from the terrible moment of the 'question of the quantity of truth' (p. 567) and tea will be served at five.

The tea party which is the occasion of farewell unfolds as if 'under menace of some stiff official visit', compared with awaiting the visit of Royalty. An agitating prelude about lying to Charlotte is without consequence. At a number of points we have edged towards conflict, but the fatal word has not been spoken nor has the destructive implication been followed up. If there are final assessments they have only an oblique relation to the conflicts that have preceded them. There is a repression of language which enables a new opening towards sexuality. And the tension is to be contained in a formality which brings us close to an aestheticism which is otherwise hesitant and reticent. The sense of accounts closed may be contained in Mr Verver's surprising utterance in French: 'Le compte y est . . .' (p. 574) which James has teased out with 'and who shall say where his thought stopped?' The 'it is finished' hovers in the charged but composed occasion: 'the splendid effect and general harmony: Mrs Verver and the Prince fairly "placed" themselves, however unwittingly, as high expressions of the kind of human furniture required aesthetically by such a scene. The fusion of their presence with the decorative elements ... was complete and admirable; though to a lingering view, a view more penetrating than the occasion really demanded, they might also have figured as concrete attestations of a rare power of purchase.' (p. 574)

As her mind moves from objects of art to the beauty of scene and of persons, and to persons as objects, the interplay between the 'gravity, that was an empty submission to the general duty of magnificence' and the perception of them as effigies at Madame Tussaud's is hard not to take as a thunderous irony. Are they indeed living beings in the Verver universe? Has some terrible reduction to the inanimacy of a possession reached its logical and grotesque consummation? Our minds are directed away from this to the generality of effect. Charlotte is 'incomparable', 'great', 'too splendid'. One is parting in awareness of Charlotte's 'value', of Verver's 'ability to rest upon high values'. Tumultuous emotion and depths of irony are subsumed into aesthetic generality and ceremonial posture. One might wonder what emotion lies behind the surface of another scene of parting, Watteau's *Pèlerinage à l'île de Cythère*, where the melancholy tones of departure from the shrine of love are suffused in a golden glow.[15]

For Maggie, 'it had been for the sake of this end. Here it was then, the moment, the golden fruit that had shone from afar'. (p. 579) And James has achieved, perhaps read within, that perfect ambiguity of formalities which blocks off the possibility of interpretation. If the darkening tone of the caging of Charlotte and the brilliance of the surfacing of Maggie's consciousness are in effective equilibrium, that balance is further qualified by the ironies we have just observed. It is in this sense that the project of finding any feel for the appropriate relations eludes us, disappearing in that cloud of qualifications. 'Appropriateness' itself remains as an understanding of the 'great game', as the necessary condition of any form of life that a civilized man might wish to live.

Chapter 16

Fictive Resolutions

If we wish to try to measure the conflict between dark tonalities and romance in the conclusion of *The Golden Bowl* we can see both the abyss of discrepancy and the clear perfection of formal unity. Nowhere else in James are questions of void and value, of what may define the civilized, so fully integrated into the literary form. The loss and the triumph are fused, are part of each other, logically, emotionally, narratively. But we are still free to ask whether such a fusion creates an intolerable imaginative conflict. Such a demand is to live with the triumph and terror, to see them fully in their incompatibility and to feel the pull between them. The question is whether this falsifies James's project of formal arrangement, by which the complete effect of the novel is to be apprehended, and whether 'the whole chain of relation and responsibility' is stretched beyond endurance. Is contradiction so deeply part of the *Bowl*'s character as to create what Paul de Man would have called an 'unreadable' novel?

We have seen the difficulty easily and lying on the surface. De Man's 'unreadable' novel is one where 'the imperatives of truth and falsehood oppose the narrative syntax and manifest themselves at its expense. The concatenation of the categories of truth and falsehood with the values of right and wrong is disrupted, affecting the economy of the narrative in decisive ways ... The ethical category is imperative (i.e. a category rather than a value).'[16] For de Man, the very failure of order and understanding is the modern condition – an approach that has no part in James's own concept of 'the prodigious form'. Yet, if we wished to analyse these conflicting signals in the manner that de Man applies to the distinctive ambivalence of Rousseau, we could easily see that the mass of incompatibilities that compose *La Nouvelle Héloïse* or the implied contradiction in *La Profession de Foi* are at least roughly analogous. As an incarnation of conflict, where two incompatible possibilities embody their points of difference, the 'unreadable' *Golden Bowl* seems naturally to beckon – however maddening James might have found the self-cancelling notion of 'unreadability'.

Certainly the double dimension, the almost schematized opposites, propose a quality of division that is clearer and more dramatic than either text of Rousseau. For the pull in opposing directions that is often merely implicit in

Rousseau comes through with a precise tearing effect both in *The Ambassadors* and in *The Golden Bowl*. The 'all comically, all tragically' may have the lightening effect of a throwaway, but the fullness of irony plays directly on our desire to see things clearly and to see them whole. And by evoking the question of genre, James sets the two great perspectives to bear with a painfully conscious light. That conflict of perspective in the Bowl is defined without the terms, but with equal clarity: the Prince sees first the disappearing carriage, and then only Maggie.

There are however good reasons for thinking that such a use of de Man's term would be less than helpful. For one thing, many of the senses of 'unreadable' imply an overly reductive definition of 'readable'. The highly determinate senses of 'readable' would be exactly those that pointed a moral in the way of assimilating to external convention, to social codes, or to literary types that fix our expectations to either a genre or a mode. The unreadability that rescues us from such fixed terms of play may turn too easily to the impossibility of reading in a manner that either rejects any possibility of interpretation, or insists on the innate fallibility of any interpretative hypothesis, or makes of 'impossibility' a mode of interpretation in its own right. And while all of these modes may have a localized acceptability, the total implication perhaps does not.[17] Especially, I think, in a case where the terms of that 'unreadability' are so clearly marked, and the conscious balance between those terms so meticulously set out. The circumstances are almost the opposite to that of Rousseau, where the multiple elements may be placed in so many and divergent relations with each other. And James would have firmly resisted the suggestion that any one reading was as 'good' as another. Mona Ozouf has remarked that 'The uncertainty in which James leaves his readers, and the major difficulty of the problem he presents, is to cultivate uncertainty while avoiding imprecision; and this should be understood not in the least as a weakness in the work, but as a mature decision.'[18] James's art is of clearly drawn tensions and controlled alternatives.

Nussbaum's brilliant analysis[19] of the novel's conclusion draws heavily on the use of 'pity' and 'dread'. These are the indications of tragic depth within Maggie's final triumph. The consummation of triumph is the acceptance of the tragedy it contains, for Maggie in terms of the perceived loss, for the Prince in the blindness of unperceiving heroism 'violating love for the sake of love'. Such a tightening of paradox effaces the identity of genre expectations. In effect we sense simultaneously all of the greatness and terror of tragedy, of having passed through the moment of sacrifice to the kind of knowledge, in Maggie's case at least, that the tragic experience conveys.

But how does one use this tragic knowledge in the world of romance that seals the conclusion? Is this knowledge effaced as Maggie buries her eyes, or simply put aside, marginalized or bracketed off by the necessity of the fulfilment that such a romance entails? It is difficult to find its place in this new order of things even if it is the foundation of that order. More than the antinomies of pure reason, the antinomies of literary form embody those cross-purposes of knowledge and feeling that the 'prodigious' means of the novel point up. But does it reconcile? What can one do, finally, with 'love's knowledge'? To take to heart what here is its bitter message might poison the age of gold into which one now enters. We could easily feel the temptation to think that *The Golden Bowl* asks too much, that the opposites held in balance are deeply incompatible and that we have reached the possible limits of the novel as the vehicle of that conflict.

These antinomies are placed at their grandest and most abstract when considered as the problem of genre. And they are posed equally, if in different terms, by *The Ambassadors* and *The Golden Bowl*, where the equilibrium is attained by different paths. The one has proceeded through essentially comic means to a bleak and dour view, where perhaps comedy still governs one's sensibility, even in sacrifice. The other projects a golden glow over its strange mixture of triumph and terror. It is, for both, the nature of their strange equilibrium, to which a critical response wishes to find a general guidance. But how far would terms of genre help us in reading this equilibrium through? Certainly, to the extent to which the notion of tragedy may imply loss and waste as well as the underlying chaos of the destructive or the unresolved, these elements may be suggested; but they are entirely controlled by a formal fastidiousness that keeps them under the surface, muted and contained by a pervasive decorum, expressed as in any civilized world by a propriety of manners, by the indirectness in which all losses are concealed.

This could of course suggest a quite modern sense of tragedy, a deep and terrifying emptiness which lies beneath our quotidian efforts to make a reasonable and satisfying narrative of our lives. In *The Wings of the Dove* the moral deceptions and self-deceptions which surround the fate of Millie Theale are in the end suitably self-destructive or self-corroding, yet Millie's death, her tragedy one could rightly call it, is not the result of things that happen to her but of things that don't. The absence of emotional fulfilment is a precise area of Jamesian knowledge, a dimension of humanity that is re-explored, most powerfully in 'The Beast in the Jungle' which is the most extreme version of that absence, of the failure of love through a remorseless egoism and failure of self-knowledge. We have noted the use of the jungle imagery in the closing sections of *The Golden Bowl*, where Charlotte is characterized in an alarming sequence of animal figures – strong enough to convey the sense of her own submission to those forces in the self that alienate, empty and destroy. If the jungle metaphor is partly exchanged for the cage, the effect is not thereby weakened. There is a tragic vision and it is Charlotte's tragedy no doubt, but it is far from shaping our sense of the whole.

A corresponding movement in James's final tales has been seen to offer a more positive view of the possibility that human feeling can transcend and triumph over circumstance. In both 'The Jolly Corner' and 'The Bench of Desolation', a cold but distinct solace follows trial and vicissitude. But only the Prince and Maggie are the incarnation of a golden glow. We could use the term 'romance' of such a plot if it were not crevassed by our sense of cost and pain. But this simply underlines the futility of hoping to see the novel under the predominant sign of any genre, system of tropes, or other so identifiable rhetorical structure.

What we must take as the 'prodigious form' does not through this become a 'loose baggy monster' or the kind of omnium gatherum which accepts the human condition as the mixed bag that it is. For the measure of the experiment has been given to us in entirely precise, even especially rarified terms. One equilibrium has been painfully and elegantly constructed. It has been as painfully and discreetly destroyed. Another equilibrium will follow, but not in the action of the novel. It is the reader's equilibrium, his understanding of what this destruction quite precisely entails, the delicious and bitter mixture of glory and humiliation, so conjoined that they are part of each other. The parting of the ways is a crossing point for ourselves, where all of these elements are so held together that we recognize a fusion of the delightful, the intolerable and the necessary.

We may as readers fail the test this imposes and follow the inclination of our instincts, to read in virtue's triumph, or to see in the fate of American City, a cruelty beyond the claims of justice. To do either is to fail ourselves in the novel's presence. The very tightness of form in holding these opposing responses in view of each other denies the exclusive legitimacy of either. And insofar as the effects of the dual movement of the conclusion ironize each other, there is that conjunction of a rigorous determinacy with the tension of opposites that will see in their mutual subversion a principle of coherence.

Will that ironizing mode of understanding support our recognition that something has happened, that Maggie's growth of self-awareness has resulted in the practical and calculative use of her power? Or that the domination of an existential will is simultaneously the domination of those vast and impersonal powers that flow from the dark centre to which Verver and Charlotte return – powers that are in their impersonality alien to the nuanced judgment and personal feeling that compass the values of the Jamesian world, and which he will find in *The Ivory Tower* ineluctably corrupt? The equilibrium which is imposed on our own judgment is that of distancing. We may observe a phenomenon with a mixture of pleasure and regret, and James has made our mental balancing easier through the mask that power wears: the sweetness of Maggie, the gentleness of Verver, the vagueness of American City. But if we recognize the terror we also recognize its modulations, its subjection to our ability to invent civilizing forms, the very thing that our arts, at their best and most responsible, can do for us. And, above all, what the novel can do in adjusting the unbearable perspectives.

Yet to see this as the moral task of literature would be to point us towards codes, towards normative models that the vast Jamesian imagination would in turn put in perspective. Yes, of course there are codes, and of course the very idea of manners implies the existence – not necessarily and always for the better – of a normative view of the social order. Two versions of such normatives, quite different ones I think, enter *The Golden Bowl* in the Assinghams, and the perspective on both of them gradually fixes the limitations; the tonalities lend themselves to a touch of ridicule. Which is not to dismiss the implicit codes in question, but to see not only around them, but around things of that kind.

'One learns correct judgments,' Wittgenstein noted. 'There are also rules, but they do not form a system, and only experienced people can apply them right ... What is most difficult ... is to put this indefiniteness, correctly and unfalsified, into words.'[20] They may do for limited and uncontested occasions; but the necessary presupposition of *The Golden Bowl* is precisely that we have a conundrum that stretches our horizons, that makes mayhem of our usual conventions and categories, yet uses the very notion of such conventions as the necessary buttress to the human condition's susceptibility to conflict. But if such a novel is prescriptive in any way, let alone conveying a 'universal prescription',[21] such prescriptive force does not arise from what we could conceivably describe as a moral law, but from a form of intelligence that would make of our laws, codes, conventions and practice part of the contingent flows in which no one rule, or form of rule, is determinant, where the peril of mutual ironizing is open to all, and the attempt to reason one's way to ethical or aesthetic conclusions may find that ethics and aesthetics are one.

One consequence however does not follow from this. There is a rich post-Romantic tradition, at least from Schopenhauer to Malraux, which sees the work of art as a rectification of life – and another of equally romantic descent, from, say, Shelley to Camus, which sees this rectification in terms of revolt – as a way in which our imaginative constructions can rise above the normal terms of the human condition to create forms of order and intelligibility which transform the chaos or banality of our quotidian lives. This claim to formal shaping and the perspective of reflective understanding is a feature of the museum, where the dialogue, in a fancy of Malraux's which has become a commonplace, is between the works themselves, a continuous interrogation which is implicit in the forms being taken from their living contexts to inhabit a timeless world. There is some such awareness in the thought of Wittgenstein – perhaps indebted to Schopenhauer – concerning the work of art being even *sub specie aeternitatis* which is also the meeting point of the aesthetic with the ethical. And these juxtapositionings are at several points connected with the transcendental.

But there is little trace of any transcendental conception of art in James. Least of all with respect to the novel. However we are to account for the strange phenomenon, the suggestion of timelessness that the Museum creates, the novel is wholly embedded in the contingent and the temporal. In the form of order that it creates, the recognition of that contingency is always ironically present. Perhaps in the wholly simplified view of the fairy tale the abandonment of any form of verisimilitude might efface that contingency, but would hardly answer to James's own sense of the novel. The effect of romance is to subordinate the contingent to the formal design, to see the created world from the outside.

Wittgenstein remarks that: 'The usual way of looking at things sees objects as it were from the midst of them, the view *sub specie aeternitatis* is from outside.'[22] James's novels have the view from the midst. *Aeternitas* does not fit the novel in the sense that James conceives it. In Japanese art the notion of *wabi* implied the imperfection through which an otherwise perfect artefact enters into time. And in the golden bowl itself an imperfection becomes the source of unsolicited knowledge that destroys an established equilibrium. Perhaps the ideal of perfection that is most moving in James is that Edenic vision of the four, bound by the reign of a *société choisie* that Eros will destroy. The breaking of that vision condemns to separation, the most painful imperfection of all. And yet it is through this breaking apart of a magic circle that Maggie and the Prince enter into a form of life that we recognize as fulfilment. In some way perfection denies, and Maggie's own pursuit leads into ambiguity. If fallen from the unsustainable harmony, another life is available by way of lost perfection. And through this fall one couple enters into time and into history. Insofar as there is a pursuit of perfection, the novel indicates its tangled path through the flawed and uncertain world. The closure of *The Golden Bowl*, the marker of the final embrace, may be a personal signal, cast its special glow, yet even in its resolution accept that imperfection, that *wabi* intrinsic to the novel's prodigious powers.

Notes to Part Four

1. In speaking of the Ververs, I normally mean Adam and Maggie. James quite carefully speaks of Mr and Mrs Verver to underline the formal relation of Adam and Charlotte, with perhaps a small touch of ironical distancing.

2. Putnam, 1983, pp. 193ff.
3. Putnam on 'rules' argues (a) that insofar as they are considered in terms of their deontological purity – cf the case of torture – they simply have no place in the novelist's world. A novelist is into that tissue of relations where we cannot see them in other than consequentialist terms; (b) that insofar as they use the guidelines that shape our moral sense, that provide a narrative indication of moral values, those guidelines will of course admit of complex cases, even exceptions. They do not enable us to resolve complex cases but they create the moral feeling which enables us to see through these problems.
   But then are we not swerving in the direction of pragmatic instruments?
4. Krook, 1967, pp. 270–274.
5. Nussbaum, 1983, p. 125.
6. Foucault in discussion with Paul Rabinow and Hubert Dreyfus, April 1983. Reprinted in Rabinow (ed.), 1984, p. 353.
7. This discussion of Foucault with reference to *The Golden Bowl* was first published in Righter, 1989, pp. 262–281.
8. Berlin, 1990, p. 13.
9. Righter, 1989, p. 268.
10. Gardner, 1983, pp. 181–182.
11. Righter, 1989, pp. 269–272.
12. Nussbaum, 1983, p. 40.
13. *op. cit.*, p. 200.
14. Righter, 1989, p. 280.
15. I follow this reading of Michael Levy, 1961, *Burlington Magazine*, pp. 180–185. And see the discussion of Pierre Rosenberg in the catalogue of *Watteau*, Edition de la Réunion des Musées Nationaux, Paris, 1984, pp. 396–401.
16. De Man, 1979, p. 206.
17. For a further discussion of de Man's case, see 'The Monstrous Clarity' in Righter, 1994, pp. 134–143.
18. Ozouf, 1998, p. 287. (Rosemary Righter's translation. This book, published shortly after my husband's death, has affinities with his own interest in James that seemed to justify the inclusion of a comment that he would have enjoyed.)
19. Nussbaum, 1990, pp. 136–137.
20. Wittgenstein, *Philosophical Investigations*, trans. Anscombe, 1953, II, xi, p. 227e.
21. cf. Martha Nussbaum who, discussing R.M. Hare's remark to her, 'What are novels anyway but universal prescriptions?', concludes that because novels present characters and events as 'something that *might happen*', their 'doings and imaginings take on … a universal significance'. Nussbaum, 1990, p. 166.
22. Wittgenstein, *Notebooks, 1914–1916*, p. 83.

PART FIVE

Form and Contingency

17.   From Portland Place to American City
18.   In the Museum
19.   The Elusive Synthesis
20.   Coda: The 'Complex Fate'

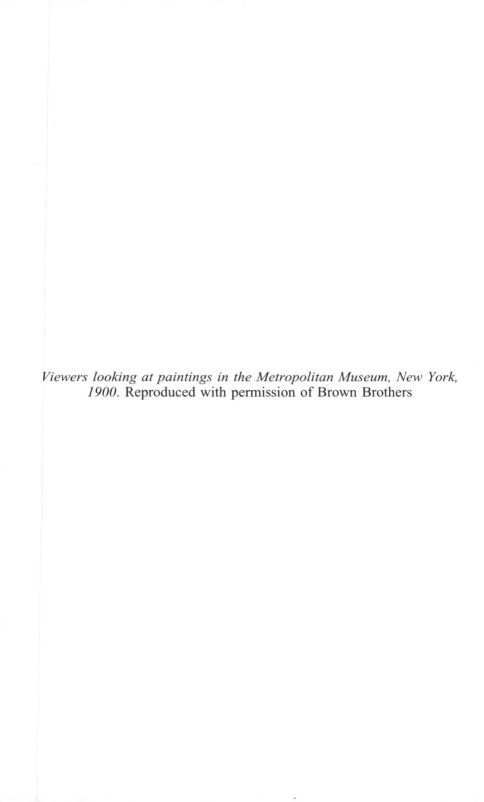

Viewers looking at paintings in the Metropolitan Museum, New York, 1900. Reproduced with permission of Brown Brothers

Chapter 17

From Portland Place to American City

If the conflict of values that James seems to project and then sometimes to withdraw does not materialize in the substantial way that some readers have expected, neither does the problem vanish with the novel's resolution. In the final pages, it is true, Maggie notes of what they may know of each other that 'It isn't a question of any beauty ... it's only a question of the quantity of truth.' (p. 566) Here the validity of two forms of assessment is neatly framed. But the consequences lead not to separation but to accommodation.

The real separation is that effected in the final crossing of the Atlantic. And the real difference in values lies between Portland Place and American City. Of course such a difference does not consist in either 'quantity of truth' or the 'touchstone of taste' but in the form of life which will be consummated in those places.

Of Eaton Square we have seen almost nothing and insofar as the Ververs are placed, it is at Fawns, the country house where part of the collection is stored and which seems to represent a conventional version of pastoral. There are lawns, benches, hedges. The garden is the scene of encounter; from the terrace, Maggie observes the party at bridge. But this too seems a setting that one abandons without pain. It will be Portland Place that represents continuing forms of life, the London world of the Prince and Princess. Yet except for the underlining of the presence of barely identified objects of art, the emphasis on luxury and the grandeur of the concluding scene, there is little that distinguishes it. There are a number of powerful evocations of place in James, of the grip that a particular house may have on the development of a life or the form of an imagination. But Portland Place has a certain neutrality, even a faint lack of allure. In a scene where the Prince and Charlotte are waiting for the others to return from Regent's Park, the glamorous pair on the balcony contrasts with the blankness of the house and the monotony and propriety of Portland Place itself. (p. 393) And James has focused in his Preface on the problem of representation. 'The thing was to induce the vision of Portland Place *to* generalise itself ... All of which meant that at a given moment the great featureless Philistine vista would itself perform a miracle, would become interesting, for a splendid atmospheric hour, as only London knows how; and that our business would be then to understand.' (p. 26)

Here then is where the final embrace takes place and where a form of life is to unfold. What then are we to understand? One thing is clear: there is not only a separation but a gulf. The form of life to be pursued in Portland Place is utterly unlike and totally opposed to that of American City. We are in fact told very little about these things. I have already mentioned the absence of any external features to the Ververs' lives. There is no social or cultural context to give Portland Place that distinctive feel, to reveal its character in any far-reaching and decisive way. On the other hand, again on the basis of much trust, we are clearly intended to understand some essential things about the setting in the 'Philistine vista'. The house is, for all that, the place of civilization in which the appropriate virtues can flourish, whatever they may be. The London of politics, power, industry, commerce, Dickensian fogs, clubs and muddy lanes, is far away. It is not merely that this world is luxurious and leisured, but that in such a world, where not only work but every other form of activity seems alien, is the inner life, the cultivation of the finer grain, to be possible.

Yet we are far from being convinced that such an inner development is part of the character of the Prince and Maggie. His very accommodation to the 'American' is doubly suspect; both in putting accommodation before any personal assertion of value and in failing, beyond the occasional throwaway, to articulate in any way the 'touchstone of taste'. We see his possession of rare books and prints, indeed he is shipping them to Portland Place in one of our last glimpses of him. But this indication has no more than the effect of décor. What interest would he find in them and how would they add to any inner richness or any quality that life might have, beyond the proper equipment of a grand gentleman's household? If the life of Portland Place represents a world where civilization's values may thrive we see little of what might fill it beyond a certain stylish correctness, considerations of social form, and the implication that for the blessèd ones it is a place where love can flourish. And it will be a love which is suitable, fully legitimated, institutionalized, fitted to all of the proper forms of social life, without conflict or destructive side effects.

Earlier I mentioned how far *The Golden Bowl* departs from direct representation of the 'international theme', the conflicts and partial understandings by which the American in Europe undergoes an inner change and is transformed in his outlook and knowledge of both self and the world. *The Ambassadors* is of course James's fullest development of that theme, although there too it can be radically ironized as in the last incarnation of Chad Newsome. But there are others among the later tales in which 'Europe' is represented as an escape from some nameless horror in one's own country. In the story of that name, in 'The Jolly Corner' or in *The Ivory Tower,* the picture of European life is almost a void, except that there one has been able to live free from the hardening and consuming effect of the world of commerce and ambition. And the failure of inner effect or transformation is given in the little vignette of Miss Mumby in *The Ivory Tower*: 'Miss Mumby had been to Europe, and he saw soon enough that there was nowhere one could say she hadn't gone and nothing one could say she hadn't done – one's perception could only bear on what she hadn't become.'[1]

Perhaps this particular failure to show the effect, in the Florence of 'Europe' or in the even less defined Europes of Spencer Brydon or Graham Fieldes, is merely the novelist's economy. But if one asks what the process entailed and how the civilizing effect came about we are left with an unexamined assumption. It is simply not the focus of such stories, which are rather designed to set off the complex and devastating pressures within American life which destroy and impoverish.

Of course there is no suggestion that the Ververs have been corrupted or limited in any sense by their American past. The continuous emphasis is upon an unqualified innocence, of the perfect sweetness of character almost unmarked by experience. But Maggie, the object of the one important inner transformation, seems unmarked by Europe as well. If we have occasionally kaleidoscopic flashes of cultural objects to indicate Mr Verver's character as collector, this touches on Maggie's very lightly. Martha Nussbaum notes the 'inveterate tendency of both father and daughter to assimilate people, in their imagination and deliberation, to fine *objets d'art*'. There are certainly some striking examples of this, not only in the early scene where the Prince is seen as a museum piece, a moment of *plaisanterie*. (p. 49) And certainly the aesthetic characterization returns vividly, as an essential feature of the tableau, in the final scene where the two collectors take hold of their choice possessions. The pictures, 'the sofas, the chairs, the tables, the cabinets, the "important" pieces, supreme in their way, stood out, round them, consciously for recognition and applause'. (p. 574) But 'the whole nobleness' of the collection is not a markedly pervasive aspect of Maggie's thought process and much of the aestheticizing of the final scene is not from Maggie's point of view but is impersonal – and ironical – narrative.

For the transformative aspect of Maggie developed through the second volume, the vocabulary mixes a practical and often astutely psychological observation with a continually sharpening moral sensibility. It is the progress of knowledge, of her own hypothesis and observation, with an extending sense of what is owed to her. To this extent too, innocence must be gradually qualified. But there is no strong sense that Maggie will devote whatever inner resources she has to aesthetic contemplation. No indication of any such kind is given. I have depicted the Ververs, perhaps too dismissively, as high-minded hobbyists.

And this certainly is too weak a description of Adam's grand design which was 'positively civilisation condensed' (p. 142). But if we are trying to glimpse the civilized world of Portland Place that design hardly touches upon it. There are some 'good things', certainly, and they are no doubt what the Ververs owe to themselves. The Prince's inheritance will doubtless create similar embellishments, as *Le Figaro* and other journals will continue to lie on the library table. Do we need fuller indications than this about the form of life which Portland Place will embody?

Of course, in a sense it is foolish to extrapolate, to consider the dramatic, social and intellectual dimensions of the future. James's ritual drawing of the curtains has completed the action. But the consequences of separation cannot be totally dismissed. And there is surely an implied schematism which imbues the true conflict of values. Europe is a world worth living in. It offers a life which is essentially private, inner, humane, with a quiet and civilized intercourse possible with reasonable persons, where these superior beings may be at ease. James may not know what will happen beyond his final curtain, nor is he meant to know. But he does know its conditionality.

Perhaps he knows far less about American City. The creation of wealth was less intelligible to him than its leisured consumption. And the recognition of this on occasion made him uneasy. But he still powerfully suggests what perhaps he doesn't know. The terror and darkness were registered by Fanny Assingham. And it is a place of hate. They clearly loathe Mr Verver there and make cruel jokes about him. (p. 509) For him it was the years of 'calculation', of 'forging and sweating'. (p. 142) But these were things 'he had to believe he liked'. And a part of a traditional American story. The making of vast sums of money and transforming it into social and cultural goals is part of a very American kind of transformation – almost a mission. In James the making of that money is essentially blanked out by the uncertainty about origins. The wealth, for James, is anonymous, an unknown power, totally isolated, neutral and void. In Mr Verver's project that dark and alien power *becomes* something. It becomes part of 'civilization'. It is put into a different form which operates as a cultural lever. If one of James's couples is turned inwards in the absorption with personal values, the other is forced outwards into a plan of social actions. Even if American City abolishes the inner and reflective dimension it makes possible a public creativity. (Whether the inner world is conveyed as being fully as empty as the outer is a judgment we need not make.)

Certainly a portrait of American City would evoke both terror and unintentional comedy. We see the great figures of American industry transformed into the beneficent creators of cultural institutions. The names of Andrew Carnegie, J.P. Morgan, of the Mellons, Rockefellers, and so on, will become attached to these towering and wealthy institutions that evolved a powerful life-form of their own. Here is a vast social theme, one of the great patterns in the use and distribution of American wealth, the creation of those educational paths which were pictured in Mr Verver's imagination as a limitless good. Are we to accept this at face value? There are points at which James suggests misgivings. But insofar as we can be guided by expressed intention there is no way in which we could doubt Mr Verver's *bona fides*, his intrinsic worthiness, his established goodness, sweetness, and dearness. The grand benevolence of the project could not be questioned.

American City is therefore the *fons* – (one cannot but admire Gore Vidal's play upon Fawns/*fons*, however unlikely[2]) – the source and origin of that wealth and power which will revert to it. What is taken in terms of gold will return. But for the individual nucleus of feeling and sensibility, the trans-formation entails a destruction which makes American City the city of death. The lived experience itself will be displaced into the artifice of the Museum. Charlotte will no longer live but will be the commentator and interpreter who presents and makes sense of these alien objects to the wilderness and its bemused inhabitants. But it will be a curiously 'second order' activity, based on the objects themselves and their detachment in the Museum. For culture must be introduced and no doubt made palatable. And for such an activity inner selves are not required. Nor is the knowledge which involves our perception and understanding of each other. In fact its absence will be required, for its presence would put in question the whole process, the tissue of choices, the commitments, the loyalties and their fallibility, the unpredictable flow of consequences which animated the now vanished community. Is this absence in the great project, this stillness of inner selves, also part of civilization? If so a deeper paradox lies at the centre of *The Golden Bowl*, one which embodies James's lifelong obsession with the relations of life and art. Art is somewhat offstage in *The Golden Bowl*, a concept and ideal which often seems to connect through a chain of many links. But the path to the Museum has landmarks that will point, however indirectly, toward that complex relation.

One aspect of American City however appears only in figural form yet lies close to the surface of the action and remains implicit in its efficient cause. As the origin of the Ververs' enormous wealth it is the necessary condition of what happens. One has noted James's reticence about the sources and features of their wealth, his withdrawal from any fuller portrayal of any aspect beyond the assurance we have seen that some such thing came about. There is the clue that Mr Verver had, even then, to do not with the relatively creative process of actually manufacturing something but with acquisitions, 'the creation of "interests" that were the extinction of other interests', and that the wealth-building activity was of a 'livid vulgarity'. (p. 142) There is just the hint that Mr Verver's talent lay in what would now be called asset-stripping. But it is the merest hint. We see only the consequence, the wealth, yet that consequence implies the cause. And the refusal to represent the cause in any substantive way – something wholly reasonable in terms of James's artistic economy – turns to the figural and suggestive, in the omnipresent image of gold.

There is however no golden glow over American City itself. The years there were years of darkness. Images abound of darkness, burial, blindness which will contrast with the light of the grand design. They touch even the Prince, and even in the first flush of Maggie's love for him. She has spoken of how the grandest works in the Verver collection are in vaults, and promises him 'you shall not be buried ... until you are dead. Unless you call it burial to go to American City'. (p. 50) A daunting little aside, the Prince might think, on what it means to be a *morceau de musée*. And with this night of the soul Charlotte, revealed in 'blackness' at the moment of the resolution to return, (p. 512) will in her doom have a rapport.

Yet the pervasiveness of the image of gold is such that it is clearly intended to cast a magical, if sinister, glow over the whole of James's masterpiece. There is the bowl itself, alluring though flawed. The solicitors at the beginning have just sealed the contract of the Prince's marriage; he is floating in waters 'poured from a gold-topped phial'. (p. 48) When he talks to Fanny of the voyage ahead, she assures him that he has reached 'the port of the Golden Isles'. (p. 60) Are they the same Golden Isles that Verver has come to rifle? Later, the Prince and Charlotte are joined by a 'majestic golden bridge' (p. 268) and at another point float in a golden mist. In posing the question of where one is – Maggie's intervention for Verver – the alternatives are a balloon whirling through space 'or down in the depths of the earth, in the glimmering passages of a gold-mine'. (p. 375) And in the same scene where the Ververs return from Regent's Park to find the Prince and Charlotte waiting for them, their park-bench conversation has begun with Maggie's intentness on preserving the 'treasured past' of her relation with her father like 'a framed picture in a museum'; and as they sit lulled (deceptively, of course) by their happy confidence, Verver is seen 'to *imitate* – oh as never yet! – the ancient tone of gold'. (p. 384)

There are many more examples and it almost seems an obsessive use of figure which picks up the height of value, the deception and the sinister depth by turn and does not construct a clear tonality of metaphor. The dark source in American City is hardly a consistent indicator. At least two patterns of substitution seem to indicate a deeply traditional ambivalence by which crowns of gold are symbols both of transcendental glory and of the basest vanity. James is unlikely to have any schematic symbolism as a controlling principle. Allure, danger, deception, even cruelty are unevenly mingled. The effect is partly one of dissolving the cutting edges of metaphor into tone, partly one of so engaging the figurative element that its double pull or multiple presences are never absent.

So in one sense the range of figurative substitution holds back or even masks the 'truth' of American City, a truth that we shall never see. We could not be brought too close to it, to see it plain, for that would be too crass and destructive altogether – we catch only its flickering and ambiguous reflections like those of Plato's cave. Perhaps in the company of our civilized and proper characters anything else would shatter the delicate tissue of continuities by which their elegant and closely examined interplay is left in equilibrium. Only through its product, at many degrees of distancing and refinement, can American City be palpably present.

But gold also suggests the fulcrum of a number of transmutations which do not end in the alchemist's triumph but in those objects which are created out of it. So American City will be the beginning and the end. The wealth created will pass through an elaborate sequence of processes that will end in the objects of art in Mr Verver's Museum. This transit, this transmutation will embrace and relate the brute thing which for James can only be obliquely indicated, so almost embarrassing is its conversion into social action. For Mr Verver: 'His greatest inconvenience, he would have admitted had he analysed, was in finding it so taken for granted that as he had money he had force. It pressed upon him hard and all round assuredly, this attribution of power. Everyone had need of one's power, whereas one's own need, at best, would have seemed to be but some trick for not communicating it.' Yet, he has come out 'at the top of his hill of difficulty ... the apex of which was a platform looking down, if one would, on the kingdoms of the earth and with standing-room for but half a dozen others'. (p. 133)

James's effort to undercut the reality of power by the lack of its appearance, yet to assert the vast scope of Verver's greatness is continuously modified by expressions that put his gentleness, sweetness, and so on, in the foreground. So the power fades from view, yet remains an active presupposition without which the terms of play are impossible. The figural man of gold is a man without a history. His birthplace is unknown, his 'adoptive' connection with American City obscure, his marriage mysterious; his power and persistence are conceded – 'in what', asks Fanny, ' – great patient exquisite as he is – did he *ever* break down?' (p. 445) – but held limitlessly benign. The material of wealth is to undergo an alchemical change in which its base elements become the stuff of civilization. This of course tempts the term 'allegory'. But the terms which would make allegory intelligible dissolve around us; as with the invitation extended by gold itself the coordinates shift, enter into conflict, and fail to shape an intelligible whole. It is hardly Maggie's standard of the 'quantity of truth' but of facing such conditionality that truth fails to attain a convincing shape, that the persuasive terms are not met.

Now at one level this seems a Jamesian general strategy, to leave aspects of character, dimensions of causality, figures in the backdrop essentially vague. In the grand *chiaroscuro* some things have been carefully drawn into focus, into the fullest light that the narrative can bring, others given the intriguing half-light that both draws and restricts us, and much left in darkness. In many of the novels, however aware of Jamesian highlighting and omission, we are finally unworried. In *The Portrait of a Lady*, *The Ambassadors*, even *The Wings of the Dove*, these choices, and the consequent grey to dark, pose certain puzzles that may for a moment hold us yet nevertheless resolve themselves. In *The Turn of the Screw* the principle of uncertainty itself controls the narrative. But in *The Golden Bowl* the 'scuro' has a magnetic power. American City acts both as hypothesis and form of life. We must accept it as point of departure, which involves us in legitimate if limited curiosity, and as destination which provokes our deeper probing of the implications. James undoubtedly intends the act of closure to be as definitive as the curtain's fall but has failed to exclude the provocation. Thus the interpretable space in a variety of ways forces itself upon us. The strategy requires its complement.

Yet without an extravagant reinvention of American City there are two features that are quite straightly understood. The great Verver aesthetic project will unfold in a wilderness in which there will be no civilized human inter-course. The fellow-citizens will be harsh, brutal materialistic philistines, and as we have seen, wholly ill-disposed towards Mr Verver. One's existence is only conceivable if sealed off from the community in hermetic isolation. However assiduously one may preserve one's enlightening taste, it will be for others and not with others. The Ververs will be alone. Their wealth, establishment, servants and so forth will perhaps insulate them, or provide the mediation through which the quotidian aspects of the task unfold. Charlotte's voice will no longer be involved in the exchange implied by personal feeling or the intellectual enterprise of understanding and interacting with others. It will be heightened in its expository mode. It will speak to the natives but not with them. Which is in effect to treat others as distanced both by their own uncultivated natures and by the nature of the project from which they are to benefit. They are the object of it all. Objects, even. And they will be addressed by other objects, by the objects of the great Museum.

Hence objects will speak to objects in a created and artificial encounter. As the walls of the Museum rise there will be a place, no doubt alien to its surroundings but whose importance derives from that alienation. The civilizing mission is one which comes from without and risks the continuance of that otherness in its very establishment. And the fulfilment of the project is the creation of something which lies outside of time and process. An effect of the double isolation, of the nature of the object of art, is a distancing from the palpable and passionate aspects of the human condition, to enter into a world half alien jungle, half deracinated object. Divorced from the world of love, the entry into American City is the entry into the city of death. Outside of history, frozen in the conventionalized and falsifying postures in which the code of manners has enveloped them, the civilizing mission of Mr and Mrs Verver looks strangely cold and abstract.

A double pattern is observable and each aspect involves a paradox which is consequent on the total narrative movement. The perfection which has been the aim of Maggie's life, a totality governed by one's sense of the good, will unfold in the contingent world of Portland Place. The appropriate setting is life itself, with all of the uncertainties that are necessarily part of it. Perfection itself paradoxically belongs to the world of movement and change, and the form that Maggie has found of the good life must partake too of an intrinsic impermanence. We can imagine, as Tolstoy does in the final epilogue to *War and Peace*, this perfect domesticity having its development, evolution and vicissitudes.

In American City a contrary movement has taken place. Charlotte's beauty with its depths of moral flaws will become one with the Verver project, with the timeless world of the Museum. To her and to Verver nothing can happen. As protected and petrified zombies they will stalk the alien world bearing their message of an incongruent cultural value. If, like Lydgate's in *Middlemarch*, their design is fraught with the stresses and abrasions a hostile community may invent, Charlotte and Verver will be untouched. Their moment of conflict and change is buried in the past and the commitment of the present is external. Like flies in amber, like the objects in museums, torn from their context and purified by the artifice, a living death embodies the arrest of time.

But does the fate of Charlotte and Verver have a point beyond the clearing of a path for Maggie's domestic bliss? That it should be seen as the punishment of the challenge of illegitimate eros has seemed natural enough, like the allegorical triumph of sacred over profane love. But why should the force of this punishment, so vividly expressed by Fanny Assingham, coincide with the fulfilment of Adam's dream? We are given the force of that vision equally compellingly. Beyond the 'forging and sweating' lies the grand design in all of its nobility: 'It hadn't merely, his plan, all the sanctions of civilisation; it was positively civilisation condensed, concrete, consummate, set down by his hands as a house on a rock.' (pp. 142–143) The comparison with St Peter may be unintentional, but the greatness of the plan, its beneficence, its intrinsic value, its transformation of power are beyond question, as is the urgency of the mission: 'the higher, the highest knowledge would shine out to bless the land. In this house, designed as a gift primarily to the people of his adoptive city and native State, the urgency of whose release from the bounds of ugliness he was in a position to measure – in this museum of museums, a palace of art which was to show for compact as a Greek temple was compact, a receptacle of treasures sifted to positive sanctity, his spirit to-day almost altogether lived.'

We see scope, grandeur, the overwhelming importance. Yet in some way the immediacy of the project seems even more attenuated than his appealing image of emulating the snail – 'the loveliest beast in nature' – would suggest. Has the perfection of his finely tuned equilibrium, that perfect life with its hidden flaw, deflected him? Certainly the hyperbole of the passage is quite uncharacteristic of his normal modesty. This extravagant glory is quietly morcellized in the tender and precious moments with Maggie and the Principino, with 'easy weeks at Fawns'. In dissolving this rhetoric James may be directing us towards humbler and more intimate values. And the plainness of Adam Verver is ambiguously related to the headiness of his vision. (p. 146) Is some falsifying power of the imagination suggested by the contrast? And is that falsifying power reanimated in that touch of public grandeur, that small element of flash that we see in Charlotte as she assumes her role of *châtelaine*? That would set the homeward path onto a vein whose authenticity would be that small degree shakier. Yet the public voice of the expositor and the provincial dreams of glory can hardly be meant to undermine the value of a man whose every word and moment of presence has seemed the bedrock of truth itself. The conflict that these authentic and personal values suggest has a shaping effect on James's concept of art, including his own.

Chapter 18

In the Museum

In a letter to Grace Norton in December 1903,[3] James expressed rather pungently a negative view of writers on art:

> I read over your letter and I came upon the Berensons, whom I don't know, and as to *him*, confess to know him by others, (and by his association with that 'writing upon art') pedagogically, which I have long since come to feel as the most boring and *insupportable* identity a man can have. I am so weary, weary of pictures and of questions of pictures, that it is the most I can do to drag myself for three minutes every three years into the National Gallery.

Such an impassioned dismissal may reflect only a passing mood and is but one aspect of James's long and complex involvement with the visual arts. Although it repeats a sentiment expressed in 1895, to Ariana Curtis, that he was 'fearfully tired of pictures and painting. I've spent myself too much on them in the past. I seem to myself to have got all they can give me – to have seen all I *can* see & to know it beforehand.'[4] But its date places it in the course of the writing of *The Golden Bowl* which was begun earlier that year and finished in May 1904. It would be crass to ask directly whether such a view qualifies the glory of Mr Verver's project and civilizing mission. There may be just a flash of irritation at the mention of Berenson. Or a serious reservation about the writer of art criticism.

Of course, Mr Verver is neither a professional connoisseur nor a writer but a wealthy collector, and this of a quite distinctively American type. Perhaps it will be Charlotte's explanatory voice that takes on such an insupportability. But there are at least two quite separate forms of comment elsewhere in James on the tycoon as collector. The most direct comparison is in three letters which comment on the Venetian palace and museum built in Boston by Isabella Stewart Gardner, for which many pillaging expeditions to Europe had ransacked the Golden Isles. The other is the comedy devoted to the conflict between heritage and wealth in what must be one of the weakest of James's works, *The Outcry*.

Mrs Gardner is a recurring presence in James's life who is personally treated with a certain affectionate irony as if endearing aspects were mingled with a certain falsity of tone. The touch of guying in some of the letters may both distance and perhaps lightly dismiss while maintaining an interchange of cheerful badinage. And this elaboration of gentle mockery enters when he tells Charles Eliot Norton that he is off to Dover to meet 'our celebrated friend ... Mrs Jack Gardner who arrives from Brussels, charged with the spoils of the Flemish school ... I must rush off, help her to disembark, see all her Van Eycks and Rubenses through the Customs and bring her hither, where three water-colours and four photographs of the "Rye school" will let her down easily.'[5]

Some of the pose is clearly defence against a forceful deployment of energies: 'not a woman, she is a locomotive'. And the *grande dame* manner also lent itself to the unintentionally comic. Yet in a letter to Paul Bourget in 1905, James writes of the project at Fenway Court:

> You must hear from me of Mrs Gardner, who is *de plus en plus* remarquable [sic] and whose *palais-musée* is a really great creation. Her acquisitions over the last ten years have been magnificent, her arrangement and administration of them are admirable, and her spirit soars higher still. Her spirit is immense, and proof against time and fate. It has greatly 'improved' her in every way to have done a thing of so much interest and importance – and to have had to do it with such almost unaided courage, intelligence and energy. She has become really a great little personage.[6]

The rhetoric of this seems overcharged with its grand generalizations about time and fate. Which frames the more oddly the diminutive on which it ends. And the glimpse of Fenway Court, the 'palace of art', to another correspondent produces again 'that she is even more than I thought, a great and extraordinary little woman'. Is the irony a leavening touch intended to be taken so, or is it merely a cosy Jamesian *façon de parler*? The unease before energy and managerial skill, the force of personality, falls back before admiration. And yet ...

With Mr Verver, the powers are applied invisibly; the cloud-capped towers rise without a whisper of locomotive power. But what is clearly put is the affirmation of the 'interest and importance' of the 'great creation'. Do we admire the character of the creator, the sense of doing and making, in some way more than we value the object of it all? Does this acceptance of interest and importance oppose his earlier scepticism to Grace Norton about the pictures and galleries and writing about art? The connectives are never drawn in a way that would be indicative and one must look, for any evaluation, to James's larger sense of the power and limits of visual art.

The omnipresent awareness of works of art in James's *oeuvre* is obvious, yet so extensive that its active presence undergoes a complex metamorphosis. The occasions of that presence have been exhaustively, if sometimes suppositionally, catalogued in the work of Adeline R. Tintner.[7] James's own writings on art are only partially indicative. They are of two kinds. One is embodied in his travel writings which necessarily present the art object as part of the sense of place and one's personal circumstances in responding to it. The duality comes out in *Italian Hours*, over Titian's 'Assumption' in the great Venetian church of the Frari. As travel writer, James dutifully notes it as 'one of the mightiest of so-called sacred pictures'[8] – while elsewhere there is also the wry note that every response is not always so suitably elevated and that indeed 'it is one of the possible disappointments of Venice, and you may if you like take advantage of your privilege of not caring for it'. To which ironic give-away he adds, 'we must moreover notoriously not expose our deepest feelings' on the subject.[9] But at yet another point, his 'deepest feelings' do come out, in the course of a hyperbolic rush of enthusiasm for Tintoretto: 'no painter ever had such breadth and such depth; and even Titian, beside him, scarce figures as more than a great decorative artist'.[10] The travel books are rich in such observations and the conditioning of the sense of place is important. While most such evocations are much earlier than *The Golden Bowl*, there are also later occasions. The magnificent evocation of Rome in his biography of William Wetmore Story shows his sense of place at his most compelling, perhaps endowed with the special eloquence of memory.[11]

But however important this may have been to James we have already noted how weak the sense of place is in *The Golden Bowl*. The Preface refers rather skittishly to Coburn's photographic illustrations for the New York edition, ironically commending both Coburn and himself for finding 'reproducible subjects ... the reference of which to Novel or Tale should exactly be *not* competitive or obvious, should on the contrary plead its case with some shyness, that of images always confessing themselves mere optical symbols or echoes, expressions of no particular thing in the text, but only of the type or idea of this or that thing'. (p. 24) As for Fawns, it is the most loosely evoked of country houses. The connections suggested by Mrs Tintner with Waddesdon or Mentmore are both thoroughly tangential and beside the point. It is precisely in the avoidance of such baggage that *The Golden Bowl* achieves its effect. Even objects themselves are largely absent, except for the occasional passing moment; distantly as with Charlotte in the gallery, fleetingly with the early Florentine painting, of which all we know is that Verver held it in 'unqualified esteem' (p. 573), vaguely as one sees objects as décor, and strangely sensuously with the Damascene tiles. And American City is more powerful, more palpable in its absence than any of these *mises-en-scène.*

The other writings that directly engage with objects of art are the reviews for American magazines. Mostly dating from the 1870s, they make the natural enough assumption of value for both object and commentary. A late essay on Sargent makes certain gestures towards the notion of pictorial language, but here as in the earlier essays the effectiveness of portraiture is the predominant interest. The excitement in interpretation is largely in the understanding of persons and the power of their representation – for it is as representation that painting comes alive to him, and the primary function of representation points to the thing represented. It is the servant of life, as is the novel itself, and the novelist himself, embarked in 'the great game'. (p. 20) Even if it involves distance or coldness, the transmission of life is its essential attribute and the most intense stylization is meant to effect that transmission, not to qualify it. How then does this primacy affect our understanding and valuation of the 'palace of art'?

One theme or sense of conditionality which certainly connects the earlier travel writings with those of James's later feeling as developed in *The Outcry* is a strong sense of the value of works in their context. The great paintings of Delacroix are partly made for a setting outside of which they could not be other than diminished. Venetian painting reflects the light, the characteristic colours, forms part of a total ensemble with its native city. And even if some of the objects in question in *The Outcry* are Dutch and Italian, they form part of the accumulation of a great country house, where these objects have long since been domesticated. They have become, along with the structure itself, its surroundings, its furniture, the portraits of ancestors, other personal belongings, part of a living whole. And Ottoline Morrell noted James's horror at the transformation of Waddesdon from a house to something 'inhuman' like 'a private museum'.[12] If this is his response to the atmospheric changes in a particular house, how is the Museum to be seen, above all in American City where it is stripped of context of any kind, and belongs to the territory of the pure idea? Is the ideal construction part of the dehumanizing process that leads the life-conveying arts into the City of Death?

Such a portentous question would take us far from the amiable comic terms of *The Outcry*. Originally written as a play which was never produced and turned into a novel two years later (1911), it remains unpalatable in its novel form and is a model country house comedy. Its highly localized nature was spelled out by James to Harley Granville-Barker who was seized by the dotty idea that it might be produced in Moscow. Such a comedy of manners would not translate. The 'interest and irony relate to England and her art wealth and the US and their art grab and their grab resources'. And it is a comedy of manners to the point of highly conventional stylization. Berenson's biographer Samuels, Edel and Tintner all regard it as a serious exploration and vindication of the connoisseur, his perception, skill at telling true from false, and so on. This, I think, plays a bit heavily with the tone and with the comic conventions the play employs. The great house, its master, his independent-minded daughter, the schemers out for a profit, the grossly comic American millionaire are cardboard cutouts from a long tradition of comedy. The young hero with bicycle-clips and spectacles hovers uneasily between comic stereotypes, 'new' man with a technical expertise, and 'decent chap' with appropriate moral fervour who is also going to get the girl. Not a very Jamesian figure, and without any trace of the internal development that constitutes the normal interest of James's fictions. Does he bear any element of the 'insupportable identity' James had attributed to Berenson and his sort?

Of course the plot follows the 'outcry' about the sale of certain masterpieces from English collections to the United States in 1908. The whole question of what constitutes an artistic heritage comes into question. The role of the 'bloated' millionaire is to create an intolerable tension in the established order of those who have great houses, many possessions, immense pride and the occasional need for cashflow. The man of large chequebook knows what they are in it for. Does this imply that James sees the mixture of hypocrisy, cash hunger and relative indifference to the artistic heritage as constituting a vein of rot in these grand inheritors? A wry, ironic conclusion would guy the taking of the matter quite so seriously. In any case, James's twist of plot avoids the shame of picking up the cheques.

The case would be exacerbated by the brashness and vulgarity of the great collector, whose passion for possession assimilates the passion for publicity which affirms the greatness of a work and of course its value. The scrambling of the identity of a painting with its rarity, with its value, is a rich source of comic confusion in which aristocratic reserve and passion for the truth regardless of value are drawn into ambiguous play. But I have noted that this social context is quite absent from *The Golden Bowl*, as is any sense of the responsibilities of those possessors in the Golden Isles whose goods are part of Mr Verver's wagon train. Perhaps the exaggerated character of Mr Bender makes the grossness of the enterprise excessively lurid. Certainly there could be no greater contrast in style or manner, or simply in the opposition of a brutish acquisitiveness and the visionary beneficence, with the creator of the Museum of Museums.

In one, the naked exercise of the power of money is unleashed with barbaric force, if with comic consequences. In the other, power is so deftly concealed, so mildly embodied, so selflessly expressed. But is that power in any substantive way different, or the Museum of American City a place uncorrupted by power? Mr Bender too would wish to involve a greater public, in a world saturated by advertisement. And indeed the painting at issue already faces the alternative of the gapers of Bond Street. The quiet of Lord Theign's great house, or in the end the public life of the National Gallery.

The value of such a public existence seems established, if with the greatest reluctance. To have belonged to the Medicis or Gonzagas, who commissioned them, or to a great collector, Arundel or Mazarin, or their latter-day descendants – all of whom conceived of a private or semi-private pleasure – seems neatly to catch James between the romantic beauty of a privileged past and the appalling vista of a public future. Yet the public future may have honourable intentions, and still be the product of the baseness of those who sell their heritage and the grossness of the despoilers who play upon them. It is probably impossible to discern a consistent view and James seems torn by the contradictory elements in the historical moment. The great works of art of the past could no longer belong to a long vanished context, nor perhaps could the collections in the great houses, their refuge sometimes for centuries, be sustained. The descendants of the great collectors were hardly the same men and the social and economic pressures that transformed their world made the home of their works of art precarious. The issues do not bear solely on a grand masterpiece although it is possible to focus on one. (In *The Outcry*, it is a little 'landscape' by Vermeer.) The drama that *The Outcry* (written after J. Pierpont Morgan's bid in 1907 for the hugely valuable Rodolphe Kann collection) records is the agonizing over social transformation; but it is defused by the comic mode and by an uncharacteristically banal romantic conclusion.

Perhaps another aspect of James's involvement with the visual arts has an important if oblique bearing on the project of American City: his friendship with Hendrick Andersen. The passionate aspect of this involvement seems to have begun without much attention to Andersen's artistic limitations; but he slowly grew to find the sculptor's aesthetic a serious obstacle to understanding. There are two phases of what amounts to exasperation, the first an attack on the excessive character (and quantity) of Andersen's nudes.[13] (There is an amusing passage in the Story biography which treats Story's struggle with the nude as a matter of social adaptation to the tastes and market of the time.) It is difficult to see whether James was wearied by the excess concentration on the nude, hence by the nude itself, or simply by the excessive mass and lifelessness of Andersen's own. Certainly it was a revulsion from the 'mania for the colossal' and '*la folie des grandeurs*' which was to be realized in Andersen's vision of a World City (letter, 14 April 1912).

There is certainly a passionate warning here against the temptation and danger of the grandiose, but also a further warning against the abstract form of a dream. It is continued more explicitly in a letter of 4 September 1913, in which the emphatic language is repeated in his refusal to enter into 'projects and plans so vast and vague and meaning to me simply nothing whatsoever'.[14] He proceeds to an attack on the use of 'World' as indicating a kind of meaningless universalizing, contrasted with 'the realities of things, with "cultivating my garden" ' which suggests the localizability of the human consciousness, of its proportion, sanity, sense of reality. The world as it is is dense, detailed, complicated and not to be seen in terms of the 'loosest simplifications', or above all under the 'dark danger' of 'megalomania'.

Now American City is not the World City, nor is Mr Verver's project totally out of proportion to his means. It is precisely means which we are assured he commands. But in the eloquent passage in which his dream is conveyed – 'it was positively civilisation condensed, concrete, consummate ... a monument to the religion he wished to propagate, the exemplary passion, the passion for perfection at any price' (pp. 142–143) – of course he has used the word 'concrete'. It is a physical construction he intends, but so too was Andersen's fantasy. And there are phrases which come close to suggesting a mystical sense of the mission which will be consummated in the 'palace of art'. Certainly it is neither a form of personal aggrandizement, nor of possession. Although the daughter of the great house in *The Outcry*, in saying 'Yes, we've got some things', (p. 117) echoes Verver's satisfaction in his moment of departure to Maggie, 'You've got some good things', the sense of personal attachment hardly intervenes. Nor does the sense of suitable décor, although passing allusion is made to the grandeur of the tea service.

Nothing in his project will resemble that highly personal museum palace of Mrs Gardner nor the richly decorated tycoon's house of Henry Clay Frick, both Mr Verver's exact contemporaries. Nor can the modern American collector simply take at his ease what just happened to be around. He inevitably constructs according to a vision, an imaginative figuration which will have its concrete realization. The repulsion that this came to effect for James is clear from another letter to Andersen (25 November 1912) in which it is the very imaginative scope of such projects which is precisely their failing, and the 'dream' is likened to that of a fairy tale prince who, if he were 'locked up in a

boundless palace by some perverse wizard, and, shut out thus from the world
and its realities and complications, were able to pass his time wandering from
room to room and dashing off, on each large wall surface as it came, "this is the
great Temple of the Arts" ' and so on to Religion. The very idea lacks contact
with 'the world of such sharp intricate actual living facts and bristling problems
and overwhelming actualities' and James continues with an apologia for his
own form of art. 'I live myself in the very intensity of reality and can only
conceive of any art-work as producing itself piece by piece and touch by touch,
in close relation to some immediate form of life. Andersen's 'colossal
aggregations' are 'brilliant castles in the air'.[15] Of course the problems of the
creative process as such do not affect the Ververs, but James conveys the unease
with grandiosity of vision, which might be linked in the case of the Museum by
the lack of any shaping of the content of presumed perfection.

Perhaps the absence of any sense of the form of realization in Mr Verver's
design adds a sense of purity to his impersonality, even to the point of
suggesting the abstract. At one point Verver congratulates himself that 'no
pope, no prince of them all had read a richer meaning' than he 'into the
character of Patron of Art'. (p. 146) Yet we are far from visualising the
contents, the character of his Museum beyond its ethical and didactic function.
It is directed at American City with all of the fervour of an essay of Emerson or
even a tract of Samuel Smiles. And we may suppose that, whatever objects the
Museum contains, they will be equally alien and confrontational in one sense,
and equally resolute in the devotion to self-improvement in another. The
aesthetic dimension of *The Golden Bowl* has entered into the ethical. Put at this
level, the conflict of values between the aesthetic and the ethical is
reformulated. And insofar as history enters into American City it is not that
of persons but of vast impersonal forces. This project propels us out of the world
in which the Jamesian novel operates. As the carriage disappears down Portland
Place the world of dialogue ceases and we cannot imagine its reinvention across
the dark fields; or even how, in the Museum itself, speech will turn into the
lecture, into information and public service. And back in Portland Place one of
the great passions of the novel is consummated: possession.

We can compare this transformation with some characteristic features of
James's own discussion of art. I will suggest, however oddly, some collective
elements that bear upon our case. For all that James's life and writings were
saturated with the presence of works of art, their perception is highly selective.
I have mentioned the writings on art and the essay on Sargent, and the
paramount importance to James of representation. But representation is not,
except in an extended sense, conceived in terms of realism. Physical

resemblance is only a path to inner dimensions and qualities which it is precisely the artist's perception that brings alive. Much of James's reflection on his own art is concerned with the methods by which indirection brings one closer to the representational truth. With the visual arts the method is not spelled out or directly in question. But the end product is observed with such a success in mind. Above all with portraiture, which is James's most immediate interest. It is the power of the portrait to catch the living quality which matters, as the novelist catches the 'living' quality of an imagined person. So of a Reynolds: 'we should not scruple to say that *character* plays up into the English face with a vivacity unmatched by Titian's heroine – character, if we are not too fanciful, as sweet and true as the mild richness of colour, into which the painter's imagination has overflowed'.[16] What follows is in effect a double reading of the qualities of the subjects' character and of their revelation on the canvas. This method is followed in his extensive treatment of Sargent, whose portraits reflected James's own social world. (He spoke too of the embarrassment of so liking Sargent's portrait of himself.)

If this preoccupation with the inner character of pictorial truth seems uppermost it is connected with the scenic and atmospheric, above all as a frame for human action and feeling; and some of the better art commentary is found in the travel writings where, as in the essay on Venice, the qualities of setting, light, colour, the general framing of perception become part of the conditionality of life as a whole. And atmosphere becomes a subtle and indirect form of representation, the capturing of those intangible aspects of our mental landscape, which bears its own relation to the novelist's art. I do not mean such slight suggestions to imply particular limits to James's interest in the visual arts but to indicate an underlying attitude. And its constant feature is a concern for life, for the living character of the thing represented. The failure of Andersen's sculpture lay not only in the mannered excess of his nude figures but in their lifelessness – something shared with the decorous Story.

It is this concern with the immediacy of living quality that creates a puzzle in *The Golden Bowl*, where the awareness of art objects is so thin and intangible. Art itself has become abstract and impalpable, the suitable subject of a socially worthy venture but strangely bloodless and evanescent, while the idea of it provides the springboard – or is it the escape route? – which will open up the necessary exit from conflict, almost the point of departure from that matrix of feeling which composes the human situation. And the concrete human world evoked for Andersen vanishes through that exit. The Museum will be the place where not only have the passions of the characters become *morceaux de musée* but the works of art themselves will speak with an attenuated voice. James's whole sense of the nature of the artistic enterprise underwrites the fatality of that attenuation; the Verver project places means and art in the bracketing off of Museum walls. The public fortune so contained within those walls will become the stuff of scholarship and classification. It will also lie outside the human frame.

So civilization's means produce their own necessary consequence. And the contrast is with another model of civilization which the action of the book has embodied: the regulation of life by a code of manners that allows the resolution of conflict, the assumed equilibrium between conflicting desires, the deflection of our fears. Here is the stuff of life subjected to that ordering process that James has spelled out with marvellous precision and restraint. This model creates a semblance of intelligible unity within the living context. The other has displaced the civilizing impulse to the impersonal demonstration that the Museum encapsulates. And American City will embody a paradox: the life of the people will no doubt sweep on, itself the impersonal force that admits neither the world of manners nor the conditions of friendship. Unlike the magical circle, there is no community in the human sense. What then will be the effect of the 'open doors and windows' of the palace of art on 'the bondage of ugliness'? James has not told us of course, but certain implications are hard to avoid. For Museum and Community cannot be one. They are divided by cultural presuppositions: the objects it receives have been alive, but their living power is cut off in their alienation, in their embodiment of the world from which they have been sundered. Another life however they may gain, one which belongs to a museum culture, to 'art history', to the world of forms. But this 'life' is hardly recognized in any of James's writings on art or in the presence of the art object in his fictions. There, a density of real involvement, as in the letter to Andersen, is the necessary condition of any thing of value. If proof against time and fate, the Museum will lie outside of time and the 'fate' of American City is Charlotte's living death.

Perhaps our awareness that the original title of *The Golden Bowl* was to be 'Charlotte' makes the handling of the terms of her fate consequential enough, however much the centre of consciousness of the book has shifted to Maggie and the elaborations of her moral triumph. Whatever suppositions we might bring to this, there is still something uncanny in this disappearance into a darkness marked only by its grandiose dream. One may compare it with another 'fate', that of Isabel Archer.[17] For here the form of life can be spelled out. For Charlotte it is absent. That is, in the conditions of Isabel's life we can see what form a living death will take. We understand about Osmond, his connections, the nature of the social circle, the surrounding conditions. We can see it all.

With Charlotte it is wholly obscure, as if our understanding and perception stopped at the threshold of such a destiny. It is a fate for which no form, no language quite exists, a dissolution of all that has been.

I am aware of the large literature and many disagreements that surround the conclusion and the relation of tone to form. Here it is a question of the characterization of American City. It is interesting, in taking a stance on the conclusion, that Edel yields to a powerful and amusing temptation. Charlotte is not heading for a prison: 'We know that she will ultimately be free, like James's other American wives, to travel, to build houses, to acquire art treasures, or other lovers. She can become Mrs Touchett or resemble the real-life Mrs Gardner.'[18] He is of course writing another novel, and the temptation comes to us all – it is part of the essential incompleteness I have mentioned – to treat these characters as Dumas did his musketeers or Balzac many of the characters in his *Comédie*. But James has imposed a closure, and for his characters two different kinds of direction are pointed, in the domestic world of Portland Place, rich in the density of the quotidian, and the blank dark oubliette of American City. Of the latter he may have said very little, beyond conveying its otherness, but I think he intends us to take it seriously, both as project and as fate.

If the pursuit of perfection leads to the void it has been imperfection that has given shape to life. The catalytic bowl itself, its hidden flaw, has produced the truth – as in the concept of *wabi* where the imperfection of an object is its guaranty of authenticity, its entry into the phenomenal world, into life and into time. Perfection belongs to the gods and, if man should reach for it, it would be at the cost of his humanity, in a form of transcendence which the phenomenal object of art cannot reasonably attain. Perhaps it is fanciful to see such an imperfection in the bowl itself as the necessary threshold of the human truth, but the alternative, the hypothesis of flawlessness, of an unblemished community of four, suggests an inhuman perfection, a timelessness in which no true work of art participates, least of all a novel. Civilization is not an abstract idea, a gilded paradigm, but the considerate rule of the manners, perception and discipline that enable man's passions and interests to attain a reasonable if necessarily imperfect harmony.

James prefers the word 'civilization' to 'culture' and it makes a frequent appearance in *The American Scene*, where in a variety of ways, direct and indirect, he asks what civilization is. But the question always has a context, whether a New York dinner party or a swamp in Florida; there is always the necessary vantage of a 'particular attaching case'. So such a project as Arnold's, where culture is seen as the 'study of perfection', having its origin in a 'love of perfection',[19] would be alien to the Jamesian sense of the possible.

Of course, Arnold too provides his own version of contexts; perfection is used as a foil to moral uplift and other forms of Victorian heaving and striving, or to the aspect of Victorian life contained in the maxim 'every man for himself'. For the comedies of self-improvement and of rampant individualism must be contrasted with the classical purity of the ideal, with the social and intellectual touchstones.

The novelist might feel a flicker of suspicion about the notion of disinterested pursuit, and the possibility of any realization that did not alter, transform or qualify. Even the pursuit of beauty, such an essential part of Arnold's vision, must for James work through complex circumstance and mediation, which are, alas, the condition of any grand design, conditions that alter the most ideal conception, or the most extravagant deployment of means. Of the future of beauty in America 'I had felt myself catching this vibration, received some vivid impression of the growing quantity of force available for that conquest', so that 'you wonder' what is wanting for 'the aesthetic revel', why some 'great undaunted adventure of the arts' should not 'take place in conditions unexampled'. But somehow 'the universal organising passion, the native aptitude for putting affairs "through" ' does not, for 'all that waiting money and all the general fury', lend itself to the aesthetically creative. The right form of enquiry, he finds, is 'What is wanting in the way of taste ... – that small circumstance alone being *positively* contributive. The others, the boundless field, the endless gold, the habit of great enterprises, are, you feel, at most, simple negations of difficulty.'[20]

James mixes a number of possible goals, from the conditions of an artistic renaissance to the creation of an informed body of good taste. And certainly Arnold would have agreed that neither of these, nor any aspect of his cultural ideal, the pursuit of perfection, could be approached by way of wealth. (Above all, one uneasily supposes, by way of new, brash, untutored wealth.) But there is also a deep and far-reaching difference. For James the postulate of an ideal of perfection would not fit with the novelist's sense of pervasive contingency. And Arnold's evocation would approach that ideal with an impossible directness. James would of course assent that it is used as a measure of social and institutional failure, or class-bound limitations and other – wholly contingent – benightedness. But that ideal could hardly fail to carry a transcendental shadow, and even the refuge of 'the Great Good Place' carries, *pace* Auden, none of that baggage.[21] And the force of the Goethean sense of the uplift of the ideal, even in the form of the Eternal Feminine, could only enter *The Golden Bowl* in a qualified way. Neither Maggie's nor her father's pursuit of perfection would quite accommodate it. They may retain it within themselves of course, at the risk of creating an irony that is too dry altogether.

The symbols of the world of art do not entirely adhere to the notion of any purity in the object which belongs to a world of the ideal. Any symbolism invested in a sacred object is at least partly clouded by its place in a complex and ambiguous action. If one thinks of Maggie's pagoda – which exists only in the mind's eye – or of the ivory tower itself, one thinks less of an object of art than of a figurative device which works as a feature of narrative. Objects, imaginary or otherwise, are invented for the richness and complexity of their case. And if one turns to the experience of the art object one finds it interwoven with experience of every other kind. Perhaps James's childhood experience of the Louvre, above all of the Galerie d'Apollon revisited in later life in a famous dream, represents more powerfully than any object evoked the grandeur of the artistic enterprise.

> I have dim reminiscences of ... visits ... during which the house of life and the palace of art became so mixed and interchangeable – the Louvre being, under a general description, the most peopled of all scenes not less than the most hushed of all temples – that an excursion to look at pictures would have but half-expressed my afternoon. I had looked at pictures, looked and looked again, at the vast Veronese, at Murillo's moon-borne Madonna, at Leonardo's almost unholy dame with the folded hands, treasures of the Salon Carré as that display was then composed; but I had also looked at France and looked at Europe, looked even at America as Europe itself might be conceived so to look, looked at history, as a still-felt past and a complacently personal future, at societies, manners, type, characters, possibilities and prodigies and mysteries of fifty sorts.[22]

But largely the effect lies in its scale, in its sense of the ensemble, the totality, in which one's awareness can open to the full sense of glory, a transformation of oneself by a contact with the artistic world which goes beyond aesthetic appreciation to involve the entire self and its possible world.

Will such a vision be possible in Mr Verver's Museum? The totality would necessarily be of another kind, not caught up in an historical vision, or forming part of the world which its images represent, but with its very identity marked by its apartness, by its presentation of a 'culture' necessarily different. Can the experience of that culture be the beginning point of self-understanding, either for an individual or for the culture itself? Only through the acceptance of difference as the beginning point of knowledge, with the consequent forms of substitution, displacement, metaphorization that are a necessary part of such a perspective. So the culture-hungry citizens of American City may follow three courses. They may view the objects as alien and enter the museum as a place of otherness, regarding its contents as so many curiosities, like the reconstruction of dinosaurs or the freaks at the county fair. Or they may regard the presence of objects of beauty – for we must assume that there are some of these – so as to put in question the values of a community sunk in ugliness. (As Mr Verver has assured us that it is.) What should follow would be an exercise in social transformation, an evangelical call (Ruskin comes to mind) for the creation of an authentically aware social body, granting that such a re-creation must be on the ground of difference, in wholly American terms. Or they must accept that the act of contemplation in the face of these masterpieces forces the consequences of difference upon the viewer. Which may reduce them to dream, to a spiritual refuge, or may provide the moment of leverage in which the 'restless analyst' is born.

Chapter 19

The Elusive Synthesis

If one deep truth shown by the American journey that inspired *The American Scene* was of the necessary limit that the country imposed on the possibility of interpretation, there was, somewhere in the 'great margin', a sense of a supreme challenge to representation. The whole transformation of American life, the creation of a new form of power in the great tycoons, meant a new form of dramatic presence – perhaps a dimension of character – which the new wealth opened to the novelist. We have already seen a passing but uneasy mention in *The American Scene* of the alteration of Newport. And omnipresent there is at least *one* 'lesson of Balzac',[23] that money lies at the heart of so much of social behaviour. But Balzac's world of property, enterprises, inheritance, lawyers, speculators, and so on was transformed for James in his American journey, by the scale of the new America's social and economic transformations and its volatility. It was enormous quantities of money, made quickly, expended on the goods, houses, projects we have noted: grand, lavish, often vulgar, and impermanent.

To grasp the effect of such a world on the American character, to see those effects as they move between generations, clearly had its innate fascination. But this exploration has omitted the makers in their raw excesses of power. The process of making is alien to James, as is the empty habitat of the businessman, cut off from the culture and language which belong to the civilized world. If the active world of Gaw and Betterman[24] is hidden from us, it is the same with Adam Verver. One notes that there is that degree of opacity in Verver which makes feeling and motive difficult to reach. The financial world of Gaw and Betterman is as obscure as whatever activity went on in American City. James tacitly places this world of action and of strife outside his imaginative range. It is money as transmitted that interests him, its reflected power in the lives that depend upon it. And of course wealth and power in all its purity, in its dissembling, in its delayed and indirect action, in its seductive capacity to refashion its recipients and aspirants. Above all in its power to bend the imagination, intellectual gifts and moral sensibilities, by an insinuating magnetism.

If this reticence before the rawly acquisitive poses an ambiguity in James's work as a whole, a sketch or outline may give at least a partial perspective.

Wealth is of course necessary to the good life. Yet the making of wealth requires an effort and turn of character that excludes the leisure on which the good life depends. For the contents of such a life consist in reflection and the intelligent conversation which follows from it. The subject matter may vary: character and personal relations, and their form as literature presents them; the arts themselves; history and the great public issues of the time; above all those most compelling aspects of the affective life and their effect on character. This is perhaps close to the famous formula of G. E. Moore that the good life consists of personal affections and aesthetic enjoyment, the essentials of the Bloomsbury ideal. But James goes beyond such a spare formula. Like Aristotle, he realizes the need for certain conditions. Wealth, a good bearing, even a fine appearance are important ancillaries. For such a life is absolutely dependent upon leisure, and leisure with such a reasonable level of affluence as to enable one to avoid anxieties, to travel in comfort, to attend the theatre and other cultural matters, to entertain one's friends and to indulge in the occasional act of generosity.

All is relative to your position in life. Great wealth is not necessary for persons of more modest needs. To have grand properties and great debts like Prince Amerigo is perhaps rather special. But for such a position his course is quite conventional. The notion of a rich American heiress was a common-place. In 1900 some 400 wealthy American girls were married to European titles, a list which included some of the most illustrious families. A century later, the habit lingers on, as with the marriage in July 1995 of the prince of a dilapidated exiled royal house[25] to the daughter of a self-made American billionaire. The point is that this in no way reflects on anyone's character; it is simply one way of solving an inherited problem. The oddity of Prince Amerigo is to involve himself in an inner way with the American sensibility, and that sensibility not in the form of the new Newport, but of a restrained moral consciousness and aesthetic commitment. The voice of an older America is grafted onto the new, for in the conventional distinction between 'old' and 'new' money, Verver is the newest of the new.

So to ask if the Prince is in any way corrupted by Verver's wealth is to approach the matter mistakenly. The curiosity, if not the corruption, lies in the passivity before the working of the whole Verver establishment. For Charlotte it is different: in being both female and without a fortune she is extremely dependent and vulnerable, although her expectations of Verver do not seem to exceed those possible to any affluent husband. And what young woman of brilliant talents and appearance would fail, even if more disguisedly in this age than then, to think of that affluence as part of any reasonable plan of life. But Horton Vint is corrupted by Graham Fielder's money, and part of that corruption, which involves the whole changing *mise-en-scène* of *The Ivory*

Tower, is that he is in the business of money. For the Prince and Charlotte it is an expectation appropriate to their position and form of life. For Vint it is a temptation and it is seemingly natural to exploit old friendship. But he is clearly intended, in an almost simplified and allegorical fashion, to represent the new consciousness of the business world. If, rather than embodying the new wealth, he is parasitic on it, this deviousness and manifestation are part of it all. Gaw and Betterman have been involved in their own deviousness; there is a Balzacian *déformation professionelle* in the pursuit of wealth which makes it an end in itself and wholly alien to the good life. Wealth is appropriate to the Prince and even to Charlotte as a condition of being themselves but those selves are not devoured by that wealth, nor are their lives essentially concerned with it.

When we turn from the conditions necessary to great persons such as the Prince we can see the rather diffuse but nevertheless distinct image of those whose civilized life is based on a reasonable degree of affluence. Marie de Vionnet or Maria Gostrey are models of the modest scale. But the danger that Moore's aesthetic contemplation will sink into a frivolous aestheticism is also quite alien to James. His touch of unease with William Wetmore Story clearly reflects a doubt about a life devoted to an art that, lacking the necessary level of talent and inspiration, is weak enough to put in question the whole conscious design. And there is the occasional expression of horror at idle-minded cultural or literary chat. Criteria for deciding what is the real thing may be impossible to state, but it is necessary that we can understand these differences and apply them. James's equilibrium between a seriousness amounting to severity, and the notion that whatever the good life contains is expressed in form, varies from case to case and context to context. But it can be recognized, even, perhaps above all, when the form of life is, as in the case of Lambert Strether, out of reach.

The radically altered America that thrust itself into the foreground of James's interpretative quest as he recorded *The American Scene* is the intractable material dominating his last unfinished projects. Few writers, as I have observed, have written so penetratingly about the 'new America' of the 1900s. But the 'current of feeling, observation, etc., that can float me further than any other' marooned the 'restless analyst' in a landscape that appalled as well as fascinated him. The great jostling bustle challenged the Jamesian sense of history, cultural and personal, introducing a vast mass of material that he could not quite, as novelist, make his own. Beyond observation lay a further imaginative effort. This new America imposed a sharp shift of perspective, introduced further incommensurates, through which he was to wrestle with the creation of a semblance of intelligible unity and moral identity. There is a troubled sense, clear in his dialogue with himself in the late notebooks, that the knowledge available to him was inadequate.

The eloquence of the unfinished arises so powerfully from the grandeur of these late projects. It is not the contingency or folly through which the second part of Gogol's *Dead Souls* was lost that moves us, so much as our sense of the tragic loss of something transcendental and incalculable – even if the vanished manuscript might have been ludicrous or incoherent. James's four last incomplete projects are different in kind, but there is no doubt of the scale, importance and reach of the conception in each of them. And nothing is more alien to James than a fashionable post-modern valuation of the fragmentary, the discontinuous, the disseminated. The aim of everything was completeness – a completeness seen in the fullest understanding and perfection of form.

An exception to this might seem to be *The American Scene*, where the unwritten second half appears simply to have slipped away from him with the awareness that the Western part of his American journey evoked none of the intensity of the physical and social terrain that called directly on the memory of the personal past. And the chronicle of America observed did not lend itself to the artist's sense of the whole. Of course it was in the context of *Notes of a Son and Brother* that he ascribed to Henry Adams the 'inexhaustible' sense of the artist's role and powers. All these works place their point of reference in an imagined or constructed past, where the mixture of memory and an impassive nature outside present knowledge provide a continuous play of perspectives. There are brilliant examples of this combination of perception and limits at a number of points in *The American Scene*, where he has stepped beyond the comparative frame which is given by the authority of memory. And if the autobiographies are in the end an attempt to see his life steadily and whole, the fact of their incompleteness is due to the contingent cause, and the breaking off in mid-sentence had to do not with the problems of shape or substance, but with the fortuitous intervention of the gods.

The two great unfinished novels, *The Ivory Tower* and *The Sense of the Past*, pose problems of another kind: whether a certain view of self and experience can find an intelligible imaginative form. These novels do not break off, but are abandoned in the face of problems for which the appropriate solutions have not been found. Our evidence in both cases is fragmentary and the attempt to return to *The Sense of the Past* indicates the value placed on some unfinished business, on an awareness of connections which have not been fully articulated, perhaps on the invention of a necessary memory. Here the return is to an absent self, which is the hypothesis necessary to explain and shore up the possible present, to a past which may have posed some limit to the imaginative powers themselves. As surely did, in a quite different fashion, the continuation of *The Ivory Tower*, which was faced by the construction of an America which James did not really know or understand. The reality was perceived early enough, but the detail to fill it out, to give his development the necessary density, must have seemed at the limits of his knowledge, to be an America which would require more than the passing visit to bring fully to life. Betterman and Gaw, *The Ivory Tower*'s crumbling millionaires on their Newport verandahs, are no more than caricatures.

'I want to steer clear of the tiresome "artistic" associations hanging about the usual type of young Anglo-Saxon "brought up abroad"; though only indeed so far as they *are* tiresome.'[26] This of the projected image of Graham Fielder, the rather diffident protagonist of *The Ivory Tower*. And James notes, of this young American brought up entirely in Europe and summoned back to inherit his grim uncle Betterman's fortune: 'Of course the trouble with him is a sort of excess of "culture".' But what this culture implies is something that James has failed to fill out. We are given an inviting picture of a kind of person but without any vivid sense of how that kind is to come to any very concrete picture of activity or commitment: 'I can see him as more or less covertly and waitingly, fastidiously and often too sceptically, conscious of possibilities of "writing".'[27] But no very clear decision is revealed and James clearly wishes for his protagonist a kind of negative capability, 'exposed and assaulted', so deeply fastidious as to avoid any recognizable form of practice.

'His "culture", his initiations of intelligence and experience, his possibilities of imagination, if one will ... make for me a sort of picture of a floating island on which he drifts and bumps and coasts about, wanting to get alongside as much as possible, yet always with the gap of water, the little island *fact*, to be somehow bridged over.' This is the perfect model of the conscientious and sensitive disengagement forced on the man who hopes to live the best form of life, but whose engagement with the world's demands upon him is marked by that little 'gap' and his own awareness that a gap, some form of inner distancing, is essential to his nature.

Like the 'superfluous man' of Russian fiction there is the awareness of being outside all the events which surround you. But unlike a Russian world of idle landowners, eccentric officers and *désoeuvré* intellectuals, the American setting does not lend itself to the incongruity which is even absurd – merely to that tiny sense of distance which fences off the self-isolating life. And this marks Fielder as the victim of those who are willing to take action in their own interest.

Another feature of this gap is its difference from the Gidean 'disponibilité'. For Gide, the young protagonist who stands back from the world's demands upon him, does it of his will to understand, to assess, and to find his way to the desired conclusion, usually in terms of experience itself. But Fielder's is a cast of mind which he cannot help; it is not directed to any purpose, not even a detachment which might create a sense of perspective and hence of understanding. It seems rather to work against understanding, to mark out the world of Newport, the vast inheritance, as something beyond Fielder's Europeanized sensibility, except insofar as he slowly grows to see the moral deformation that great wealth induces. But there too, the 'gap' is to prevent him playing other than a passive role.

It is perhaps possible to extrapolate too much from James's notes, but they are of course our only indication as to the development of this novel and they become rather thinner and more uncertain as they progress. Perhaps the 'successive aspects' would have gradually given solidity to a character who is uncommonly pale and elusive from the opening pages and the notes. But a feature of the whole seems clear: the mismatch between the civilized expatriate and the 'American scene' – the bridge of understanding operates only at the level of moral repugnance. The presence of Rosanna Gaw as the naturally decent warm-hearted American idealist, devoted from her teens to the younger 'Gray', seems intended to make a resolution possible in which the abandonment of both wealth and America for some small, modestly conceived version of the good life in an act of refusal becomes the only possible humane escape.

This would of course treat Europe as refuge, as escape from the problems America poses, an avoidance of the implied force in that vast reservoir of potential. The novel's unfinished state deprives us of seeing how the terms of it would have worked. Part of the problem of projection lies in the pallor and sketchiness of Fielder himself. He is intended to have his own form of perfection, as the conversation with Betterman implied, in language that reminds us of Verver and the Prince: ' "I've got you without a flaw. So!" Mr Betterman triumphantly breathed. Gray's sense was by this time of his being examined and appraised as never in his life before – very much as in the exposed state of an important "piece", an object of value picked, for finer examination, from under containing glass.'[29]

This may only be a manner of speaking, but the resemblance to the *morceau de musée* makes one think of the perfection or imperfection of the object of choice. The dying millionaire has wanted an heir unlike himself, who will stand outside 'the hustle', who will direct his wealth to other kinds of end. Therefore we need not think about the Balzacian plots and struggles, for we have the wealth as a finished product, clear of its turbulent sources. Betterman enacts precisely the picture of *The American Scene*: 'I *was* business, I've been business and nothing *else* in the world. I'm business at this moment still – because I can't be anything else.' But he wishes to cut the link. To Fielder he cleans the slate of all of that: 'It's none of your affair.'

Indeed, there is nothing for him to actually *do*. Betterman makes it clear: 'Do? The question isn't of your doing, but simply of your being.' To which the reply that 'Don't they come to the same thing?' gets the opaque return: 'Well, I guess that for you they'll have to.' Does this suggest in fact a reversal of man's usual fate, and that for Gray Fielder being will be his form of doing? We must think of what sort of contract with the devil such 'decontaminated' wealth might imply. It seems that James wants to pitch the conditions towards such a decontamination, to reach the independence shown by Gray's mother, and Gray's own distance from the dark heart of it all. It underlines the degree to which Betterman's gift has a fairytale quality of pure gratuity, and hence of moral liberation. The devil, if devil it is, asks for nothing; Fielder has only to be himself. If the gold of the Rhine goes from thief to thief, the American gold has only a special guarantee of its innocence – like that indeed of Mr Verver?

Yet, in this case at least, the American gold carries all of the destructive weight of a culture whose ultimate iron it is. Gray will seem to take up the challenge: 'I want ... to like my luck. I want to go in for it, as you say, with every inch of such capacity as I have. And I want to believe in my capacity; I assure you on my honour I do. I've lashed myself up into feeling that if I don't I shall be a base creature, a worm of worms as I say, and fit only to be utterly ashamed.' (p. 963) All of this 'with a wondrous candour' to Horton Vint, the man who will betray and exploit him, for whom money is a natural aim. If the Kingdom of Ends were devised in American terms it would be conceived as such, and Gray's candour is that of one to whom it does not come naturally, who must make the adjustment, 'develop my capacity' to face the fortune which is alien to instinct and sensibility. But the warmth and enthusiasm have the sheen of innocence. He is on the fatal point of asking his friend to act for him, which will be the mainspring of a sequence that we shall not see through to the end.

The failure to carry it through to the end may of course relate to fortuitous matters: James's declining powers; the disturbance occasioned by the outbreak of the war; the priority given to the autobiographies. But it is also possible to think that there are causes that are intrinsic to the project itself.

There seem to me to be two areas in which contradictions arise. One lies in James's uncertainty about aspects of his material. He has, in one circumstance or another, confessed that the workings of the business world are to him impenetrable – the actual processes, the way in which people think, the way in which that thought is turned into a series of operations which have causal effects. The very process by which Horton Vint eases himself into control and Gray is marginalized may have posed a problem of representation. Of course it is the effects on several lives that matter, and the choices that follow from them, and the moral assessment of it all. One could omit the workings of the action – it is precisely here that Balzac's fascination with process is alien to James. And to show the knock-on effects of a *fait accompli* would have been consonant with his methods.

Yet the project seems to have intended some grasp of the new order of American life. To show the world of financial manipulation, the mind and workings of Horton Vint and those who thought like him would have brought James closer to a transformation that both fascinated and appalled. To indicate Gray's Europeanized sensibility properly would require some real knowledge of, and representational power over, its opposite. The schematism seems to require it and James's *données* to be incomplete without it. Above all it is the new America that must be given and not effectively shirked. And in another fragment that James did complete we seem to come to the threshold of something James has not done before. In 'A Round of Visits', the fascination is there, but we hardly attach the story to more than the shadowy drawing rooms of the victims.

The other intrinsic difficulty may lie in the character of the protagonist. In the passage about the indeterminate nature of his own intellectual qualities, the civilized sensibilities are rather vaguer than one might expect from the finished text, and no doubt the development would have given more colour. But would the 'gap' that he has described be also a challenge to representation? The sheer pallor and negativity could have their use in a shorter fiction but, like John Harmon in *Our Mutual Friend*, it seems a frail thread for such an extended design. And James's method is so much more intimately concentrated on a narrower range of action than is characteristic of a Dickens plot.

One feels the attraction powerfully. Fielder becomes the focal point of the action and attention of others. James slips into an extravagant series of comparisons with a monarchical presence at the centre of a world which is 'in waiting'. The sense of excitement rises, self-awareness intensifies: 'History and the great life surged in upon our hero through such images as these at their fullest tide, finding him out however he might have tried to hide from them.' (p. 986) Perhaps the irony seems heavy-handed, with that hint of a childish *folie de grandeur*. But these elated moments are more symptoms of the 'gap' than any sort of bridge over it. James's real difficulty with his hero is in making him distinct enough.

Fitzgerald noted of *The Great Gatsby* that it had a flaw which none of the critics had noticed: there was no indication of what had happened in Gatsby's life from the rediscovery of a rapport with Daisy to the accident which led to his death. There is sometimes an analogous void, a curious gap in James in which assumptions are made about the civilized pleasures of a form of life, the quality of experience that it involves, but where this plays no part, or very little, in the developing action. What have Graham Fielder or Spencer Brydon been doing that marks the difference from an alternative American life? There is not a strict and structural relevance. With accumulated cases, one has a certain curiosity about what would fill this assumption out – as James does not do. A fiction which valorizes the very form of life that seems inaccessible to representation depends heavily on the use of that foil to put something else into relief. In certain respects, *The Ivory Tower* belongs with a series of later tales, notably 'The Jolly Corner', which do not require a further representation to make their point, because they are so deeply immersed in an American context. The recovery of a European culture or sense of the past could exist as a mere postulate for the sake of the dramatic conflict in question.

The case is almost the opposite of that conveyed in *The American Scene* where the American cultural failure is figured as the pallor of the marks on the etcher's plate. Here it is the Europeanized American whose character is less clearly marked, whose diffidence and withdrawal are at least products of an evolution that precedes his American situation. And if the American moment precipitates the *folie de grandeur* it is not the characteristic and durable mode. James appears to have given thought to the effects of the 'gap', to have realized the danger to the full representation of such a person, and to have compensated by the occasional flicker of a powerful sense of self. But what the result does not convey is the essential form of the conflict between the power of the great American economic machine and the inner form that Europe's civilizing process has created. As with Chad Newsome, there is a curious hollow in the centre of the portrait – although, of course, this is a far less vivid representation, partly perhaps because the European setting in which Chad was seen gave the more vivid particulars.

This failure to represent the European *formation* of his 'hero' is partly a matter of scenery. Having posed a cultural contrast, one of the poles is only shakily indicated, the odd pointer being considered sufficient. The dramatic development is the American dimension, where certain types – Cissy Foy and perhaps the Bradhams – would seem familiar from a number of Jamesian contexts. But the creation of a new American innocence out of European experience must be balanced by a greater and facile knowingness, the kind that is at home with facts and figures to see off the 'blatant ass' (p. 920) that Gray sees as himself. And, as noted, the build-up of this world, the necessary recontextualizing, is incomplete.

But if you postulate the world, not merely of Newport, but of the active components of the American scene, in the first decade of the twentieth century, as a primary given, there is a vivid dialectical play between engagement and detachment. In *The Ivory Tower*, *The Sense of the Past* and 'The Jolly Corner' we feel this as the primary context, but one which is less than fully present. Neither is the alternative world developed as a context. The terms of a dilemma are set but not given a substantial solidity. Hence the action focuses on a small area of human contact, on the narrowly conceived tensions within a tiny compass. We are accustomed to this through *The Golden Bowl*, a process of stripping down, of suppressing context to focus on the relations of a few figures through whom the totality of context is implied. The effect of the method is clear enough, but the question seems open as to whether it can account for the America that was so deeply experienced. And the Europe that is implied as the alternative pole.

A realization of another and highly experimental kind is attempted in *The Sense of the Past*. If *The Ivory Tower* confronts the new America with Europe, the implicit and no doubt final avenue of escape, *The Sense of the Past* enacts both the international comparison and one of past and present. It involves a quite different artistic method, one that seeks – and fails – to establish a direct connection through the ghostly *alter ego*. For this last Jamesian enterprise combines the two elements, in a vision of himself in a Europe that is to be possessed through losing oneself in an historical identity that fuses both continents. It is a very different work from *The Ivory Tower*. The latter is a novel of manners evolving from a conflict with the mode of life of modern America, almost reworking a morality play. This journey into the past is an elaborate fantasy, an imaginative stretch that seems in part an allegory, in the special de Manian sense of constructing a schematism where meaning will never find its coordinates.

This is of course not to say that James wishes this vanishing of identity into the indeterminate, except insofar as Ralph Pendrel, his protagonist, is in search of a self that may not find its acceptable version in either the present or the past. Of course the conception is more diffident than this. The hero's life has been confined by family circumstances to New York, and to what seems like a rather restricted circle. The interest in the past does not seem so much personal as the kind of generalized conception that would be appropriate to one who has written a modest tome called *An Essay in Aid of the Reading of History*. One in effect starts at a high level of generality; the question of history looms from outside, from an awareness of the problem as a whole cultural situation might reveal it. The essay is also the trigger which brings about the inheritance by which history becomes a living personal matter. The house which Ralph Pendrel inherits in London is the direct consequence of what is in effect an academic enquiry.

If the consequence of the great American exposure, the economic enterprise, the moral coarsening of life will be to drive Gray Fielder back to a Europe which, however indistinct, is a refuge, Pendrel's point of departure is a journey of discovery, a discovery of a Europe that exists in a wholly personal experience, transmitted intentionally and meant for him alone. The opening also has the form of a fairy tale, or an episode from the Arabian Nights. The great heiress, 'princess', object of desire, sets a condition for the diffident, scholarly Pendrel. Of course he must make the visit to Europe, so long postponed out of consideration for his failing mother. He must as an historian use it to deepen his sense of the past, to find himself in the extended process of doing so. But then he must return. Aurora, a widow, has lived in Europe, and for reasons, some of which remain mysterious to both character and reader, wishes to abandon it forever. Some tantalizing episode in her past is hinted but not revealed.

To both find oneself and return with oneself means in effect that the past must become present. The young historian – he and Aurora are 30 – is to inherit a house in London from a distant relation. It is literally his past that he is to inherit. To bring it back to New York – even if indeed rather a Whartonish 'old' New York – would create the synthesis that no other James novel has quite attempted, and on which *The Ambassadors* has thrown a sceptical perspective. The synthesis would bring 'home' the personal adventure into the past and reconcile it with modern life, as lived by an observable 'modern' society, helped perhaps by the thought that it is not quite the dim provincial backwater of Woollett or a distant shadow like American City.

The entry into the past poses what was perhaps James's worst case of 'damnable difficulty'. The notebook entry of August 9th, 1900[29] spells out much of the original problem of representation. A request from Howells had mentioned an 'international ghost'. James wished 'something as simple as *The Turn of the Screw*, only different and less grossly and merely apparitional'.

This seems to have suggested a return to a project James had already begun. And he noted in his revision plans of 1914 the similarity to 'The Jolly Corner', the notion of the apparition suggesting a solution to the entry into the past. As in 'The Jolly Corner', the selves that meet in the present had two different pasts. And one feature that the apparitional element seemed to present from the start (1900) was 'terror', somehow vaguely related to 'the quasi-grotesque Europeo-American situation'. But this allusive account, turning over ways in which the subject might evolve, is inconclusive.

In the end James moved from terror to an almost bizarre form of assimilation. Pendrel enters the house that he has inherited in an intense and exploratory frame of mind. His imagination fastens on a portrait which appears to undergo subtle changes as he looks at it, and alters its character between his visits. Then it turns its face; and it is Pendrel's own that looks out. In effect Pendrel vanishes into the house and, by way of the portrait – although the manner of this is, unsurprisingly, not entirely clear – into a remote past which is his own. So one passes from a character looking into the past to a full evocation of that past and his place in it. At such a point terror is replaced by a full assimilation, and the subsequent scenes employ a change of method. For James embarked on a new kind of novel, a true historical novel which reads rather like a particular version of Jane Austen. The language is not archaized, but there is a degree of increased formality. And the circumstances of 1820 involve their own version of a plot. His distant cousin in that incarnation produces a further complication of romantic involvement.

Yet clearly the intention was there to evolve a double consciousness: the awareness of 1910 would play upon the world of 1820; however the world of 1820 would have a consciousness of its own which would in turn play upon that alien element (and hence an unease that does not amount to 'terror') which has reached them from 1910. An awareness of such a world was to be transmitted. One understands the damnable difficulty, and the degree to which this gradually loomed large enough to frustrate the development of the whole. How could it be shown, not merely told? The move into the past had effects that were perhaps difficult to control. In some ways the 1820 Pendrel seems more at ease in his London world than the Pendrel who set out from 1910 New York. Certainly the conversations with his cousins, the Midmore sisters, have a fluency and assurance that is quite lacking in the anguished and contorted interview with Aurora. The involvements, even the misunderstandings, operate at a degree of distance which deprives them of the extraordinary tension of that opening.

This might indicate that the Pendrel of 1820 was at least a man who had escaped the New World destiny and felt wholly at ease with himself. But the opposite becomes true. The more deeply his relationship with the two sisters, and ultimately the younger one, evolves, the more he has a strange awareness of the pull of his later self, and the need to live in the present. But the form which that present should take is not clear to James. The indications in his notes show that Aurora will, in spite of her resolutions, return to London, that through means that James had not fully worked out Pendrel would return to the world of 1910, perhaps simply recovering his identity within the house, and becoming able to walk through the door again into contemporary London. It was clearly intended by James to be a romance, but the ground on which the union with Aurora will take place has not been determined. There is no indication that Aurora will insist on her original terms – she had left herself an out in saying that she would only return if she really wanted to. So the future may just as well lie in Manchester Square as in New York.

The 'ghosts' are not exactly ghosts, for they inhabit a world of their own into which Pendrel is mysteriously drawn. Too literal an account of this world would destroy James's effect. He makes a bold transition from the presence in the house to the house's past. We are simply displaced from one book to another. It is not indicated that this is a dream or Pendrel's fantasy world. In spite of the shift in language, closer to historical romance, there is no indication that within the fiction one world is more real than another. Pendrel lives in both. And he brings the two worlds together in what seems intended to be a synthesis of past and present, in a personal connection with the past. But it is the very directness in the connecting of two identities that posed an insuperable artistic problem. Largely, the sense of discontinuity is built into the perception because the object of enquiry is the hidden aspect of a person shaped in that slightly 'other' cultural ambience, where the rules of play are, to a somewhat indeterminate degree, different.

To what extent can we see James creating an allegorical structure in which the problem of American identity is resituated, its commitment to Old World and New, to Past and Present? There is no doubt some such intention, although the notebooks, as usual, do not generalize very fully about such interpretation. Of course in the novel itself the terms of interpretation come from the present. It is the awareness of the claims of the present that are felt in the past and both Aurora and the Ambassador who has acted as Pendrel's confessor and adviser provide (or were to provide) the final framework of the action. And perhaps there is an intended acknowledgement that however deeply we plunge into the past there is a present which is all we have. As a fictional device the world of the Midmores of 1820 becomes a form more of revelation than of an alternative world. The essential factor must be that if one vanished into the 1820 plot, the loss of coordinates would be such as to destroy the interest of the thing, and to ramble into the kind of historical romance that would be little more than a curiosity. The interest of it all lies in the tension between two worlds. And, at a further step, in the interpretation of that interplay, in terms of the new America which James had discovered between the original attempt on the story and the revised projection of 1914.

That he has chosen a double form, one based in the psychological conflict of the young New Yorker, the other an historical romance that seems quite alien to it, is not so much a confusion as a measure of ambition. Does it push the necessary coherence of the prodigious form beyond the possible? Certainly the problems of 1900 were far from solved and introducing the Midmore world required a different mode of representation that pressed at the limits of possible coherence.

Does one therefore want to say that this was an error in terms of the artistic strategy or that there were substantial issues which could not be given their final and satisfactory shape within the terms of a single work, or at any rate as they were considered in his own mind? It is of course impossible to say when this was one of the two major works – the other was *The Middle Years* – that were cut off by James's final illness. The indications of the scenario and of the notes become vague on a number of points, the most important being already noted: the return of Pendrel to the present with the consequent fusion of the two plots, and the relation of Europe and America in the form of life that will be represented by the marriage of Ralph and Aurora. A synthesis is indicated, a meeting point of multiple worlds, but some crucial terms of this synthesis, alas, elude us.

Chapter 20

Coda: The 'Complex Fate'

It is possible to see the terms of this synthesis, as changed between 1900 and 1914, through the problems posed in *The American Scene* and not quite adjusted to the demands of a particular fiction. The sense of size and scope and emptiness and movement, and the sheer vertiginous contingency built into the conditions of American life, appalled and challenged. One feature of the most prodigious form, at least in the Preface to *The Ambassadors*, was the mixture of scope and personal order. Here is the supreme instrument for interpreting ourselves in all of the vastly multifarious aspects of our social and our inner worlds.

In *The Golden Bowl* the necessity of manners, of a codified form of *politesse* provided the only possible escape from an irresolvable dilemma. To impose on oneself the necessary areas of silence, to maintain a correct and distinguished bearing in the face of adversity, to know how to at least manage, if not conquer, the rough matter of experience, to understand that suitable arrangement is civilization's answer to violence and chaos – these are certainly the Master's response to conflicting values. It is not to praise social manipulation and hypocrisy, for one sees easily their corruptive effect. It is simply to recognize the moment when that conflict of values is such as to make no reasonable solution possible without loss; and loss must be managed without the recognition that it is so. It is a representation of what Isaiah Berlin has called a tragic view of life. But the rule of decorum does not admit of tragedy. To do so would be to open ourselves to the destructive effects of an inner violence, to accept the chaotic and meaningless character of our lives. Life may have no meaning, but our mixture of perception and discipline may give it distinction, the semblance of intelligible unity and the kind of order that enables us to avoid the precipice beneath our feet, to create a viable form of life beyond the wholly mundane. The catastrophe of American City will be itself a part of the good life, lived in a mixture of generosity and opulence, of pain and self-denial.

One thing James seems to have abandoned, in the years that these last projects declared themselves, is the concern with power in the raw sense that the New World had posited. From the sanitized power of Mr Verver to the crass figures of Newport, the glory of great wealth has been so attenuated as to leave nothing but the ugly aftermath in human casualties. The emptiness of the power of wealth is markedly clear.

Above all the new American wealth is without personal value. The frail beneficiary may be victimized, but the substance is external to the private condition. The great mills of finance and industry churn on in a manner that may shape the working of the world, and may alienate and expel its own children, but which has ceased to enter into our real world insofar as culture and reflection have shaped it.

Power and imagination have parted from each other. Yet the fragility of those who have lived in its wake and then abandoned it is marked by the contrast with the vast, mindless machine that will roar forward according to its own laws. The man of sensibility will be left aside to his own destiny of isolated observer, crank, bohemian, in whatever ivory tower he can construct for himself. The reflective life will be like flotsam on the surface of the world.

But how can this parting of the ways between the great powers operative in the social order, and the private, the reflective, find its voice? The novel, as James has said through a variety of indirections, is the only vehicle capable of rendering this enormous conflict. And its own form is the analogue of the social code that produces, not rules, but their softer and less rigid version in decorum, elaborated through unspoken and indirect means – exactly the means that are required to bring about the novelist's control of the ragged edges of the world. Its very combination of multiple strategies, its mixture of ease, latitude and rigour give its fusion of representational freedom with the presence of form its unique power.

If that power operated at its highest level in *The Ambassadors* and *The Golden Bowl*, a breaking point appears with the American experience, a moment in which the synthetic force that holds the elements of the vision together is profoundly tested. If it was in the realization that the world was too large, too diffuse, too chaotic to yield to the powers of arrangement, it also acknowledged the necessity that this awareness imposed: to find a perspective that could contain and control the vast uncharted thing. The terms of 'the complex fate' had changed. The form of American choice had to be reformulated for an age which could not recognize the restraints that played upon Lambert Strether, where the possibility of finding the vanishing and shared decorum began to fade. It was to find the terms of play of the new America – if any such terms might be thought to exist. But what abyss opens before *This Side of Paradise*? And Fitzgerald is perhaps the most Jamesian of later writers in his concern with the lost rules of lost games.

But this would be in a mode where its predecessor's decorum, with its elaborate internal tensions, is also lost. One may ask desperately about the rules of the game when every element of life seems to run awry. Perhaps we can see some movement in that direction in *The Ivory Tower*, if only tentative and fragmentary. But the very social process which James approached was inimical to his art. The notion of that variety of elements that the new America had thrown so chaotically together, and on so vast a scale, meant that even the ingenuity of the 'most prodigious form' was insufficient. And this may also account for the elaboration of hypotaxis that makes the work something of a strain to read. It is perhaps not a case of the 'final manner' becoming that touch more final; the historical sections of *The Sense of the Past*, written after *The Ivory Tower*, are in rather arch and mannered prose, perhaps thought appropriate to an imagined time, but are not excessively complex or protracted. It is rather that the language gropes towards fixing the quality of relation that eludes it. Perhaps against the atomic fragments that swirl off into the void, Jamesian syntax could provide for civilization its last defence.

There is an analogy in I.A. Richards's view of poetry as the mode of organization of feeling, which gave to our sensations and mental processes the kind of order and distinction that rescued them from ugliness, banality and mere utilitarian employment. The line, of course, runs back to Arnold's felt necessity of the cultural role of poetry in the decline of faith. For Richards this was perhaps an overly tidy, almost mechanical set of correlations between linguistic traits and mental states. And the notion of order in our mental processes might need adjustment for the indirection of Jamesian strategies. But in his treatment of Coleridge,[30] Richards had an historical moment, his own historical moment, fully in view. Of course it is not a question of place but of a change in the working of language itself, through an evolution of consciousness which itself is not alien to James and touches the development of the Jamesian novel's treatment of the inner state.

It is not merely the 'how' instead of the 'what' and 'why', as Richards puts it, but an awareness of the power of language in its reciprocal action in relating culture and the mind. James's passionate involvement in the 'how', shown in its most explicit form in the notebooks, is at one level a matter of craftsmanship. But at another it is a belief in the powers of language to shape the human world. Representation is the mirror in which we can find that pleasure in our intelligent and civilized selves, uncovered in the arrangement that an evolved art allows us: the awareness of relations, the delightful and precarious movement of mind involved in an approach to self-knowledge, a self-knowledge which is based in the control and exploration of language. Hence any kind of Jamesian aestheticism is founded on this supreme and wholly central form of description. If for Richards the model of civilized mental and emotional organization is the closely wrought short poem, it is obviously for James the extension to the most fully representational form, an extension which may push the language of art to its limits.

If the model of inner order is the closely wrought poem, the danger of the historical is shown through the novel. For the modern novel shows a detachment from the objects of consciousness in favour of the concentration on consciousness itself. Richards's example of this 'modification of consciousness' compares Defoe's lack of interest, when he describes things, in 'the reverberations of their *sensory* qualities in the percipient's mind', with Joyce's *A Portrait of the Artist as a Young Man*. Crusoe's eyes, he remarks, 'look outward', whereas those of Stephen Dedalus, walking on Sandymount strand, 'see symbols of his own moods'.[31] And there is allusion to 'something new in the modes of perception' of Virginia Woolf. It is the separation of consciousness from the observed world that Richards indicates as the source of its dissolution.[32] This no doubt underrates the capacity of modernist novelists to employ and explore this movement from the excess of consciousness to its dissolution. But it is a crisis of language which he fears, in which that shaping power is lost in dissolution, in a fragmentation process in which nothing could intelligibly connect, where things 'fall apart' in a syntactical entropy.

The resistance to such a falling apart in that fusion of manners and syntax may look like a Jamesian response to the process of historical deliquescence, like Conrad's well-rigged ship. While aspects of James's exploration of consciousness have their affinities with modernism, the rupture of syntax, the breaking of continuity would have seemed yielding to a mental retrogression unworthy of art, and a vehicle for the truth only at its most mundane level. England of course was protected, and the great modernist works in the English language are by American or Irish writers. Virginia Woolf is the most marked exception. Yet does the final moment of cross purpose, of the embrace of impossible projects, show the limit to which his method had brought him and the implicit, if uneasy, awareness of what lay beyond it? Whether through contingent factors or internal difficulty the project begins to fail. One sees that in the last two novels the failure is different in kind. For a variety of reasons the fictional method that produced *The Golden Bowl* had achieved its maximum point of tension and could not adapt to radical change in its form of enquiry, nor to the new mass of undifferentiated material that lay before it.

If America took James over the edge of those reasonable defendable coordinates which made the cultural elements in such contrasts as past and present, Europe and America, it is quite clear that the new novels' role is different, their response to the historical moment more direct. And in the absence of completed texts, we cannot judge the full scale of a Jamesian response. There is however in absence its own eloquence. And in the testimony that points towards what is missing: the scenarios and notes which represent James's process of thinking it out and which Matthiessen calls 'James's colloquy with himself'. Part of the delight in these is at a fairly direct level: James constantly interrogates himself on movements in the plot, in time and place relationships, or simply the mechanics of how things will work. The continuous trying on process subtly alters and colours the conception, for which the means of realization take on a life of their own.

With *The Sense of the Past* there is much concern with the verisimilitude to be worked out within the two time schemes, and what sense of difference the narrative could bear. Eloquent notes also reveal the appeal of this glance into the 'phantasmal' past as a counterweight to 'our present disconcerting conditions' of 1914, and the marvellous reflective process of resituating oneself before the complex demands of one's subject. In fact, one is trebly situated – in 1820, in the prewar stability of 1910, and in the turbulent moment that was the writer's own. Also, the sense of the future within the past, which is barely foreshadowed in the finished chapters, but is part of the past's perception of an alien in their midst. There is the awareness of the dangers of the 'precise milieu and tone' required in the 'old world' atmosphere, above all in effecting the transition to the past. Perhaps it is the compression of this which adds to the eloquence, and the powerful sense of the terror involved in the displacement into the past. It is not a cure for the lost soul of the present. Rather 'the miraculous excursion into the past . . . that he has so yearned for, what it does for him most of all, he speedily becomes aware with sick dismay, is to make him feel far more off and lost, far more scared, as it were, and terrified, far more *horribly*, that is, painfully and nostalgically misplaced and disconnected, than had ever entered into the play of his imagination about the matter'.[33] This loss of self is to be consequential in ways undreamt of, in that Ralph is to feel 'immersed and shut in, lost and damned, as it were beyond all rescue'. And there is the passionate need for escape, by means of 'some effective password or charm'.

More startling is the indication of what might be the route to escape, and certainly a palpable form of personal triumph. The hero of 'The Jolly Corner' has found his ghost and routed him, as James himself had done in the dream of the Galerie d'Apollon. Here the ghost is effectively the totality of the past from which the necessary 'password or charm' is more difficult to dramatize, and in fact James never reached the point of doing so.

Indeed this is not entirely the novel as we have it. But the passionate account of being lost, damned, shut up without 'password or charm' shows a vivid horror of the temporal displacement, something perhaps suppressed in the subsequent narrative. But the value implied, a passionate engagement with the present, points the way out of the strangely marginalized moment of imagination.

Where is this moment of truth? It seems to efface the Atlantic, and to bring us to a shared present. Perhaps the terror is both universalized, for all men, and particularized in each person's own past and present. James is bridging more and greater gaps in a series of problems where the demands on his powers are increasingly extreme. And is the final 'password' or form of charm missing in such a way that the last lesson of the Master is something about the limits of language, and of representational powers? If so, it puts no limits to the reflection on the 'how' and the final movement of mind is towards relations that are so stretched that one suggests there is no risk too great. And if one's powers fail one has at least acted so as to deny the possibility of the limit.

Notes to Part Five

1. James, 1951, *The Ivory Tower*, Mattheissen (ed.), p. 905.
2. Vidal, 1985, p. 15.
3. Edel, 1972, *Life*, Vol. V, p. 386.
4. Tintner, 1993, p. 157.
5. Edel, 1969, *Life*, Vol IV, pp. 124–125.
6. Edel, 1972, *Life*, vol. V, p. 254.
7. *Vide*, especially, Tintner, 1986.
8. James, 1986 (edn), *Italian Hours*, p. 25.
9. *ibid.* , p. 18; and James, 1958 (edn), *Art of Travel*, pp. 401ff.
10. James, 1986 (edn), *Italian Hours*, p. 58.
11. James, 1903, *William Wetmore Story*, Vol. II, pp. 205–211.
12. Quoted in Tintner, 1986, p. 242.
13. Edel, 1972, *Life*, Vol. V, pp. 473–474.
14. *Ibid.*, pp. 477–478.
15. *Ibid.*, pp. 641–642.
16. James, 1956 (edn), *The Painter's Eye*, pp. 69–70.
17. There is a sense in which for Isabel Archer, heroine of *The Portrait of a Lady*, Europe is a living death as American City is for Charlotte.
18. Edel, 1972, *Life*, Vol. V, p. 221.
19. Arnold, 1960 (edn) *Culture and Anarchy*, pp. 44–45 and 48–49.
20. James, 1946 (edn), *The American Scene*, pp. 444–445.
21. Pace Auden's observation that what James, 'in his own discreet way', was presenting was 'a religious parable ... a spiritual state which is achievable by the individual', with the money required for membership of the 'Great Good Place' a symbol rather than a cause of that state. (Auden, Introduction to *The American Scene*, p. xxii).
22. James, 1956 (edn), *Autobiography*, Vol. I, pp. 198–199.
23. The title of James's lecture series given during the great American journey.

24. The embittered, dying former business partners with whom *The Ivory Tower* opens.
25. That of ex-King Constantine of Greece.
26. James, 1951 (edn), 'Notes for *The Ivory Tower*', p. 1026.
27. *Ibid.*, p. 1027.
28. *Ibid.*, pp. 918–920.
29. James, 1955 (edn), *Notebooks*, pp. 298–301.
30. Richards, 1934.
31. *Ibid.*, p. 222.
32. *Ibid.*, p. 225.
33. James, 1955 (edn), *Notebooks*, pp. 361–367.

Bibliography

Arnold, Matthew (1960 edn), *Culture and Anarchy*, Cambridge: Cambridge University Press.

Auden, W.H. (1946), Introduction to *The American Scene*, New York: Charles Scribner's Sons.

Berlin, Isaiah (1990), *The Crooked Timber of Humanity*, London: John Murray.

Edel, Leon (1953): *Henry James: A Life: Vol I, the Untried Years* (1953), London: Rupert Hart-Davis.

Edel, Leon *Vol II, The Conquest of London* (1962), London: Rupert Hart-Davis.

Edel, Leon *Volume III, The Middle Years* (1962), London: Rupert Hart-Davis.

Edel, Leon *Volume IV, The Treacherous Years* (1969), London: Rupert Hart-Davis.

Edel, Leon *Volume V, The Master* (1972), London: Rupert Hart-Davis.

Edel, Leon (1985), *Henry James: a Life*, London: William Collins.

Eliot, T.S, (1975), *Selected prose of T.S. Eliot*, ed. Frank Kermode, London: Faber and Faber.

Foucault, Michel (1984), 'On the Genealogy of Ethics', in *The Foucault Reader*, ed. Paul Rabinow, New York: Pantheon Books.

Gardner, Patrick (1983), 'Professor Nussbaum on *The Golden Bowl*', *New Literary History*, 15(1), pp. 179–184: Charlottesville, The University of Virginia.

Holland, Lawrence Bedwell (1964), *The Expense of Vision: Essays on the Craft of Henry James*, Princeton: Princeton University Press.

James, Henry (1986 edn), *The Ambassadors*, London: Penguin Classics.

James, Henry (1946 edn), *The American Scene*, New York: Charles Scribner's Sons.

James, Henry (1951), *The American Novels and Stories of Henry James*, ed. F.O. Matthiessen, New York: Knopf.

James, Henry (1958), *The Art of Travel*, ed. M. D. Zabel, New York: Doubleday.

James, Henry (1956 edn), *Autobiography: A Small Boy and Others*, ed. F. W. Dupee, New York: Criterion Books.

James, Henry (1914), *Autobiography: Notes of a Son and Brother*, London: Macmillan & Co.

James, Henry (1987 edn), *The Complete Notebooks of Henry James*, ed. L. Edel and L. Powers, Oxford: Oxford University Press.

James, Henry (1923 edn) 'Crapy Cornelia', in *The Finer Grain*, London, Macmillan.

James, Henry (1986 edn), *Italian Hours*, London: Century Hutchison.

James, Henry (1951 edn), *The Ivory Tower*, ed. F. O. Mattheissen, New York: Knopf.

James, Henry (1984 edn), *Letters*, ed. L. Edel, Harvard: Belknap Press.

James, Henry (1955), *The Notebooks of Henry James*, eds. F. O. Matthiessen and K. B. Murdock, New York: George Braziller Inc.

James, Henry (1911), *The Outcry*, London: Methuen.

James, Henry (1986), *The Painter's Eye*, ed. J. L. Sweeney, London: Rupert Hart-Davis.

James, Henry (1903), *William Wetmore Story and His Friends* vols I and II, Boston: Houghton, Mifflin & Co.

Krook, Dorothea (1967), *The Ordeal of Consciousness in Henry James*, Cambridge: Cambridge University Press.

Levy, Michael (1961), 'Departure from Cythère', *Burlington Magazine*, CIII, No. 698, London.

Man, Paul de (1979), *Allegories of Reading*, Yale: Yale University Press.

Nietzsche, Friedrich (1983), *Untimely Meditations*, trans. R.J. Hollingdale, Cambridge: Cambridge University Press.

Nussbaum, Martha (1983), 'Flawed Crystals: James's *The Golden Bowl* and Literature as Moral Philosophy', *New Literary History*, 15(1), pp. 25–50.

Nussbaum, Martha (1990), *Love's Knowledge*, Oxford: Oxford University Press.

Ozouf, Mona (1998), *La muse démocratique*, Paris: Calmann-Levy.

Putnam, Hilary (1983), 'Taking Rules Seriously', *New Literary History*, 15(1), 193–200.

Richards, I.A. (1934), *Coleridge on Imagination*, London: Kegan Paul.

Righter, William (1989), 'Golden Bowls and Golden Rules', *Philosophy and Literature*, 13(2), 262–281, Hanover (PA): The Sheridan Press.

Righter, William (1994), *The Myth of Theory*, Cambridge: Cambridge University Press.

Righter, William (1996), 'Strether's Reasons', paper presented at the Symposium with Martha Nussbaum, Centre for Philosophy and Literature, University of Warwick, UK.

Rosenberg, Pierre (1984) 'Les Tableaux de Watteau' in *Watteau* (Catalogue of the Exhibition), Paris: Edition de la Réunion des Musées Nationaux.

Tanner, Tony (1987), 'Proust, Ruskin, James and "le désir de Venise" ' in Perosa, Sergio (ed.), *Henry James e Venezia*, Florence: Leo S. Olshki Editore.

Tintner, Adeline R. (1986), *The Museum World of Henry James*, Ann Arbor: UMI Research Press.

Tintner, Adeline R. (1993), *Henry James and the Lust of the Eyes*, Baton Rouge: Louisiana State University Press.

Tocqueville, Alexis de (1948 edn), *Democracy in America*, trans. Henry Reeve, New York: Knopf.

Vidal, Gore (1985), Introduction to *The Golden Bowl*, London: Penguin Classics.

Wittgenstein, Ludwig (1914–16), *Notebooks*, trans. and ed. by G.E.M. Anscombe, Oxford: Basil Blackwell.

Wittgenstein, Ludwig (1953 edn), *Philosophical Investigations*, trans. G.E.M. Anscombe, Oxford: Basil Blackwell.

Index

accommodation 107
action, power and 136–43, 149–150
Adams, Clove Hooper 28, 82
Adams, Henry 5–6, 10, 14, 196
aliens (immigrants) 7, 25–6
Ambassadors, The (James) 6, 8, 18, 22,
    45–94, 113, 152–3, 159, 160, 176, 207
  comedy of moral terms 64–71
  distancing and Strether's decision
    making 73–8
  incommensurability 79–85
  international theme 57–8, 80–81, 170
  nihilism and decorum 86–94
  Strether's encounter with Mme de
    Vionnet in Nôtre Dame 49–55, 91
  Strether's struggle with the problem of
    interpretation 66–9
  transformations and place 114–15
  transformation of Strether's sensibility
    56–63
American City 115, 125, 169–78
  Museum of 6, 41, 173, 176–7, 179–92
American Scene, The (James) 6, 7–8, 9,
    22–43, 94, 193, 195–6, 201, 207
Andersen, Hendrick 184–5, 187
animal imagery 111, 116, 145, 160–61
Aristotle 194
Arnold, Matthew 28, 189–90, 209
art
  collections 40–1, 43, 171, 179–92
  and life 125, 162–3, 187–8
Aspern Papers, The (James) 20
assimilation 7–8, 26–7
asymmetry 125–35
Auden, W.H. 190, 212
authorial voice, modification of 153
Autobiography (James) 9, 11, 15, 191, 196
awareness *see* consciousness

Balzac, Honoré de 102, 189, 193
'Beast in the Jungle, The' (James) 90, 160
'Bench of Desolation, The' (James) 161
Berenson, Bernhard 179, 183
Berlin, Isaiah 6, 79–80, 93, 147, 207
Bloom, Harold 38
Boston 25, 33–4, 38, 41
Bourget, Paul 180
Britain 37–8
  see also London
Brooks, Van Wyck 16
business 32, 42, 172–4, 193–5, 199–200

California 35
Cape Cod 23–4
Carnegie, Andrew 172
Charleston 35
cities 20, 33–4
  see also under individual names
Coburn, Alvin Langdon, 123
Coleridge, S.T. 209
collections and collecting 40–41, 43, 171,
    179–92
comedy 64–71, 79
community 27–8, 188
  and symmetry in *The Golden Bowl*
    125–35
completeness of *The Golden Bowl* 100
composite light 12–13
Concord, Massachusetts 37–8
conflict
  in *The Golden Bowl* 158–63
  see also value conflicts
Conrad, Joseph 152, 210
consciousness
  double in *The Sense of the Past* 204
  in *The Golden Bowl* 108–9, 115
  heightened in *The Ambassadors* 49,

58–63, 72–3, 74–5, 76–7, 89
  modification of 210
context 152
continuity 37
  and process 5–6
cosmopolite 13
'Crapy Cornelia' (James) 18, 20
cultural institutions 172–3
  see also museums
Curtis, Ariana 179

De Man, Paul 158–9
death 125
  living death 176–7, 188–9
decorum
  The Ambassadors 91–4
  The American Scene 24
  The Golden Bowl 90–91, 133, 150–51,
    154–5, 207
  see also manners
Defoe, Daniel 210
Delacroix, Eugène 182
democracy 30–31
Dickens, Charles 200
disinterest, moral value of 74–8
distancing 75, 84, 150–51
diversity 26–7
DuBois, William 34
Dumas, Alexandre 189

Edel, Leon 11, 12, 183, 189
Elias, Norbert 93
Eliot, George 15, 177
Eliot, T.S. 5, 90
Emerson, Ralph Waldo 5, 13, 38
Enlightenment 5, 50
equilibrium 125–35, 161–2
Europe 5, 6, 8
  impact of James's memories of 9–21
  migration to America from 25–6
  representation in Portland Place 169–78
'Europe' (James) 18
experience 191
  in *The Ambassadors* 58–63

Fawns 100, 103, 106, 109, 111, 117,
  137–8, 169, 173, 178, 181

Fenway Court 41, 43, 179–80, 185
figure 116–18, 174–5
Fitzgerald, F. Scott 208
  The Great Gatsby 200
Flaubert, Gustave 58
Florida 35
form, sense of 24
Forster, E.M. 152
Foucault, Michel 142–3
Frick, Henry Clay 185

Gardner, Isabella Stewart 41, 179–80,
  185
Gardner, Patrick 151
generality 152–4
genre, problem of 158–63
ghosts 202–5, 211
Gogol, Nikolai 196
gold, image of 116–8, 174–5
Golden Bowl, The (James) 6, 8, 16, 20, 22,
    68, 87, 95–192, 202, 207, 210
  American wealth 193–5
  anomalies of place and time 112–20
  character of Adam Verver 109–11
  community and symmetry 125–35
  decorum 90–91, 133, 150–51, 154–5,
    207
  depiction of Charlotte 102, 110–11
  fate of Charlotte 188-9
  fictive resolutions 158–63
  incommensurability 144–57
  internalization of Europe 17
  Museum of American City 6, 41, 173,
    176–7, 179–92
  nature of Prince Amerigo 103, 104–11,
    113, 170
  Portland Place and American City 115,
    169–78
  representation of principal characters
    99–103
  transformation of Maggie Verver 114,
    136–42, 171
  Verver's history and wealth 173–6
Gould, Jay 110, 120
Grant's tomb 34, 39
Granville-Barker, Harley 182

Harrison, Frederick 15
Harvey, Colonel George 22, 44
Hawthorne, Nathaniel 12, 21, 38
heiresses, American 194
Holland, L.B. 115
hotels 36–7
houses, and rooms 20
Hugo, Victor 56

immigration 7, 25–6
imperfection 163, 189
incommensurability
    The Ambassadors 79–85
    The Golden Bowl 144–57
Independence Hall 34, 38
international theme 5, 170–71
    The Ambassadors 57–8, 80–81, 170
    The Golden Bowl 103, 112–20, 170
interpretation 108–10, 116
Italian Hours (James) 181
Ivory Tower, The (James) 18, 28, 42, 94,
    101, 148, 161, 170–1, 193, 194–5,
    196–202, 208–9

James, Henry
    attitude to money and wealth 21, 42–3,
        172–3, 193–4
    concept of history 5–8
    memory and reflection 9–21
    phases in absorption of European culture
        and cosmopolitanism 18–20
    powers, limits of 86, 100–101
    and 'the prodigious form' 7, 144–5, 147,
        148, 158, 161, 205, 207, 209
    and the visual arts 40–41, 179–85, 191
    see also under individual works
James, William 28, 82
'Jolly Corner, The' (James) 18, 110, 118,
    161, 170–71, 201, 203, 211
Joyce, James 210

Krook, D. 57

language, power of 209
Leavis, F.R. 50, 56, 94
Lee monument 39
Lévi-Strauss, Claude 24, 93

life, art and 125, 162–3, 187–8
living death, America as 176–7, 188–9
London 11, 20, 34
    in *The Golden Bowl* 20, 169–78
Louvre 10, 13, 191
love 125, 140–41, 151

Malraux, André 162, 163
manners
    The Ambassadors 88, 90–3
    The American Scene 23–6, 41
    The Golden Bowl 150–51, 162, 188,
        207
    see also decorum
marriage 67–8
Matthiesson, F.O. 16, 210–11
Mellon, Andrew William 172
Melville, Herman 24
memory 7, 9–10, 33–5
    annihilation of 26
Metropolitan Museum 41, 167
Middle Years, The (James) 11, 206
modernism 7, 210
monumental, the 14, 34, 39–40
Moore, G.E. 194
morality
    The Ambassadors 64–78
    incommensurability in *The Golden Bowl*
        148–54
    triumph of the will in *The Golden Bowl*
        136–43
Morgan, J. Pierpont 172, 184
Morrell, Ottoline 182
Morris, William 11
Mount Vernon 34
Mulberry Street 3
Museum of American City 6, 41, 173,
    176–7, 179–92
museums 40–41, 43, 162–3

narrative, and philosophy 154–5
'native tradition' 5, 7, 8
New England 5, 29, 37–8, 82
New York 20, 24, 25, 34, 39, 42
Nietzsche, Friedrich 14, 15
nihilism 86–94
Norton, Charles Eliot 11, 112, 180

Norton, Grace 44, 179, 180
Nôtre Dame encounter 49–55, 91
novel
  'prodigious form' 7, 144–5, 147, 148,
    158, 161, 205, 207, 209
Nussbaum, Martha 77, 99, 107, 142, 154,
    159, 164–5, 171

obligation 142–3
'Occasional Paris' (James) 13
Outcry, The (James) 179, 182–4, 185
Ozouf, Mona 159

Palm Beach 35
Paris
  The Ambassadors 20, 49–55, 56–63, 83,
    92
  encounter in Nôtre Dame 49–55, 91
  Louvre 10, 13, 191
pastoral 58–9
perfection 189–90
  The Golden Bowl 125–35, 141–2, 148,
    163, 177
  imperfection 163, 189
philosophy, and narrative 154–5
place
  anomalies of place and time 112–20
  representation of 19–21
poetry 209
Portland Place 115, 169–78
Portrait of a Lady (James) 5, 6, 14, 176,
    188, 212
portraiture 187
power 148–50
  and action 136–43, 149–50
  and wealth 207–8
Princess Casamassima, The (James) 20
process, and continuity 5–6
Pullman car 35–6
Puritans 5, 12, 50
purpose 117–18
Putnam, H. 130, 132, 133, 154–5, 164

realism 186–7
reconstruction 56–63
representation 182, 186–7, 209
residual will 138, 139

Richards, I.A. 209–10
Richmond, Virginia 34, 39
Rockefeller, John D. 172
romance form 148
Rome 11, 181
Rousseau, Jean Jacques 24, 158
Ruskin, John 11

sacrifice 79, 134–5, 144, 145–7
Santayana, George 6
Sargent, John Singer 182, 187
  In the Luxembourg Gardens 47
scale 27, 28–30, 42
Schopenhauer, Artur 162, 163
Schopenhauerian will 131–2, 136, 138, 139
self, desire and 73
self-denial 74–8
self-discovery 58–63
sensation 51–3, 58–63
Sense of the Past, The (James) 6, 7, 112,
    196, 201–2, 202–6, 209, 211
sexuality 131
Sherman monument 39
Solomon, Solomon J., *A Conversation
    Piece* 97
Stephen, Leslie 11
Story, William Wetmore 19, 21, 44, 181,
    195
subjection, mode of 142–3
'successive aspects', law of 153
Swinburne, Algernon Charles 15
symmetry, community and 125–35

Temple, Minnie 11
Tennyson, Alfred Lord 15
Thoreau, Henry 38
Tintner, Adeline R. 181, 183
Tintoretto (Jacopo Robusti) 181
Titian (Tiziano Vecellio) 15, 181
Tocqueville, Alexis de 23, 28, 29
Tolstoy, Leo 177
tragedy 79, 160
Tragic Muse, The (James) 80
transformation 112–20
Turn of the Screw, The (James) 90, 176,
    203
Twain, Mark 24

unreadability 158–9

value 56–7, 76–7
value conflicts
  The Ambassadors 79–85
  The Golden Bowl 144–57, 169–78
Venice 20, 181
Vidal, Gore 100, 104
vision, grandiosity of 185–6

wabi 163, 189
Waddesdon Manor 181, 182
waiting, role of 56
Washington, D.C. 32–3, 39, 40

Watteau, J.A. 156
wealth 137
  American 21, 193–5, 207–8
  creation of 172–4
Wharton, Edith 16, 21, 102–3
Whistler, James McNeill 57
will 131–43
William Wetmore Story and His Friends
  (James) 19, 21, 44, 181, 195
Wings of the Dove, The (James) 20, 68,
  114–15, 160, 176
Wittgenstein, Ludwig 162, 163
women, American 32
Woolf, Virginia 210